NAPOLEON'S
GREAT
ADVERSARY
Archduke Charles
and the
Austrian Army, 1792–1814

NAPOLEON'S GREAT ADVERSARY

Archduke Charles and the Austrian Army, 1792–1814

Gunther E. Rothenberg

SPELLMOUNT

Staplehurst

British Library Cataloguing in Publication Data:
A catalogue record for this book is available from the British Library

Copyright © 1982, 1995 by Gunther E. Rothenberg

ISBN 1-873376-40-5

First published in 1982 by B. T. Batsford Ltd
This edition published in the UK in 1995 by
SPELLMOUNT LIMITED
The Old Rectory
Staplehurst
Kent TN12 0AZ

The right of Gunther E. Rothenberg to be identified
as the author of this work has been asserted by him in
accordance with the Copyright, Designs and
Patents Act 1985

Typeset by CentraCet Ltd, Linton, Cambridge
Printed in Great Britain by
Mackays of Chatham plc

Contents

List of Illustrations

Black and white photographs

Between pages 64 and 65

Between pages 128 and 129

Maps

Preface

FOR the price of a half-hour tram journey a modern visitor to Vienna can visit two significant Napoleonic battlefields in a single day. A few miles to the east of the city, on the north bank of the Danube, the beginning of the broad Marchfeld leads to the villages of Aspern, Essling and Gross Enzersdorf, scenes of great strife on 21 and 22 May 1809, and then again on 5 and 6 July that same year. Essling still contains the much-contested granary that General Boudet's infantry held throughout the earlier engagement, and barely half-a-mile away the outline mounds of the French battery position guarding the Mühlau salient can still be traced from which the French guns pounded the flank of FML Klenau's VI Korps at 10 a.m. on the climacteric second day of the battle of Wagram. A wooden bridge nearby leads on to the Island of Lobau – used by the French as their forward mounting area for both battles, and signposts draw the visitor's attention to the sites of Napoleon's headquarters, the French magazines and their field hospitals near which Surgeon-General Larrey commandeered and slaughtered the horses of senior officers to provide broth – boiled in cuirasses set over fires – for the 10,000 French wounded after Aspern-Essling. Despite the peacefulness of the modern scene, it does not take much imagination to evoke the scenes of carnage and gallantry in the mind's eye.

Aspern-Essling was Napoleon's first true defeat in battle, (his repulse from before Acre in 1799 was the raising of a siege; the severe casualties of Eylau in 1807 at least left the French in possession of the battlefield). Wagram proved his last decisive battle-victory, leading to a favourable peace a few months later. Both battles in the spring and early summer of 1809 exemplify the scale and determination of the Austrian resistance to the ambitions of the man, whom Thomas Carlyle would later dub 'the sheep-worrier of Europe'. As Professor Rothenberg points out in his introduction, Austrian resistance led to wild fluctuations of martial and political fortune, to say the least. The Habsburgs proved the most determined and implacable of Napoleon's continental opponents, although from 1810 to mid-1813, a form of uneasy alliance existed between France and the

9

Austrian Empire. But it is strange that so little attention has been paid to the organisation, leadership and achievements of the Austrian army over these dramatic years – at least in the English language. This book therefore fills a most significant gap in the scholarly literature devoted to the Napoleonic era.

In his earlier years at least, Napoleon was a realist. He well recognised the nature of the struggle he would face in imposing his will on Europe. 'Between old monarchies and a young republic, the spirit of hostility must always exist,' he declared at the time of the Peace of Amiens in 1802. 'In the present state of affairs, every peace treaty means no more than a brief armistice; and I believe that my destiny will be to fight almost continuously.' And so indeed it was to prove. Of the ancient European monarchies, Austria was to prove second only to Great Britain in offering prolonged and determined opposition to Revolutionary, Consular and ultimately Imperial France. Between 20 April 1792, when the idealistic but rash Girondin government declared war on 'the King of Hungary and Bohemia', (the secondary title of Emperor Francis), and the final collapse of Napoleon's power on 18 June 1815, Europe knew over 23 years of tension and hostilities. The pauses represented by the barely 14-month Peace of Amiens and the 11-month sojourn of Napoleon on Elba following his first abdication were little more than exhausted breathing spaces. Great Britain, although somewhat hesitant to enter the struggle at its outset, defied France for all of 21 eventful years – defiance made practicable by the barrier of the English Channel and the protective screen of the hard-pressed Royal Navy; for long years before 1808 her land forces were excluded from the continent in practical terms, but she remained both the inspiration of European resistance and the paymaster of Europe – continually building up new coalitions on foundations of golden guineas. For the sustained land-fighting through thick and thin however, the palm must surely be awarded to Austria, who was at war for a total of thirteen and a half years. Over this period of time, she experienced having her capital twice occupied by enemy armies, saw large regions of territory in north Italy, along the Adriatic coast, on the Tyrolean frontiers, in the Low Countries, and near the Rhine torn away by four unfavourable treaties of peace dictated by the conquerors, while Napoleon's own assumption of Imperial dignity in 1804 forced the Holy Roman Emperor Francis II to designate himself Francis I of Austria and (admittedly not before time in many respects), following Austerlitz, to renounce the old title in 1806. An even stranger twist of fate would make him Napoleon's father-in-law just four years later – an unnatural dynastic alliance, which would lead to large sections of the Austrian army finding themselves fighting the troops of their erstwhile ally of the Third Coalition, Tsar Alexander, deep in Poland and Russia in 1812.

The fluctuating fortunes of the Austrian army, its recurring reconstructions after undergoing cataclysm at Rivoli, Marengo, Austerlitz and Wagram, make for fascinating reading in the pages that follow; and hovering over the whole military scene is the brooding and somewhat enigmatic figure of the Emperor Francis' talented but mercurial brother, the Archduke Charles, destined to fight against the French on many occasions between 1792 and 1809. He won successes at Neerwinden, Wetzlar, Amberg and Würzburg, Ostrach and Stockach, at First Zurich, Second Caldiero and above all at Aspern-Essling, (in this case against Napoleon in personal command). He also had his failures – Fleurus, in Italy in 1797, and above all at Wagram – but no European general had more experience of the realities of early nineteenth-century warfare than the sometime epileptic Erzherzog Karl, Field-Marshal, Archduke of Austria and later Duke of Teschen and the succession of white-clad Austrian armies that he was called upon to lead.

Dr David G. Chandler, Retired Head of the Department of War Studies and International Affairs, the Royal Military Academy, Sandhurst.

The Austrian Empire 1792–1814

Introduction

FROM 1792 to 1814 the Austrian army was the largest force continually engaged against the French Revolution and Napoleon and carried most of the burden of the war on land. Though repeatedly defeated, it always rose again. In 1809 it inflicted the first setback on Napoleon himself and in 1813 contributed the largest contingent to the allied effort in Germany. Even so, the army has been neglected by English-speaking historians. Although there exists a very considerable literature dealing with the battles and campaigns of this period, most of this has been written from the viewpoint of the French. Except for the works by Duffy, Maude, and Petre, who each devote some pages to the Austrian army, little has been done and there exists no booklength study of this force during the wars of the French Revolution and Napoleon.

However, it is both possible and necessary to look at the other side of the hill and this volume attempts to provide such a picture. As all armies, the Habsburg army was a reflection of its society and, perhaps, more than most, it never freed itself from the influence of the political, economic, and social system of its day. These constraints have been discussed together with a look at the institutions, leadership, strategy and tactics, as well as short outlines of the major battles and campaigns. Archduke Charles, without doubt the Habsburgs' best commander, is described at some length, as are his strategic and tactical concepts. If the narrative is not always simple or clearcut, this is because the army and its various components often were sprawling, contradictory and confusing. Moreover, the constantly rising costs of printing have somewhat curtailed the length of this book and forced the author to limit his treatment of certain details.

One further caution is necessary. Although there is no shortage of Austrian materials, above all the documents in the admirably conducted Kriegsarchiv, Vienna, the printed records must be used with caution. Following its defeat in 1866, the Austrian Monarchy set out to refurbish its military image and many of the works, especially the multi-volume biographies of the Archduke Charles published at the turn of the century, tend to be somewhat slanted. They were commissioned by the archduke's descendants and written by serving officers. By contrast, the official history of these wars, compiled by the Historical Section of the General Staff within the Kriegsarchiv, is much more objective, though the series tends to limit itself to military operations proper and provides little background. Perhaps significantly also, these volumes never got around to providing an account of Wagram. Even so, I have heavily relied on these accounts, supplemented by the documents in the Kriegsarchiv. In addition, I have found the observations by various English liaison officers, agents and envoys, enlightening.

Any book of this nature is built on the work of other scholars and I have freely drawn on their publications and advice. In particular I am obliged to David Chandler and Christopher Duffy of the Department of War Studies at the Royal Military Academy, Sandhurst, and to Drs Kurt Peball, Walter Wagner, and Peter Broucek of the Kriegsarchiv, Vienna. My debt to Dr Manfried Rauchensteiner of the Militärwissenschaftliches Institut, Heeresgeschichtliches Museum, Vienna, is evident throughout the book. In the USA I am deeply obliged to Professor Peter Paret of Stanford University and to the financial assistance provided by the Research Project on War and Society in East Central Europe, headed by my friend Professor Bela K. Kiraly. At Purdue University I am grateful for the unflagging and cheerful support of Mrs Joyce R. Good and Mrs Grace E. Dienhart, who supervised the typing and other copying necessary, and to my wife, Ruth, co-ordinator of Interlibrary Loan Services. I am grateful to Dr Johann C. Allmayer-Beck of the Heeresgeschichtliches Museum, Vienna, for providing most of the illustrations and to Mr Scotty Bowden of the Empire Games Press, Arlington, Texas, for permission to reproduce several maps. Additional maps and information were provided by Dr Robert Epstein of the US Army Command and General Staff College, Ft Leavenworth, Kansas. The new maps were done by Patrick Leeson and Derek Stone. Finally, I am obliged to Mr William F. Waller of B.T. Batsford Ltd who not only commissioned this book, but performed many services in preparing it for publication and to his assistant editor, Ms Mimi Rolbant. It goes without saying that I alone remain responsible for any mistakes of ommission and commission which exist in this work.

Note on ranks, personal names and place names

The highest rank, except that of *Generalissimus*, in the Habsburg armies was *Feldmarschall*, followed either by *Feldzeugmeister* for officers of the infantry, artillery, and engineering branches, or *General der Cavallerie*. This was followed by *Feldmarschall Leutnant* and then by General Major. Lower commissioned and enlisted ranks generally followed the common pattern of European armies and are always given in their English version.

The rendition of place names has been done with an eye to familiarity rather than absolute consistency. During the period covered here, most localities were known under German, Serbo-Croat, Hungarian, Italian, and French names. Because German was the official language of the Austrian army, the German version has been employed except when names have become part of the common English usage. The spelling of personal names also presented difficulties. It must be kept in mind that official documents as well as individuals and families often employed different versions of one name. The practice here has been to use the German version and again, exceptions have been made when the name or title has become part of English historical usage. Similarly, *Grenz* has been used as an anglicization specifically for the Military Border.

I

The Habsburg Monarchy and its Army in 1792

AT first the revolution in France caused little concern in the capitals of Europe. Rather the contrary. France was the most powerful nation in Europe and her neutralization by internal troubles was welcome to Austria, Prussia, and Russia, manoeuvring for a Second Partition of Poland, while across the Channel, Britain was looking towards a period of peace and stability. In 1791, however, this situation changed. In Paris, moderates were displaced by ever more radical elements, King Louis XVI and his Austrian-born wife, Marie Antoinette, became virtual prisoners, and the government assumed a threatening posture. Perturbed, in July 1791, the peace-loving Habsburg emperor, Leopold II (1790–92), urged European sovereigns to support the monarchist cause in France. But this was a half-hearted gesture and a few weeks later, on hearing that Louis XVI had ratified the new constitution, he withdrew his declaration. At this the aged Austrian chancellor, Prince Wenzel Kaunitz, remarked that God was to be thanked that the king of France had got everyone out of a dangerous impasse.

Kaunitz misjudged the true nature of the problem. Revolutionary France needed war. 'A people who after twelve centuries of slavery have won liberty,' Jacques Pierre Brissot, leading the Left in the Legislative Assembly, proclaimed, 'need a war to consolidate it.' The Assembly now pressed Leopold II to disperse the small concentrations of aristocratic French emigrés along the Rhine and after the emperor complied, demanded in January 1792 that Austria declare within a month whether the Austro-French alliance of 1756 still was valid. In response, on 7 February 1792, Austria and Prussia signed a treaty to co-operate in the affairs of France and Poland. This compact, an uneasy arrangement between two powers who had been deadly rivals for half a century, inflamed passions in Paris.

On 1 March 1792, Leopold died suddenly and was succeeded by his eldest son, Francis II.[1] Although some have suggested that if Leopold had lived there would have been no war, this seems unrealistic. It is true that Francis was young, less patient and prudent than his father, but while French armies already were concentrating along the Rhine, in keeping with the defensive posture adopted by the Habsburg Empire in western Europe, preparations for war remained at a very low level. In fact, no conflict was expected. On 21 April 1792, the young Archduke Charles, later the Habsburgs' most renowned soldier, reported from Brussels that 'no one here considers war likely.'[2]

The evening before, however, the Legislative Assembly in Paris had declared war against the 'King of Hungary and Bohemia,' a formula designed to encourage the neutrality of Prussia and other German states. Thus began 23 years of hostilities during which in terms of men engaged in combat on land the Austrian army assumed the largest burden. To be sure, between 1792 and 1814, Great Britain was at war for over 240 months, but, except for its expeditionary force in the Peninsula, engaged no major land elements in protracted action. Austria was at war with France for 108 months, compared to 58 for Prussia and 55 for Russia. While, as Albert Sorel wrote, Austria 'always was one idea and one army behind, she always had an idea and an army,' and, though repeatedly defeated, always managed to rise and fight again.[3] And in 1813–14, Austria contributed the largest contingent to the overthrow of Napoleon.

The military system of the Austrian Monarchy

In the last decade of the eighteenth century the 'Austrian Monarchy,' a convenient misnomer for the territories diligently collected by an ambitious dynasty, stretched from the Lower Rhine to the plains of Galicia and from Bohemia to northern Italy. The core of this vast empire were the *Erblande*, the hereditary lands, Upper and Lower Austria, the Tyrol, Vorarlberg, Styria, Carinthia, and Carniola, with Bohemia, Moravia, and the Austrian littoral on the Adriatic. In addition, there were the lands of the Hungarian Crown, as well as Transylvania, a large part of Galicia occupied in the First Polish Partition of 1772, the Austrian Netherlands (Belgium and Luxemburg), and the Habsburg domains in Italy, the duchies of Milan, Mantua and Tuscany. Finally, the Habsburg possessions included small enclaves along the Upper Rhine. From his capital in Vienna the Habsburg emperor, a title referring to the Holy Roman Empire and little more than titular by this time, ruled over some 5,650,000 Germans, 3,360,000 Magyars, 2,550,000 Czechs, 1,800,000 Italians, 1,600,000 Romanians, 1,255,000 Slovaks, 2,000,000 Flemings and Walloons, 1,000,000 Poles, 900,000 Croats, 700,000 Serbs, as well as a number of smaller ethnic groups.[4]

Such variety made pretty pictures, but difficult politics. The Austrian Monarchy, a dynastic collection of lands, lacked unity and purpose. The Habsburgs ruled by virtue of separate titles over territories that had little or nothing in common and their military posture was weakened by the lack of uniform political authority and administration. In many lands relics of later medieval government – diets constituted of predominantly noble estates and their institutions and personnel – competed with the central government. The invasion of Silesia by Frederick II of Prussia revealed the weakness of this system and compelled Maria Theresa (1740–80) to make administrative, fiscal, and above all military reforms, continued after 1765 by her son and co-ruler, the later Emperor Joseph II (1780–90). The estates of the hereditary lands lost much of their powers as taxes were fixed by long-term contracts and administrative authority assumed by officials of the Crown. In Vienna a Council of State, the *Staatsrat*, emerged as the major internal agency while the *Haus-, Hof- und Staatskanzlei* handled foreign relations. Its head, the *Kanzler*, also acted as the first minister of state. For the first time, with replacements and financial support assured, Austria was able to maintain a very substantial army in peace as well as war.

Even so, the reforms did not go far enough and there remained numerous restraints on the military posture of the Monarchy. Even in the hereditary lands there were difficulties. The Tyrol, for instance, preserved its ancient privilege to raise a burgher-peasant militia for its own defence and to limit recruiting for the standing army. Further afield, because of their special character and distance from Vienna, the Italian duchies as well as the Austrian Netherlands were largely excluded from the changes. When Joseph II tried to enforce reforms in the Netherlands there was a revolt in 1789 and in the end the attempt had to be abandoned.

But Hungary constituted the most critical internal problem of the Austrian Monarchy. The central issue was that the 'ruling nation,' that is the magnates, lesser nobles, and clergy who alone were represented in the Diet, rejected the control of the dynasty and furiously defended their privileges, above all exemption from all taxation in return for personal service in the obsolete feudal levy, the *insurrectio*. With national consciousness more pronounced in Hungary than elsewhere, the nobles often were able to rally the peasantry to the cause of 'Hungarian rights.'

In 1715–22, to be sure, the Diet had accepted the principle of a standing royal army, but retained control over recruitment and supply.[5] And during the Prussian Wars, despite protestations of loyalty and devotion, Hungary had provided little support. A Diet convoked in 1764 to raise the country's contribution to army finances and to convert the service obligation of the nobility into a cash subsidy refused to act. Nonetheless, Maria Theresa thought coercion unwise. 'In the Kingdom of Hungary,' she wrote, 'I did think it better not to introduce any changes. . . special considerations apply in the case of the Hungarians.'[6] When Joseph II tried to introduce reforms, the nobles revolted and had to be pacified by Leopold II with a mixture of threats and concessions. By 1792 the struggle between the Hungarian ruling nation and the Crown had resolved itself in an uneasy truce among equals. Hungary's contribution to the military establishment remained disproportionately small compared with the hereditary lands and even in time of crisis the Habsburgs had to negotiate and cajole for manpower and supply rather than to command.

Another constraint was the state of finances. Although the Austrian Monarchy's economic potential was considerable, with many agriculturally rich areas, substantial mineral resources, a good supply of skilled craftsmen and small-to-middling manufacturing enterprises, the numerous wars and the expanding military establishment were costly and had to be financed by foreign loans and by issuing paper money. First used in 1762, the amount of paper in circulation increased steadily, though until the mid-1790s it traded at par. Payments on debts and current expenditures pushed the Monarchy into a deficit of about 9,600,000 florins annually. In 1790, the deficit climbed to 27 million, sank to the 23 million the next year, and after Leopold II reduced the army in 1791, it reached a low of 4 million florins in 1792. Nonetheless, Count Chotek, the chief finance official, painted a gloomy picture. On the one hand, inflation and rising prices made higher taxes undesirable, while on the other hand the deficit made it difficult to float internal or external loans to finance the war. He recommended an appeal for voluntary contributions in kind from the provinces, coupled with another attempt to secure foreign loans.[7]

Finally, there was the emerging problem of nationalism. While nationalism still was in a nascent stage, except perhaps among the Magyars, command of an army whose regiments variously spoke German, Czech, French, Flemish, Serbo-Croat, Italian, Magyar,

Romanian and Polish could, one officer observed, cause 'singular confusion.' To overcome this, German had been introduced as the language of drill books, regulations and formal command and most officers had at least a smattering of several languages. As for the spirit of the troops, opinion varied. In 1788 a publicist pictured the army composed of 'spirited and brave Austrians, fiery and courageous Hungarians, steady Bohemians, steadfast Moravians, brave and purposeful Styrians, obliging Poles, daring Croats, boisterous Italians, and warlike Netherlanders,' but only a few years later another officer questioned whether an army of 'Hungarians, Croats, Transylvanians, Italians, Bohemians, Moravians, Poles, Wallachs, Slavonians, Austrians, Styrians, Tyroleans, Carnioleans, and gypsies could march under one flag and fight for a cause it knows nothing about.'[8] Of course, the army did fight and overall did well enough. Still, compared with France or Prussia where centralized institutions produced higher revenues and more coherent military establishments, the Habsburg state was at a disadvantage. In April 1791, just one year before the war broke out, Karl Leiberich Baron Mack, then a promising young staff officer, commented that 'lack of unity, conflicting jurisdictions, and large distances make the Austrian military system far more complex than the Prussian.'[9]

Supreme command of the army

The *kaiserlich-königliche Armee* of 1792, so styled since 1745 when the queen's husband, Francis Stephen of Lorraine-Tuscany, was elected Holy Roman Emperor, in large measure was the creation of Maria Theresa and Joseph II. Although the standing army dated back to 1649, on her accession in 1740 Maria Theresa had found many defects. 'Who would believe,' she later commented, 'that no sort of rule was in force among my troops? Every unit had a different order of marching, a different drill, etc. The same commands were differently understood in each unit . . . and the state of the army beggared description.'[10] Her military reforms, continued by her son Joseph II, enlarged the army and recast it on the Prussian model. Together with the administrative reforms, this provided the framework which enabled it to withstand the strain of prolonged conflict after 1792.

The ultimate control over the army, of course, was vested in the sovereign, though the Habsburgs seldom excelled as field commanders. Maria Theresa had shown firmness and resolution during the Prussian Wars but she had lacked the necessary ruthlessness to sack unlucky, indifferent, or superannuated generals or to impose discipline on her bitterly factionalized principal officers.[11] Joseph II, emulating Frederick II of Prussia, had aspirations to command in the field. His military talents, however, were scant and his attempt to personally lead the army against the Turks in 1788 ended in disaster.[12] Although Fieldmarshal Gideon Ernst Baron Laudon (Loudon), the ablest Austrian commander of his day, restored the situation the next year, Prussian threats, the revolt in the Netherlands, and the insurrection in Hungary prevented exploitation of his victories.

When Joseph died in February 1790, the army had not fully recuperated from the setbacks and losses suffered during the Turkish War and his successor, Leopold II, had to extricate the Monarchy from a difficult situation. In contrast to Joseph, Leopold II had no military pretensions. An enlightened rationalist, he had, when the Duke of Tuscany reduced his army to 300, barely enough to guard the city gates of Florence, his capital. Although it was one thing to rule a minor Italian duchy and another to rule over the sprawling Austrian Monarchy, Leopold felt that military expenditures, about 45 percent of the budget, were too high and late in 1791 he cut his forces, already understrength as a result of the war, by another 25,000 men.[13] At the same time he appointed his son and heir, Francis, to chair a *Militär-Hof-Commission* to inquire into the state of the army.[14]

Three months later, Leopold was dead and Francis commenced his 43-year reign. Later called 'the Good', on his accession Francis was hailed by some as a 'soldier-emperor,' though the appellation did not really fit. Born in 1768, he had received a sketchy military education at the court in Florence and in 1786, at the wish of Emperor Joseph, he was sent to Vienna. That year he made a tour of observation in Bohemia and Hungary and was tutored in regimental, staff, and command duties. In 1788 he visited the Turkish front, reportedly showing coolness under fire. He also witnessed the near disintegration of the army, a lesson that would make him even more cautious, and the next year he held a nominal command during the siege and capture of Belgrade, an experience which may have led him to overestimate the importance of fortress warfare.[15]

His grounding in military affairs was limited and in any case the requirements for a war against revolutionary France were quite different from those of a campaign against the Turks. They required changes in strategy and tactics, indeed the whole conduct of war itself, but Francis' innate conservatism, coupled with his nervous and suspicious nature, made him fear and resist innovations. Like almost all Austrian rulers since the days of the Thirty Years' War (1618–48) he distrusted outstanding soldiers and was unwilling to grant them too much authority. Most recently there was the example of Joseph II who had relegated the immensely popular Laudon to unemployment from which he was hastily recalled to save the imperial army from the consequences of an ill-conceived campaign.[16] Francis much preferred military mediocrities and his confidence in his principal officers seemed to vary in inverse proportion to their ability. Typical of this approach was the appointment of Major General Franz von Rollin, one of his former tutors, whom he selected as his adjutant general. Rollin served as Francis' representative in the *Militär-Hof-Commission*, now chaired by Fieldmarshal Count Nostitz-Rieneck. The commission sat for six years, but badly split into factions, accomplished nothing except collecting 17 cartons of documents and 554 separate reports.[17]

The emperor's tendency to distrust the military also led him to listen to civilian advisers, such as Foreign Ministers Thugut, Cobenzl, Colloredo, and later Stadion and Chancellor Metternich. And these did not hesitate to question strategy but also intervened in the direction of operations. This irritated command relationships and created conflicts with field commanders; the intermittent quarrel with the emperor's gifted younger brother, the Archduke Charles, is one example. The question of military-civilian relations was further complicated when, in 1792, Francis sanctioned the creation of a 'military section within the *Staatsrat* with duties that overlapped those of the *Hofkriegsrat*.[18]

Established in 1566, the *Hofkriegsrat*, a mixed military-civilian body, was in Christopher Duffy's words 'the most notorious and least understood of Habsburg military institutions.'[19] Often regarded as a supreme command, a function it never held, it has been charged with dilatory and bureaucratic interference in the conduct of operations. This misconception arose because over the course of centuries the *Hofkriegsrat* had been charged with many and diverse functions. While primarily an agency of routine administration and not a command and control organization, senior field commanders communicated directly with the emperor, it nonetheless did serve as a planning staff and handled replacement and logistics. It elaborated schemes and, with imperial approval, passed them on to field and regional commanders. Nominally it was responsible for officer entry and promotions at the junior levels, though the regimental proprietors had a good deal to say on this point, and the emperor reserved the right to appoint all field, staff, and general officers. It directed the ordnance, engineering, and supply departments, issued all routine orders, enforced discipline, and directly controlled the Military Border, a narrow strip of land along the southern frontiers of Hungary-Croatia where warlike soldier-peasants, the *Grenzer*, formed a screen against Turkish incursions and since the 1740s light regiments for service in the wars of the Monarchy.[20] In addition, until the middle of the century, the *Hofkriegsrat* conducted diplomatic relations with Russia and the Ottoman Empire.

Clearly these many functions were beyond the capabilities of an agency with, at least by present standards, a rather small staff – a president and a vice president as well as some thirty-odd counsellors, of whom only a handful of senior generals, designated *wirkliche Hofkriegsräte*, had much influence. In addition there was a staff of some 100 or so clerical employees. During the Theresan and Josephinian reforms efforts were made to rationalize this institution. Fieldmarshal Leopold Joseph Count Daun, president of the war council from 1762–6, replaced high-ranking civil servants with experienced generals, while Fieldmarshal Franz Moritz Count Lacy, 1766–74, organized the council into three functional departments – *publica*, military and political affairs, *oeconomica*, finances and supply, and *judicalia*, military justice. The first two, geographically subdivided into sections, were headed by military *wirkliche Hofkriegsräte*, while the justice department had a civilian head. To simplify administrative procedures, corresponding divisions were introduced in each of the twelve regional commands, the generalcies or *Generalkommanden*. This organization, introduced in 1766, remained in force until 1801.[21]

Subject to the *Hofkriegsrat*, but outside its direct chain of command, were a number of agencies including the Director General of Artillery, the Director General of Engineers, the *Feld-und Hauszeugamt*, dealing with ordnance and arsenals, the *Reichswerbungsamt*, for recruiting in the Holy Roman Empire, the *General Vicar*, Chaplain General, the *Oberste Feldarzt*, the *General-Kriegs-Commissariat*, the Commissary General, as well as civilian agencies such as the *Hauptverpflegungsamt*, responsible for provisions, the *Oberst-Schiffamt*, looking after river transport, as well as additional agencies concerned with matters of pay, the care of invalids, and contracts.

The result of all this was much confusion and an endless stream of directives, minutes, and returns clogging up the military administration at all levels. For example, in 1772 the *Hofkriegsrat* sternly directed every company on the Military Border in Croatia to maintain 72 separate files, render two weekly, ten monthly, and two quarterly reports, as well as a consolidated return every six months, all in proper form and forwarded with endorsement through proper channels to Vienna.[22] And then there was the story, well found if perhaps not true, about the enormous file generated by the Lower Austrian *Generalkommando*'s request to keep a cat because mice were nibbling at the papers in the headquarters' attic. Leopold did have good reason to ask his *Militär-Hof-Commission* 'whether the many useless, superfluous, and burdensome reports, returns, and accounts did not interfere with efficiency?' Until 1801, however, there was little change and under three presidents, Fieldmarshals Michael Johann Count Wallis, 1792–5, Nostitz-Rieneck, 1795–6, and *General der Cavallerie* Ferdinand Count Tige, 1796–1801, business continued as usual.

Direction of operations and the Quartermaster General Staff

Maria Theresa, Joseph II, and later Francis often communicated directly with field commanders. At the same time, they and their military entourage often handled strategic planning, though sometimes with the assistance of the *Hofkriegsrat*. This, however, did not compensate for the lack of a general staff in the modern sense for which the war council was no substitute. Then, too, the Austrian army still was a 'regimental' army, lacking permanent subdivisions such as brigades, divisions, or corps. Names such as 'army detachment' or 'corps' merely signified *ad hoc* arrangements. Most general officers lacked training or experience handling large formations and relied on the instructions issued by individual army commanders. All generals assigned to an army constituted the Great General Staff which, by regulation, the commander was required to consult in a formal council of war before any major undertaking.

Staff work proper was handled by the Quartermaster General Staff according to procedures laid down in Lacy's *Generals Reglement* of 1769, a compendium of standing orders, field service regulations, and staff instructions.[23] Lacy had created a small staff corps, 30 including the director in early 1792, as well as staff troops to serve as escorts, guards, and orderlies. In peacetime the permanent staff officers were employed making surveys and collecting data on potential theatres of operations. On the approach of war a chief of the Quartermaster General Staff, with the rank of *Feldmarschall Leutnant*, was appointed, staff officers were detailed to the various armies and additional officers 'who know how to draw and have some command of geometry' were collected. According to the Prince de Ligne, regimental commanders all too often recommended officers 'they want to get rid of, or the ones they wish to favour, boldly claiming that they have the necessary qualifications.'[24] Together with the adjutant general and his assistants, the Quartermaster General Staff formed the Small General Staff of each field army.

In the field the chief of staff assisted the commander in making plans, but the primary duty of staff officers was topographical reconnaissance. Maps still were scarce and none too accurate, though it does appear odd that as late as 1796 an officer had to be sent to reconnoitre the Stuttgart area, 'as unknown to us as America,' while Bavaria, a frequent scene of Austrian operations for nearly a century, was described 'as little known as Kamchatka.'[25] These and other deficiencies clearly demonstrated the need for a permanent chief of the Quartermaster General Staff, but the first such was appointed only in 1801.[26]

Of course, much of the logistic work that in our days would be handled by staff officers then was entrusted to the *General-Kriegs-Commissariat*, another mixed civilian-military body, largely staffed by former officers and headed by an active duty general. Provisions, mainly bread and fodder, were procured by the civilian *Hauptverpfle-gungsamt* which had branches in each province where an *Oberlan-deskommissar* provided liaison with the local authorities. Although, except in Hungary and Transylvania, contributions in kind had been converted into tax-based cash subsidies, the system remained complex. There were 'Netherlandish, Roman Imperial, Italian, Transylvanian, Hungarian, and German *Erblande* scales,' one officer complained, complicating troop movements and creating paper work.[27]

Strategically located, usually along navigable rivers, the main magazines, *Hauptmagazine*, were to be stocked by civilian contractors who were also engaged to carry the provisions to the forward depots, the *Fassungsmagazine*, where they were picked up by the army field trains. Because Turkey still loomed as the major potential enemy, the Austrian army maintained a substantial permanent field train considered necessary to sustain operations in a region lacking civilian resources. The permanent field train, the *Militärverpflegungs-fuhrwesenkorps*, had been established by Joseph II in 1782 with a strength of 1743 men and 1908 horses. On its war footing of 17,180 men and 34,000 horses, the corps was to provide not only the field train, but draft teams for the artillery, field bakeries, and administrative services as well.[28] This, however, proved difficult and during the Turkish War of 1788, the Austrian commissariat and transport, utilizing some 14,000 horses and the same number of draft oxen, proved unsatisfactory. Overhaul of the field train was high on the agenda of the *Militär-Hof-Commission*, though shelved when war broke out in April 1792. In any case, during the operations against France, conducted in a much more heavily populated and developed environment, the large mass of heavy vehicles often obstructed movement.[29]

Officers and men

The officer corps, multinational and of diverse social origins, reflected the nature of the Habsburg state. In the early days of the standing army, with the indigenous nobility opposing centralization, the Habsburgs frequently had entrusted high command to foreign military entrepreneurs and soldiers of fortune, Montecuccoli, the great Eugene, Browne, Lacy, Laudon, and others. Most officers, of course, came from the Habsburg lands, German-Austrians, Hungarians, Czechs, Italians, Croats, and Walloons, and some of the great families – the Esterházy, Gyulai, Liechtenstein, Lobkowitz, Colloredo, Harrach, Kinsky, to mention a few – were regularly represented in the service, but the nobility as a class did not follow military careers.[30] Aware that her army could profit from the stabilizing influence of the native nobility, Maria Theresa attempted to entice these men into her service and to this end she established an academy of nobles in Vienna. By 1755, however, she had to concede failure. 'It is unbelievable,' she wrote, 'that no one wishes to take advantage of these favors.'[31]

The upper nobility shunned the profession of arms because reforms had removed many of the financial incentives and because the nature of the profession was changing. Specialized knowledge became a prerequisite of command and armies too large to be entrusted to amateurs, however well born, brave, or rich. Most of the aristocrats had little inclination to submit to military discipline and acquire technical proficiency by hard work. Therefore Maria Theresa opened her military academies, the *Theresianische Militärakademie* in Vienna-Neustadt opened in 1752 and the *Ingenieursakademie* in Vienna, to sons of the impoverished minor nobility as well as to commoners, usually the sons of serving officers and state officials. Future officers entered in their teens and after a four-year course in military subjects as well as polite accomplishments were commissioned in the cavalry or the infantry. The curriculum at the *Ingenieursakademie* took eight years, concentrating on professional subjects, though French, rhetoric, horsemanship, and even dancing were not neglected. Because there were only three battalions of technical troops, most engineering graduates were commissioned in the 'regiments.' Still, the combined output of the two academies, about 60 a year, was inadequate even when supplemented by the handful of sons of Magyar magnates who served a military appren- ticeship in the Royal Hungarian Bodyguard, a ceremonial body, and, until 1789, by graduates of the Josephinian Orphanage in Antwerp.[32]

Gunners were trained in the Artillery Corps School near Budweis in Bohemia and since 1786 in the elite *Bombardeur Corps* formed by *Feldzeugmeister* Franz Ulrich Prince Kinsky, director of artillery, which provided theoretical as well as practical instruction for officers and enlisted gunners. In 1790 the corps moved to Vienna where the course lasted for seven years and included mathematics, geometry, physics, chemistry, as well as surveying, fortification, military admin- istration, tactics, and practical exercises. Students completing the full course, usually in their early twenties, were commissioned, while those taking the five year curriculum were appointed enlisted gun captains. Austria's artillery specialists were considered among the best in Europe.[33]

Excluding officers who transferred from foreign armies, the bulk of the Austrian officers received formal training. They entered the army in various ways, by direct commission, by appointment as a cadet, or, in rare cases, by promotion from the ranks. The first method was reserved to members of the imperial house or the high aristocracy. As one writer put it, 'the son of a ruling prince entered the service under different – more favourable – circumstances than an ordinary mortal.'[34] They rapidly passed through the ranks and obtained a field grade, if not a senior position, in their twenties. Cadets formed the most numerous group. There were *k.k.ordinaire* cadets appointed by the *Hofkriegsrat* as well as the *ex-propriis* cadets appointed by the regimental colonel proprietors. Taught the rudi- ments of their trade by experienced sergeants, they normally reached the rank of sub-lieutenant in a year or so. Foreigners, especially south Germans, were accepted.[35] Finally, there was promotion from the ranks. Given the low level of literacy and the high volume of paperwork in the army, educated common soldiers often would be appointed *Fourier*, a non-commissioned company clerk dealing with rations, quartering, returns and such. In time of war, it was not unusual for such a man to be commissioned.

Subject to *Hofkriegsrat* approval, promotion through the rank of major was the prerogative of the regimental proprietors; majors and up were appointed by the emperor. In the artillery, promotion depended on the director general of artillery, while in the *Grenzer* regiments it was handled by the *Hofkriegsrat*. Because many junior officers had no private means, and to save money officers rarely were pensioned off or invalided out, advancement in the lower grades was painfully slow. It could, however, be speeded up by purchase. Styled a 'convention,' this was a private contract by which, subject to certain safeguards, an incumbent sold his billet. Purchase applied only to the next higher grade up to the rank of captain and the transaction had to be approved by the respective colonel and the *Hofkriegsrat*. Although the practice was frequently condemned, the *Militisauar-Hof-Commission* reported in 1793 that it had advantages. It saved on pensions, invalid officers were replaced by more active men, and wealthy individuals, always useful to a regiment, might be attracted to military careers.[36]

Officers' pay and allowances were calculated on a complicated scale and varied according to the state of peace or war, the station, and the branch of service. Broadly speaking, however, the senior grades did very well while subalterns were hard pressed. Generals drew between 5000 to 12,000 florins a year, which, with various allowances in cash and kind, added up to over 16,000 for a fieldmarshal commanding an army. By contrast a sub-lieutenant had a base pay of 288 florins, doubled perhaps by various allowances on campaign. The establishment for officers at the regimental level was sparse, but there was an excess of general officers, 356 in 1792. These included 13 fieldmarshals, 18 *Feldzeugmeister* or *Generäle der Cavallerie* (full generals), 79 *Feldmarschall Leutnants* (lieutenant generals), and no less than 232 major generals. In peacetime most were unemployed, though even in war there were too many. The general staff history calculated that if actual troop commands were considered, there was one general officer for every three battalions or squadrons.[37] Moreover, the generalcy, still aristocratic for the most part, was badly divided by feuds and personal rivalries, while army commanders, all too often selected for their connections and seniority, were physically out of shape and mentally out of date.

Still, the composition of the officer corps, and indeed the nobility, was changing. Vitally concerned to secure the loyalty of her officers, Maria Theresa took steps to elevate their social status. In 1751 she ordered all uniformed officers admitted to court; a few years later she opened her new Order of Maria Theresa, a most coveted distinction, to all officers regardless of social rank or religion, and in 1757 she decreed that commoners with 30 years of meritorious service be raised to the hereditary nobility. These innovations had long-range consequences creating military families which for generations wore the uniform, and in the words of Francis II became 'patriots for me.'[38] On the other hand, however, these changes did little to alter the marked lack of intellectual activity in the Habsburg army. Compared to France, Prussia, even Hesse, the Habsburg officer corps showed little interest in military theories. While Daun already had called for more professional education 'because commanders require a good head more than a strong arm and experience alone did not provide systematic knowledge,' connections still played a major role in appointments and, except for the academy graduates, the bulk of the officers were poorly educated.[39] In 1802 one general felt it necessary to issue a plan of studies for his officers including the simplest arithmetic, because most were not academy graduates and knew very little.[40] The Austrian officer corps at all levels showed a marked inclination to cling to the methods developed during the Prussian Wars, was too devoted to routine and to look no further than orders issued by their superiors or to the appropriate army regulations.

Whatever their origin or rank, officers were a world apart from the rank-and-file. Service in the ranks was considered neither honourable nor desirable and conditions, even by the standards of the time, poor. Discipline was harsh and most of the Articles of War recommended that the offender should be corporally or capitally punished. Pay was nominal. A private received but five *Kreutzer* a day, 60 *Kreutzer* to the florin, as well as a bread ration, but deductions were made for the noon meal and for cleaning materials. The highest enlisted pay was 15 *Kreutzer* for a senior *Feldwebel* (sergeant-major). Quarters varied. Some units were quartered in barracks, mainly converted monasteries, with two men to a bed, others were lodged in 'soldier rooms' in towns and villages, while the most fortunate were billeted on individual families.

Manpower for the *k.k. Armee* was provided by selective conscription and voluntary enlistment. Only on the Military Border was service universal. In 1771, Joseph II had introduced a systematic census, a general *Conscription*, of all male inhabitants in the Austrian lands. Liberal exemptions were granted to individuals, towns, and even whole provinces. Military service applied only to the Hereditary lands, except for the Tyrol, and to Galicia. Hungary, the Austrian Netherlands, and the Italian duchies were excluded. Also exempt everywhere were nobles, officials, and tax producing elements. In practice, conscription was implemented only for the lowest classes, so that with an overwhelming rural population the ranks were filled with the poorest peasants and agricultural labourers. Serving for life or until invalided and discharged, they made steady soldiers, physically tough and inured to hardship. The conscripted lands, except Galicia, were subdivided into regimental districts for the 'German' line infantry. Considered unreliable, the Poles of Galicia were distributed among the various regiments. The eight regiments of foot recruited in Italy, the Tyrol, and the Netherlands relied on free recruiting, while Hungarian units were filled by the local authorities according to quotas fixed by the Diet. Conscription was unpopular everywhere and compulsion and subterfuges were common to meet the required numbers.

Cavalry, artillery, and technical troops recruited at large. In theory the cavalry was to take only men already trained in the infantry, but this was usually disregarded. Mounted regiments, especially the Hungarian Hussars, had little difficulty in attracting recruits. The artillery was the most selective arm, accepting only volunteers who had to be Austrian subjects, unmarried, and able to read and write German.[41]

Austria had the right to recruit in the smaller south German states and regiments would send special teams to lure suitable young men into their ranks. Bounties were offered: 35 florins for an infantry recruit, 29 for a cavalry recruit, descending to 10 or 15 florins for young men 'with prospects but below the height requirement.' One source estimated that about one half of the 39 'German' infantry regiments – German as distinct from Hungarian, Croatian, Italian or Walloon regiments – were drawn from this region and because they were better educated they constituted an even larger proportion of non-commissioned officers.[42] One volunteer remembered that he was given a cursory medical examination and then 'locked up in a large room with twenty young men in various stages of inebriation.' The next morning, and presumably more sober, the group was met by an infantry platoon with fixed bayonets and escorted to join a draft on its way to their regiments.[43] In contrast with the lifetime conscripts, volunteers signed on for limited terms, usually seven years, after which they were encouraged to re-enlist.

Finally, on the Military Borders in Croatia, Slavonia, Hungary, and Transylvania every able-bodied male was a peasant-soldier. The Military Borders were organized in 17 regiments, one independent battalion of pontooneers, the *Tschaikisten*, and one regiment of Szekler *Grenz* Hussars. With a total population of 823,850, including 101,692 men of military age, in 1799, they normally provided 56,644 men for frontier guards and foreign service, one-sixth of the total strength of the army. In 1792, however, because of losses sustained in the Turkish War and adverse economic conditions, the Military Border could raise only 13,000 men for field service.[44]

Overall the replacement situation of the army had deteriorated. In 1783 the muster rolls showed 38,847 men on indefinite furlough and 241,857 enrolled but not trained. The 1781 emancipation of the serfs in the Hereditary lands increased the number of small independent peasants, normally exempt, and also permitted large-scale movement to urban centres which again were exempt from conscription. In 1791, only 15,643 men were shown on leave and the reservoir of enrolled recruits had dwindled to 64,000. Even invalids were retained on active duty performing limited service.[45]

Combat arms: infantry, cavalry and artillery

The army was composed of 57 line infantry regiments, two garrison regiments, one garrison battalion, 17 *Grenz* infantry regiments, and 35 cavalry regiments. Artillery comprised three field regiments, one Artillery Fusilier Battalion, 13 garrison (fortress) artillery districts, and a central ordnance depot, the *Feldzeugamt*. In addition there existed small contingents of technical troops and auxiliary services. Infantry clearly was the largest arm, while cavalry had declined since the days of Maria Theresa when it had constituted between a quarter to one-third of the army. Artillery was the smallest of the three combat arms. On paper the war strength of the Austrian military establishment exceeded 359,000, but losses incurred during the Turkish War had not been made good and to save money the army had been reduced. At the outbreak of hostilities there were but 230,000 effectives.[46]

Infantry, variously designated as German (including Bohemian, Moravian and Tyrolean units), Hungarian (including Croatian and Transylvanian units), Italian, Walloon, or *Grenzer* regiments, differed in composition. The German regiments had two field battalions with six Fusilier companies each and a garrison battalion with four companies. Including a detachment of gunners and infantry to operate the three 6-pounders issued to each battalion, nominal strength stood at 4575 all ranks. Hungarian regiments were larger, three field battalions and one garrison battalion with an establishment of 5508, including again the assigned 'line' artillery. In 1792 neither type was up to full strength. Fusilier companies with a war establishment of four officers and 230 men commonly had only three officers and 120 men. In addition, each German or Hungarian regiment had a Grenadier 'division,' two companies considered elite units, dressed in high and heavy bearskin hats, which frequently were combined with other divisions into composite Grenadier battalions commanded by a lieutenant colonel. *Grenzer* regiments comprised two field battalions, six companies each, with a regimental headquarter, 256 sharpshooters armed with an over-and-under rifle/shotgun, and an artillery detachment with three 3-pounders. When regiments departed for foreign service, there remained a local reserve organized into two *Landes-Defensions Divisionen.*[47]

Except for the *Grenzer* sharpshooters whose weapons later were withdrawn, most foot soldiers were armed either with Model 1774 or the Model 1784 musket, both shooting an 18.3 mm ball, and a triangular bayonet. German and *Grenz* infantry carried the Fusilier sabre with a 43 cm blade, while Hungarian infantry, Grenadiers, and all non-commissioned officers were equipped with the longer, 63 cm blade, Grenadier sabre. Personal equipment included a cartridge box, a haversack, one waterbottle for every two men and one tent and one copper kettle for every five men. Each soldier carried 60 rounds of ammunition with 36 additional rounds carried by the 30 packhorses allotted to each battalion. There was one wagon for each company and approximately four wagons and several carts, the exact number fluctuating, for each battalion.

In the Austrian army, light infantry missions, scouting and skirmishing, commonly were entrusted to the *Grenzer*, though there were complaints that training them as line infantry had spoiled their natural aptitude for these duties. As Fieldmarshal Lacy put it in a memorandum dated 5 December 1782, 'it must be decided once and for all whether the *Grenzer* are to be considered regular troops or a mere militia. If they are considered regulars they must be properly exercised and trained and this will give them very little time to devote to agriculture.'[48] Lacy, of course, conceived military efficiency not in terms of light infantry, but in the framework of linear tactics. Nonetheless, training and organization of the *Grenzer* continued to conform with that of the line and their combat performance declined. After the first campaign against the French Revolution even General Klein, a strong advocate of the Military Border institution, wondered why as late as the Seven Years' War the semi-irregulars of the Border had provided 'a much better light infantry than the present regulated and drilled *Grenzer.*'[49] To compensate, there were a number of free corps, usually raised at the beginning of a war. Still in existence in 1792 was the Tyrolean *Jäger* Free Corps, two battalions totalling 950 men, the Le Loup Free Corps, about 1000 men, and several smaller units.[50] Soldiers unfit for regular field duties were posted to the garrison regiments, the cadre formations of the staff troops, one infantry regiment and one of Dragoons, left over in 1792 from the Turkish War, or to the Cordon Detachments, an organization controlling internal boundaries to catch deserters. These units were only partially equipped and not considered combat elements.

The mounted arm, about 40,000 strong, was organized in 35 regiments: two regiments of Carabiniers, nine of Cuirassiers, six German Dragoons, one staff Dragoons, six German *Chevaulegers*, one Walloon *Chevaulegers*, eight Hungarian Hussars, one Szekler *Grenz* Hussars, and one newly formed regiment of *Uhlans*. Because of the time required to train horsemen, mounted regiments were kept near full war establishment. Composition varied from time to time, though normally Carabiniers and Hungarian Hussar regiments comprised four 'divisions' of two squadrons each, while the remaining units had but three divisions. The *Uhlans*, not fully organized, had only two divisions. Heavy cavalry, Carabiniers and Cuirassiers, squadrons numbered 150 all ranks; Dragoons and the light cavalry, *Chevaulegers*, and Hussars had squadrons of between 170 and 180 men. Overall, the cavalry was in the process of reorganization early in 1792.

All troopers were armed with cut-and-thrust weapons as well as firearms. The heavy cavalry carried a long one-edged sword, Hussars had a distinctive curved sabre, while the remainder carried the light cavalry sabre. Two pistols in saddle holsters were general issue, and the German regiments as well as the Hussars also carried the Model 1770 cavalry carbine. Early in 1792, six men in every squadron of the carbine armed regiments were issued a short-barrelled rifled, *Cavalleriestutzen*, the Model 1789 firing a 17.6 mm ball. The *Uhlans* carried 13-foot lances.[51] Constituting the main shock element, Carabiniers and Cuirassiers, heavy men on heavy horses, retained armour, a half cuirass. Every trooper was issued one waterbottle, but cavalry carried no cooking utensils, which with the tents were carried on its packhorses, thirty-one for each squadron. Regimental staffs, about 30 all ranks, had several carts and all officers were allowed individual packhorses.

Artillery had no tactical formations in peacetime. The three field regiments served as administrative and disciplinary bodies. In war, their officers and men, 9282 all ranks, were sent to direct and serve the battalion pieces, line guns, of the infantry regiments. The *Bombardeur Corps* and the Artillery Fusiliers, together with personnel detailed from the fortress artillery, manned the light and heavy artillery reserve. These were formed into 'position' batteries, usually mixed with four guns and two howitzers. Also assigned to the light artillery reserve were the mobile *Kavallerie Batterien*, not horse artillery but light 6-pounders with officers and non-commissioned officers mounted while the crews straddled an elongated caisson, the famous *Wurst-Wagen*. The other guns, line or reserve, were foot artillery and lacked organic transport. In the field, draft horses and drivers were provided by the *Fuhrwesencorps*, at best an unsatisfactory arrangement.

Austrian artillery material consisted of 24, 18, 12, 6, and 3-pounder cannon, 7 and 10-pounder howitzers, while massive 30, 60, and 100-pounder Coehorn mortars still remained in the inventory. The heavy mortars and some of the heavier cannon were iron, the lighter guns were bronze, a mixture of ten parts tin and 100 parts copper. When introduced back in 1753, the range of Austrian ordnance probably had been the finest in Europe, but now was outmatched by the corresponding French 4, 8, and 12-pounders which threw heavier projectiles. While there was little difference in muzzle velocities, the French guns outranged the lighter pieces and their heavier shot had more hitting power. Ranges of field guns and howitzers varied according to elevation, loads, wind conditions, and the type of projectile fired, but the practical outer limits for the 12-pounders were 1200 to 900 paces, and up to 800 paces for the lighter pieces employing solid round shot. Howitzer shell had a shorter range, while case shot (canister), the name from the container of thin metal fllled with balls of various sizes, served for anti-personnel work at shorter ranges.[52]

Strategy and battle tactics

Austrian strategy conformed to the prevailing school of military thought that tried to reduce the conduct of war to a methodical, precise, and predictable pattern.[53] Moreover, it was held that in war against western European armies the issue of victory or defeat no longer depended primarily on the ability of the commanders or the quality of the troops, but, to a large extent, was a question of coincidence and logistics. Therefore Fieldmarshal Lacy advocated the so-called 'cordon system,' a defensive deployment attempting to be equally strong on all sectors of the front, reinforced by fortresses such as Theresienstadt, Josefstadt, and Königgratz in Bohemia. Moreover, the strategy appealed to Lacy's orderly mind because it left control entirely in the hands of the army commander. In a very large army a senior general sometimes might command a detachment,

Armee Abtheilung, but he had no independence and initiative was discouraged. For this reason, though personal rivalries should not be discounted, it was opposed by Fieldmarshal Laudon and this split the officer corps into opposing factions, *Lacianer* and *Laudonianer*, a rift continuing into the early years of the French Wars. Overall, the cordon system was brittle and already had failed against the Turks in 1788–9; it would prove even less effective against the mobile French revolutionary armies because it left the army outnumbered at any point this enemy chose to concentrate.

The tactical counterpart to the cordon system was the linear order of battle perfected by Frederick the Great of Prussia and widely imitated throughout Europe. The Austrian battle formation consisted of two parallel lines of battalions with each unit assigned a permanent place according to seniority. Each line, called a *Treffen*, was subdivided into a right, centre, and left. Command of the right wing was held by the most senior general, command on the left by a junior. Almost invariably infantry, supported by the line guns, was deployed in the middle to produce massed fire, while cavalry was placed at the wings with the primary mission to counter the enemy's horse. A third line of battalions, the *Corps de Reserve*, usually smaller than the first two *Treffen*, was stationed several hundred paces to the rear. The artillery reserve guns were emplaced in positions chosen beforehand and usually not moved during battle.

Battle formations of six to eight regiments in each line, with three to four cavalry regiments at the wings, required a frontage of 10,000 to 12,000 paces. Because such a wide front could not be controlled effectively by the army commander, positions in line were fixed by detailed written orders issued to each subordinate commander. In broken terrain, movement was difficult and cooperation between the two *Treffen* and the reserve sometimes impossible. The linear order was best on the defensive, but if there was a prolonged forward movement, columns could be employed until the advance guard, normally light infantry and cavalry, made contact with the enemy. Then lines were formed and to facilitate this, careful attention was given to keep the columns aligned with each other.[54]

Tactics of the individual combat arms were determined by regulations, modified by the army commanders at the outset of a campaign. Regulations for the infantry dated to 1769 and made the battalion the main manoeuvre unit. Though bayonets were fixed at all times, controlled fire was stressed. Highly complicated, the regulations recognized no less than ten types of fire for all possible, and some not very likely, occasions. The main element was the controlled volley fired by battalions, companies, and platoons. Normally each battalion had three divisions each of eight platoons. Firing in each division started with the right-wing platoon and then alternated between the wings ending in the centre. The platoon or the half-company volley was the most common, battalion volleys rare because there was concern to have some fire available against sudden cavalry charges.[55]

Cavalry operated according to the regulations of 1784 that had slightly amended the earlier regulations of 1765 and 1769. There were complicated rules for cavalry firefights, normally executed in two lines, though Austrian cavalry, light or heavy, considered shock rather than fire action as its primary mission. For combat with cold steel three ranks were formed with troopers closed up knee to knee. The charge was made with speed gradually building up from a slow trot to the gallop. At 80 paces from the enemy, the commander ordered the trumpeter to sound 'Alarm' while division commanders shouted '*Marsch! Marsch!*' Now the gallop became all out. Troopers raised sabres above their heads and fell on the enemy. The 1784 regulations for the first time discussed fencing instead of the simple downward stroke and also mentioned a massed charge by several mounted regiments, though they provided no details. According to Colonel Mack, able to speak with authority on this point, in 1789 there were few, if any, squadrons which could gallop a couple of hundred yards without becoming disordered and generally, despite its numerical superiority and the quality of its mounts, the performance of the Austrian horse in the wars of the French Revolution would be disappointing.[56]

No specific rules governed artillery in combat. Line guns were used as single pieces and during an advance were pushed or dragged slightly ahead of the line, about 15 paces, and fired after the infantry had volleyed. On occasion, heavier guns, 12-pounders and 10-pounder howitzers, were positioned in line to add weight to the fire. This had been tried with good effect in some engagements of the War of the Bavarian Succession (1778–9) and was repeated during the wars against France. Though well trained and efficient, the Austrian artillery was handicapped by pieces with projectiles, weight for weight, intrinsically inferior to that of the French, and diluted its fire by distributing most of its guns in penny-packages.

All in all, though the Austrian army had seen much action against Prussians, Turks, and Belgians, by 1792 it had become too defensive minded. The lessons of the closing years of the Seven Years' War, when Prussian infantry repeatedly had been beaten back when attempting to storm field entrenchments, had left the impression that the defence was the naturally stronger form of combat, an attitude not only held by the senior officers but absorbed by many of the subalterns. Beyond that, the army had become overly pedantic and schematic. Archduke Charles later commented that while the organization and the fighting instructions for all arms and branches were well thought out, 'their spirit had become superannuated and replaced by the dead hand of regulations.'[57] Trained in the rigid techniques of eighteenth-century warfare, the army would be repeatedly mauled by the more aggressive and elastic forces of the French Revolution and Napoleon. There was nothing wrong with the Austrian rank and file, but their commanders were thinking in terms fast becoming obsolete.

II

The War of the First Coalition and the Emergence of Archduke Charles, 1792–7

AUSTRIA'S first war against revolutionary France lasted for almost five years. During much of this time her army fought with only little support. Although Prussia joined Austria in June 1792, followed in 1793 by Sardinia, Naples, Spain, and the minor states of the Holy Roman Empire, with Britain, Holland and Portugal, this First Coalition was divided in war aims and lacked strategic coordination. At the outset a concerted offensive might have swept the disorganized French armies from the field, but the allies committed only a fraction of their forces. Austria and Prussia retained considerable forces to deal with Poland and to watch each other and Russia, while Britain's small army was mainly engaged overseas. The other states counted for little. This allowed France to recover from the confusion of the revolution. By 1793 the government of the 'Terror' created a new military system, a mass citizen army, led by aggressive leaders exploiting its superior strategic and tactical mobility.

In 1793–4 the French regained the offensive, drove the allies out of the Low Countries and crossed the Rhine. The following year the British evacuated the continent, Prussia made peace, followed by Spain and most of the minor German states. Only Austria and Sardinia were left, while Britain, one historian concluded, 'could remain at war with France in Europe only so long as Austria was willing to keep her armies in the field.'[1] In 1795, aided by renewed turmoil in France, Austria managed to hold the Upper Rhine and the Alps, but the next year the new French government, the Directory, launched concerted offensives. In Germany, Archduke Charles, emerging as a major figure in 1796, defeated the French, but in Italy, regarded as a secondary theatre, Napoleon Bonaparte burst through the Austro-Sardinian cordon, shattered the Sardinians and drove the Austrians into Mantua. After defeating four attempts to relieve the fortress which capitulated in February 1797, Napoleon exploited his success to move east and thus threatening Vienna. Rushed to the disintegrating front, Charles was unable to stop his advance. On 18 April 1797, Austria signed the Preliminary Peace of Leoben, followed in October by the Peace of Campo Formio. Austria ceded Belgium, regarded as a strategic liability, recognized the new Cisalpine Republic and French control of the left bank of the Rhine, but in return received Venice and its possessions, an actual accession of territory and population.[2]

Though defeated, the Austrian army emerged from the war with credit. Like all allied armies, its formalized evolutions and elderly generals often had been unequal to the republican armies with their emphasis on mobility, flexibility, and individual initiative. Still, the common soldiers had fought with courage and determination and for all its shortcomings 'the most formidable army which the French had to face in the last years of the eighteenth century and the first few of the nineteenth was that of Austria.'[3]

Mobilization of the Habsburg army

Fearing complications over Poland, Leopold had ordered a small increase in the number of men under arms in February 1792, but mobilization in earnest began only on the eve of war with France. The mobilization scheme had been conceived by Lacy in 1772. Sixteen days were required to notify all regiments and commands. After that, depending on the type of mobilization, regiments either moved out on their peace establishment or first were placed on a war footing. In the first instance, line regiments were supposed to be ready three days after receiving orders and *Grenzer* units within seven to 15 days. In the second case one to three months were required, though it was believed that most units would be ready within 35 days.

To bring a regiment up to war footing required manpower, supplies and transport. Officers were posted or appointed, men recalled from leave or the reserve and new recruits mustered. Enlisted men were issued new boots and uniforms and each regiment of foot drew 200 pairs of boots, 75 pairs of gaiters, 200 pants, and 800 shirts from mobilization stores. Tentage comprised 534 five-man tents per line regiment. All this required a regimental train of 16 wagons, one field forge, and 110 draft and pack horses for each foot regiment. Cavalry transport allocations were smaller and, depending on the size of the unit, varied between five and nine carts. On campaign, field wagons remained with the regimental staff; packhorses carrying tentage, cooking utensils, and extra ammunition moved with the field battalions. The transport scale was not excessive, but mobility was impaired by the officers who took from two to six riding horses into the field and in addition were permitted their own tents, carts and unlimited baggage.[4] As was contemporary practice the army moved slowly, marching no more than six hours a day.

In 1792, the *Hofkriegsrat* ordered mobilization on a full war scale. With most of the army still stationed near the Turkish border or facing Galicia, major reinforcements could not reach the Rhine until early July. Moreover, battalions and squadrons alone did not make a field army. Staff, technical and medical units had to be formed or expanded, the reserve artillery had to be organized into batteries and provided with transport, supply arrangements had to be made, field depots established, and contractors engaged. All this required time and money and strained the military administration.

Supply was the greatest problem, never adequately resolved. In the field, the daily allowance was between one-and-a-half and two pounds of bread, with loaves prepared in large brick ovens at the main magazines or in efficient mobile iron ovens at the smaller field magazines and with the supply columns. The bread ration was free, but soldiers had to club together to buy meat from the regimental butcher, a contract civilian, supervised by the commissary. Cattle depots were maintained by each army and, if necessary, the price was to be subsidized so that it did not exceed 5 *Kreutzer* a pound when sold to the rank and file. Requisitioning was permitted but strictly controlled, and the army did a good deal of foraging, especially in enemy territory, where procuring feed for their own mounts and denying it to the enemy was considered an important objective.[5] The system tended to break down under the stress of frequent movement or if the army stayed too long in a given area and exhausted its resources. Already in the late summer of 1792, Archduke Charles complained that the troops lacked food, straw, tents and clothing. 'Our misery,' he wrote, 'is great.'[6]

By contrast, mobilization of the staff elements was easier. Given the great number of unemployed senior officers, forming the Great and Small General Staffs was easy, albeit complicated by a great deal of place hunting. Already in existence was the engineering staff. Because of the importance of fortress warfare in this period, the *k.k. Ingenieurs Corps*, headed in 1792 by Director General Fieldmarshal

Count Pellegrini, was always kept at full strength, ten major generals, six colonels, 11 lieutenant colonels, ten majors, 26 captains, and 106 senior and junior lieutenants.[7] The corps controlled two battalion-size technical units, the Sappers stationed at Theresienstadt fortress in Bohemia and the *Mineur Corps* at nearby Josephstadt. Sappers were trained to build fortifications while miners were used in the defence of and the attack on fortifications. A third unit, the pioneers, assisted in their work, but rated below the sappers and miners in skill, was activated only in war time. The first of several pioneer battalions was not raised until November 1792. Finally, there was a battalion of pontooneers who in peacetime were responsible to the civilian *Oberstschiffamt* in Vienna.

Finding officers was less difficult than providing replacements for the rank and file. In 1792, only 5500 replacements were available, and though the situation improved for the next two years, as the pace of war accelerated there were barely enough to make up for losses and not enough to raise new formations.[8] Contributing was the general inadequacy of the medical services. When the wars began in 1792 the state of military medicine had barely changed in a century and medical services everywhere found themselves outmatched by the greatly increased pace of operations, unprecedented casualties, and high disease rates. In peacetime permanent military hospitals were maintained in large garrisons; on campaign field hospitals followed the army. Hospital attendants were chosen from semi-invalids, soldiers' wives, if they had no dependent children or were 'not too young and attractive.' In addition, there were *Loco-Hospitäle*, established in towns and villages near the site of the battle, where care was to be provided by local inhabitants. One Austrian officer patient who survived remembered that 'in the cold of winter men lay on cold stones, without care. There were no doctors or regular attendants and no senior officer took any measure to deal with this desperate situation.'[9] Little wonder that post-operative complications and contagious diseases killed more men than did enemy action.

In battle, casualty stations were established behind the wings of the army, manned by two staff surgeons and their assistants. Surgical procedures were limited to amputation of shattered limbs, though if there was time, surgeons might probe for and extract bullets, shell fragments, and other foreign objects. Standing orders required that 'officers, especially the seriously wounded, were to be treated first, thereafter the rank and file.'[10] In theory, senior surgeons were attached to each regiment and assistant surgeons were to be distributed down to company levels, but in practice there were far too few trained medical men.

To improve medical services, in 1785 Joseph II had founded a medical-surgical military academy, the Josephinium, in Vienna. Its director, Anton Edler von Bienenburg, also functioned as *Protochirugus*, that is chief medical officer of the army. He supervised some 120 staff surgeons, who had to be graduates of an approved medical school, and about the same number of regimental surgeons who had to meet the same educational requirement. Senior surgeons, regulations stated, had to be of good character, able to enforce general troop hygiene, and 'well versed in general medicine, especially anatomy, and trained to apply all internal and external medications, execute all major surgical procedures, and be able to supervise the battalion and company surgeons in their charge.'[11]

Battalion surgeons, *Ober-Chirugen*, and company surgeons, *Unter-Chirugen*, were not graduate doctors. At best battalion surgeons had a master's degree, while sub-surgeons, normally enlisted men, had received some on-the-job training. At that surgeons or physicians were not rated as commissioned officers but as military officials and appeared near the very bottom of the army list. Performance of the medical service in the field was poor. There never were enough surgeons or attendants, while physicians were described as afraid of contagion and close contact with their patients. At times, the service was saved from total collapse only by the assistance given by civilians, above all by the religious nursing orders. In close contact with the enemy this was not enough and the *Militär-Hof-Commission* admitted in 1795 that 'human misery exceeded the boundaries of the permissible.'[12]

The forces of the Holy Roman Empire

Although the emperor was at war this did not mean that the 300-odd states, principalities, duchies, and others, comprising the Holy Roman Empire automatically were at war too. The imperial dignity was elective and executive power, such as it was, was vested in the imperial Diet, in 'permanent session' at Ratisbon since 1661. Each state had the right to conduct its own foreign policy and make its own alliances, provided that these were not directed against the emperor or the empire. If the Diet declared a *Reichskrieg*, the 'armed estates,' that is the states maintaining military forces, were to furnish contingents according to a formula set by the imperial war constitution of 1681. The embodied *Reichsarmee* was commanded by an appointed *Reichsgeneralfeldmarschall*, assisted by a *Reichsgeneralk-riegskommissar* and a coterie of generals and commissioners, all chosen with due attention to parity between Protestants and Catholics.[13]

Although on paper the collective forces of the empire came to over 600,000, not counting the various militia bodies, if Austria and Prussia were excluded, only the Bavarian, Saxon, Hanoverian and electoral Hessian contingents were of much consequence. At that, the Bavarian army had fallen into a bad state, most of its regiments were skeleton units and its cavalry without horses. Moreover, most units from the larger states were designated as *Haustruppen* and exempt from imperial service. The quotas set in 1681 were small, only 28,000 men, though the Diet could call for greater numbers by declaring that a *duplum* or a *triplum* was needed. Larger numbers did not mean greater combat effectiveness. The various mini-armies had different training, weapons and supply systems. Officers commonly held inflated rank and were reluctant to obey 'foreign' commanders. Finally, the various princes and princelings wanted the imperial army to remain independent and they were unwilling to co-operate with the Austrians or for that matter the Prussians.[14]

In November 1792 the Diet resolved to call a triplum with all contingents to be ready by February 1793. Little was done and on 11 March 1793, the emperor called on the rulers to 'consider the present danger and to act promptly.' The appeal fell on deaf ears. Although there was no imperial army, the Diet declared war in March and empowered Francis to name a commander. He selected the veteran Fieldmarshal Josias Prince of Coburg-Saalfeld, already appointed to command allied forces in Belgium. Though Coburg was a popular choice, a German and Protestant, the imperial estates remained passive and only British subsidy payments stirred a few states from their lethargy.

The first campaigns, 1792–3

While Austria mobilized, the French had assembled three armies on their eastern frontier. Composed of demoralized regulars and untrained volunteers, these were poor troops, but Dumouriez none-theless pressed for an immediate invasion of the Austrian Netherlands where he expected to be welcomed as a liberator. Three French columns, 34,000 men in all, invaded on 29 April 1792. The Austrian defenders comprised 44 battalions and 38 squadrons, about 50,000, commanded by 79-year-old Fieldmarshal Blasius Baron Bender. Most of this force, however, was tied down in garrison and internal security duties, leaving only 20,000 men in a cordon along the frontier. Encountering the Austrians, the invaders panicked and disintegrated. There followed a pause during which command passed to Fieldmarshal Albert Duke of Sachsen-Teschen, governor-general of the Austrian Netherlands, an indifferent soldier, but well connected at court and adoptive father to Archduke Charles, the younger brother of Francis.

The French debacle convinced the allies that there was little to fear. Preparations for a major campaign were allowed to drag. In any case, Austria and Prussia were at odds and distracted by Russian activities in Poland. In June 1792, Francis and Frederick William II of Prussia decided on an advance on Paris. The plan was to invade with three armies. Fieldmarshal Duke Ferdinand of Brunswick, reputed to be the first general in Europe, was to move from Coblenz; 15,000 Austrians under Clerfayt based in Belgium were to advance south on the Prussian right flank, while 20,000 Austrians under *Feldzeugmeister* Prince Hohenlohe-Kirchberg were to move on the Prussian left flank. Duke Albert was to advance on the Belgian frontier while a contingent of French emigrés was to operate in Alsace.

From the outset the alliance showed stress. Although the Austrian contribution fell short by some 40,000 men promised, Francis resented Brunswick's role as overall commander and instructed Hohenlohe to take care that this 'will not in any way diminish our role' and that he alone remained responsible for his army.[15] For that matter Brunswick utterly disapproved of his mission. Although the allied armies were superior to the indisciplined and not very numerous French, age had led him to exaggerate all difficulties. He opposed intervention in France, loathed the French royalists, and distrusted the Austrians. The Austrian commanders reciprocated his distrust and felt equally uneasy about venturing deep into France. Moving at a snail's pace, one month was wasted getting to the border which was crossed on 19 August 1792. Longwy and Verdun, two border fortresses, capitulated. The duke, however, became hesitant, wishing he could withdraw to winter quarters.

On 20 September, Brunswick's column came up against the combined French armies, 36,000 strong, standing at Valmy and a hundred miles from Paris. Following an indecisive exchange of artillery fire, the duke halted the engagement, and ten days later he withdrew his army back to Germany. His actions strained relations with his allies, though the Austrians too had shown little enthusiasm.

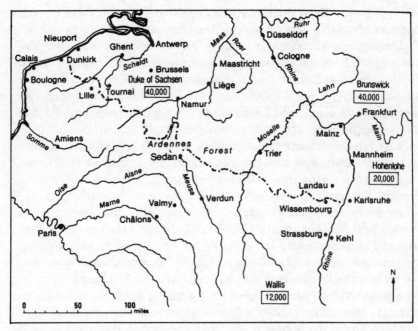

Theatre of operations, 1792–5

In the north Duke Albert had advanced only a few miles to invest Lille, while Hohenlohe had kept up with Brunswick but failed to join him as planned. In October he retired to his base in Luxemburg.

The allied repulse had enormous political and military consequences. The day after Valmy the newly elected National Convention in Paris decreed the monarchy abolished and proclaimed France a republic. Militarily, the retreat of the allied armies revitalized the French forces. From Alsace, French troops captured Speyer on 30 September, Worms four days later. On 21 October, Mainz fell into French hands and a detachment occupied Frankfurt for five weeks. The appearance of the French shattered the morale of the local governments who refused to fight. At the same time, encountering little resistance, French troops took Savoy and Nice from Sardinia.

Substantially reinforced, Dumouriez returned to the Austrian Netherlands in mid-October, forced Duke Albert to retire from Lille and to look to the defence of Belgium. with most of his forces in a 70-mile cordon along the frontier, the duke concentrated 14 battalions and 16 squadrons with 54 reserve guns, to block the main road to Brussels. On 6 November, Dumouriez, with some 35,000 foot, 3000 horse, and 100 guns, attacked his position along a ridge near

46

Jemappes and forced them to retreat towards Cologne. Antwerp and Namur capitulated, and only Maastricht remained in Austrian hands.

Heartened by success, an exultant Convention voted on 19 November 'to give fraternal support to all people who wish to regain their liberty.' Then, in a show of defiance, it tried and executed the former king in January 1793. On 1 March, the Convention declared war on Britain and Holland, and on 9 March 1793 gratuitously added Spain to its enemies. But the Convention overreached itself. Soon it was split by bitter factional disputes, while a forced levy of 300,000 men to replace losses and time-expired volunteers provoked opposition, escalating by spring into armed resistance in southern and western France. By spring it appeared that France was disintegrating. The allies, however, failed to grasp their opportunity. In January 1793, Prussia and Russia agreed on the Second Polish Partition. In Vienna, Count Philip Cobenzl, an advocate of the Prussian alliance, was ousted and replaced by the anti-Prussia Baron Thugut. The new Minister brought new momentum to Austria's effort against France, he also exerted considerable, and not always beneficial, influence on strategy. Immediately, however, Poland became France's most effective ally. Greed for her remaining territory kept Russia from actively joining the Coalition, while Prussia steadily withdrew men from the Rhine for service on the Vistula. And Austria, deeply suspicious, maintained 70,000 troops to watch her northern frontier.

Even so, the Austrians and Prussians took the offensive early in 1793. The main army was entrusted to the Prince of Coburg, 70,000 men including 14,000 cavalry. It was to move across the Roer, relieve Maastricht, and then take Brussels. Brunswick, with 15,000 Prussians and some 20,000 Austrians, was to retake Mainz and clear the Palatinate, while in Alsace an Austrian corps commanded by the septuagenarian, but active and resolute, Fieldmarshal Dagobert Count Wurmser, was to breach the French fortifications to open a route into the interior of France.

Coburg clearly had the main mission, but the aged prince, a sound conventional officer, more intent on preserving his army than destroying the enemy, was not the man to conduct an energetic offensive. The same was true of his chief of staff, 40-year-old Colonel Karl Leiberich Baron Mack, a commoner enobled for bravery at Belgrade. Regarded as the 'most scientific soldier' in Europe, Mack, too, espoused the fashionable system of strategy in which the main objective was not the destruction of the enemy but control of certain topographical points. He designed intricate offensive movements by divergent columns, though he often underrated the opponent's reaction and was completely lost when his complicated schemes did not work out. For all that, he enjoyed a great reputation in the Austrian service and became highly regarded by the British.[16] Also present was the 21-year-old Archduke Charles, holding command as a major general.

The French had divided their forces to invade Holland. On 1 March, Coburg defeated their right wing at Aldenhoven and a few days later relieved Maastricht. Then, however, he halted, complaining that he lacked 'uniforms, field stores, recruits, magazine, money and even reserve artillery.'[17] The delay gave the French time to concentrate and on 18 March, Coburg with 44 battalions and 74 squadrons, 33,000 foot and 10,000 horse, met Dumouriez with 35,000 infantry and 6000 cavalry. The Battle of Neerwinden was hard fought. At one point Charles and Mack had to persuade their commander not to break off combat. In the end Dumouriez was defeated and had to evacuate Belgium. Worried about the personal consequences of defeat, he tried to rally his troops against Paris while negotiating for a convention with Coburg. The Austrian marshal would have liked to come to an agreement. His political superiors, however, disavowed any deal and Dumouriez's troops refused to follow him.

With his hopes for an internal French solution dashed, Coburg had to come up with a plan to continue the war. Meanwhile, a quarrel about rewards handed out after Neerwinden had led to Mack's temporary resignation and replacement by Hohenlohe. The campaign plan which Coburg and Hohenlohe reluctantly produced on 1 May epitomized the Austrian preoccupation with cordon deployment and fortress warfare. By mid-May Coburg expected to have 92,000 men available, 8000 Prussians, 50,000 Austrians, 14,000 Dutch, 10,000 Hanoverians, 3000 Hessians and 7000 British. Another 5000 Austrians and 8000 Hessians were expected in late June. Coburg proposed to first reduce Condé, then use 52,000 to lay siege to Valenciennes, and after the fall of this fortress, expected under the formal rules of siege warfare by the end of July, detach 10,000 to mask Lille, while the main force, 50,000, marched to besiege Dunkirk. Meanwhile a cordon of 40,000 men was to mask a front of 75 miles from Maubeuge to Ostend.

Condé and Valenciennes were duly taken and in a series of minor actions disciplined Austrian volleys and cavalry charges drove back the French. If Coburg had not wasted his time in formal sieges he might have broken into France, though Britain and Holland, both providing subsidies, were chiefly interested in the complete occupation of Belgium. Also in July, Austro-Prussian forces under Brunswick recaptured Mainz, while Wurmser fought with some success in Alsace. By the end of summer, however, the Committee of Public Safety established by the Convention managed to bring some order out of chaos and created mass citizen armies. By this time, dissension between Austria and Prussia had become so deep as to preclude further large-scale operations. Time had run out for the allies.

A new style of war

Out of bitter fraticidal struggles, the French had forged an effective military system. The replacement problem was solved by the famous *levée en masse* of 23 August 1793, creating national conscription. For the first time in modern history there arose a mass citizen army with a stake in the state and willing to fight for it. Conscripts rapidly swelled the army's ranks. By September 100,000 men were available for operations in Flanders and by the end of the year there were over 500,000 men in the French field armies, providing numerical superiority over the professional armies of the Coalition. Modified by the Jourdan Law of 1798, conscription remained the basis of France's military manpower structure for the remainder of the wars.

In Lazare Carnot, the Committee of Public Safety found a member who became the 'organizer of victory.' He assumed organization, armament, and strategic direction of the new armies, and brought new men – Jourdan, Hoche, Pichegru and Bonaparte among others – into command positions. Carnot and his generals discarded the faith in the superiority of the defence. Lacking cumbersome supply trains, the French lived off the land, bivouacked in the open, and so became capable of more rapid movement. Combining the striking power of mass and mobility, and with casualties easily replaced by conscription, they adopted Carnot's instructions to 'act offensively and in mass ... and to pursue the enemy until he is utterly destroyed.' Capabilities of the republican armies were further improved when early in 1794, the *amalgame* combined conscript battalions with the remaining veteran units into demi-brigades, which in turn formed all arms combat divisions.[18]

After the Seven Years' War the French developed sophisticated tactics, codified in the Manual of 1791, which prescribed both line and column; the line, three deep for fire action and assault, the column for the approach and for bayonet charges on fortified positions. By 1792, however, the new volunteers no longer were able to operate according to the manual. They temporarily abandoned most formal tactics. March columns were used to bring the troops into battle. Then, to overcome the massed fire of infantry in line, the most daring elements went forward as skirmishers, *tirailleurs*, on occasion supported by boldly advanced artillery. After fire had shaken the line, the remainder of the force rushed the enemy in a loose attack column. An alternative method was to fight entirely in open order, relying on individual fire and movement, personal initiative and use of terrain. These were the tactics employed in 1793–4. Of course, lacking cavalry support, a branch in which the republic was inferior, French brigades surging forward repeatedly were driven back by disciplined volleys, the bayonet, or cavalry charges. As the republican troops gained more experience and discipline, they adopted a more flexible combination of skirmishers, line, and column, supported by artillery, the *ordre mixte* later preferred by Napoleon.[19]

The new style of war, based on a transformation in the role of infantry, depended not only on military innovation but required political and social changes which the armies of the Coalition, recruited from a narrow social base and relying on harsh discipline, were unable to achieve. The Austrian service remained tied to the regulations of 1769. Infantry remained rigidly divided into 'light' and 'line' units and the light were treated as accessories, useful for the 'little war' of outposts but apart from the formal battle line. This did not solve the problem of countering the French skirmishers. Though line volleys and bayonet charges could drive the skirmishers back, this disarrayed the close order line which became vulnerable to the shock of the French columns. The situation was aggravated by the faulty organization of artillery. Except for the puny regimental guns, ordnance was massed into an artillery reserve and generally kept too far back to do much good. Proper handling, such as the provisional battery formed by Lieutenant Smola at Neerwinden, positioned forward to support the line with canister, were exceptional and caused much comment. Finally, Austrian generals would not abandon their reliance on a defensive strategy and on formally besieging any fortress which might threaten their communications at a future date.

Republican victories and the Austrian army, 1793–5

In the autumn of 1793 the tide turned against the allies. Republican authority had been restored throughout most of France; new armies were in the field. On 8–9 September the Army of the North defeated a British-Dutch-Austrian force at Hondschoote and lifted the siege of Dunkirk. The next month, on instructions from Carnot, General

Jourdan managed to concentrate 45,000 men south of Maubeuge where on 15–16 October he defeated Coburg and relieved the besieged fortress. Further south, heavily outnumbered Prussians repulsed the French at Pirmasens in September, but at the end of the month King Frederick William, convinced that Austria was behind growing unrest in Poland, left the army and scaled down operations. In Alsace, Wurmser breached the Wissembourg line, but Pichegru commanding the Army of the Moselle and Hoche that of the Rhine, drove the Austrians back across the river in late December.

For 1794, Carnot intended to mount a series of offensives to break the Coalition. His primary objective was the Austrian army in Belgium and Germany. After 18 months of war that army was in poor shape. The supply system had failed and the troops lacked food, fuel, and shelter. The Belgians were unwilling to furnish and Coburg was reluctant to requisition supplies even though, as he complained in February, some regiments 'have been without bread for several days and two contractors have been driven to suicide.'[20] Archduke Charles, promoted to *Feldmarschall Leutnant*, while also serving as governor general of the Netherlands after Neerwinden, painted an even gloomier picture. The troops, he wrote to his imperial brother, lacked uniforms, rations, and decent hospitals. Morale was low and the officers were as discontented as the rank and file. Too many promotions had gone to the well-connected on the staff of commanders. There was resentment against staff officers lacking combat exposure. Officers of the Kinsky *Chevaulegers*, he wrote, 'have sworn that the first such gentleman who delivers an order to attack will be forced to take part in the charge.' The army, continued the archduke, was becoming disaffected. Rollin, the emperor's adjutant general, was blamed for its troubles and the officers wanted him removed. Only the venerable Lacy was acceptable.[21]

The emperor cannot have been pleased with his brother's foray into army politics, but he gave a mild answer. To dampen dissensions, he announced that he would accompany the army in the field. In February 1794, Mack, who had managed to re-establish his influence and had been promoted to major general, was sent to London to announce the emperor's intention and to drum up support for a plan of operations that had 220,000 men marching on Paris with another 120,000 in a cordon from the Meuse to the Channel. As part of the plan, all French frontier fortresses were to be reduced and this called for a huge siege train.[22] No such numbers or siege train were available, especially when in March the Prussians threatened to leave the Coalition altogether and were persuaded to stay only by the

promise of increased British subsidies. Even so, they did not participate in the campaign in Flanders.

Reappointed quartermaster general to Coburg, Mack elaborated
army instructions in April 1794. He conceded that the enemy had a
large numerical superiority, though he discounted it because of what
he claimed the 'miserable quality of French leaders and troops.' The
enemy, the instructions ordered, should be attacked at all times and
in all circumstances. Even when the army was in entrenchments, at
least one half of the foot and the entire horse should be prepared to
attack. Moreover, Mack suggested that the three-rank formation
prescribed in the 1769 regulations could be modified. The low quality
of the enemy, he maintained, did not warrant a deep formation,
rather, to prevent being outflanked by the more numerous adversary,
the third rank of each battalion should be utilized to extend the battle
line. And if there was no danger of being outflanked, it could be used
in the attack. Finally he exhorted senior officers to take the tactical
initiative. 'Night actions,' he wrote, 'against an enemy lacking
experience, discipline, real steadiness, and courage, will always
succeed.' Such attacks should be accompanied by a noisy diversion,
while the main column charged in silence and with unloaded
muskets.[23]

While Mack's instructions departed from the defence-mindedness
of the army, they grossly underestimated the combat value of the
French and failed to come to grips with the problem of the enemy's
skirmishers. The two-rank formation was not proposed to strengthen
the firing line or to provide skirmishers, but merely to extend an
already overlong and brittle deployment. In the end, the system of
controlled firing, bayonet charges, and intricate manoeuvring based
on the regulations of 1769 was not that easily discarded. Neither the
steady Austrian foot nor the superb horse were used to best advantage
and it remained a general rule that in any engagement, but especially
in hilly or broken terrain, the French moved faster and made better
use of ground.

In 1794, therefore, the Austrians again were not well prepared to
deal with the full power of the French armies. The main fighting was
in Flanders where Pichegru's Army of the North, 160,000, and
Jourdan's Army of the Meuse and Sambre, 80,000, were under orders
to clear the Netherlands. The allies, commanded by Coburg, were
deployed along a wide front. On the right, around Tournai, was
Clerfayt with an Austrian-Hessian-Hanoverian force of 30,000. The
main army in the centre was composed of the Prince of Orange with
19,000 Dutch, Coburg with 43,000 Austrians, and the Duke of York

with 22,000 British troops. The left wing, from Maubeuge to Dinant on the Meuse, was entrusted to Feldzeugmeister Count Kaunitz with 25,000 men clustered at Maubeuge and Charleroi. Coburg first intended to reduce Landrecies and then commence his advance, reducing French fortresses along the way. Thus the Austrians once again had made elaborate plans for a campaign of petty sieges that could achieve no result. On 14 April, the emperor, accompanied by a large suite, arrived in camp before Valenciennes, which surrendered on 30 April.

Meanwhile, undisturbed by Coburg, the French had concentrated and on 11 May, Pichegru defeated an Austro-British force at Courtray, administered another defeat at Tourcoing, and although he suffered a check at Tournai, where, except for Clerfayt's corps, Coburg had assembled his entire field force in an entrenched camp, he continued towards Brussels, taking Ypres on 19 June. Meanwhile, striking north, Jourdan had invested Charleroi, a threat to the flank of the allied position. On 25 June the fortress surrendered and the next day, Coburg who had tardily moved to relieve the fortress, broke off battle at Fleurus, although the fighting still was undecided. Even more, he now decided to give up the province.

His decision has been blamed on secret orders from Vienna where Francis I had returned in early June. Thugut, it has been claimed, wanted to cut losses in the west and concentrate on arrangements with Russia to divide the rest of Poland. For that matter, Coburg's successor in command after August, Clerfayt, always asserted that he had evacuated Belgium only because of superior orders. However, even if he had wanted to make a stand, the army no longer was battleworthy. 'The truth is,' one British officer commented, 'that the Austrian army is incapable of further action. The men are disheartened and the officers disgusted and disunited.'[24] The allied retreat continued. By the end of August the Austrians were back in Germany, the British and Dutch in Holland.

Meanwhile, matters also had gone poorly along the Middle and Upper Rhine. A Prussian-Austrian force under General Möllendorf, a Prussian, operating west of Mainz, had done very little, while Duke Albert of Sachsen-Teschen, holding the front from Mannheim to Basle with 60,000 men, felt himself too weak to do anything. And the French, also weak, had remained on the defensive. After Fleurus, however, they were reinforced and drove the allies back across the Rhine. The regional rulers panicked and tried to come to an accommodation with the enemy. In this emergency, Austrian commanders tried to revive the old militia organization in the invasion-threatened lands, but Lacy, still very influential, warned that 'lacking proper organization and officers, such people will constitute an impediment rather than an advantage.'[25] Austria then and later was reluctant to use an armed population to fight revolution.

In October, the main weight of the French offensive switched back to the Netherlands. Pichegru invaded Holland. Indifferently defended, the Dutch fortresses fell, while the British army withdrew into northern Germany to be evacuated by the Royal Navy in April. By the time they sailed away, Prussia had left the war. After the conquest of Belgium had removed the threat of invasion from France, there was a reaction against the oppressive Committee of Public Safety which was overthrown in July 1794. The Convention continued until October when it was replaced by the Directory. Paris appeared to be amenable to negotiations and, after some delay, Prussia concluded the Treaty of Basle on 5 April, ceding the left bank of the Rhine and establishing a neutral zone in Germany north of the Main river. Soon thereafter, Spain and Portugal left the war. Austria, meanwhile, had utilized the political troubles in Paris to come to an agreement with Russia. On 5 January 1795 the two powers renewed their alliance against the Turks, agreed on an exchange of Belgium for Bavaria, and divided the rest of Poland without consulting Prussia.

The campaigns of 1795

Under these circumstances, and with both Austria and France exhausted, there was little action in 1795. In Italy, Austrian and Sardinian troops maintained their defences along the line of the Alps. Along the Rhine the armies rested. The French were reorganizing, while Thugut, who now had assumed a major role in Vienna, had no intention of commencing hostilities before Prussia had recognized the Austro-Russian settlement, and therefore kept back the best of the Monarchy's armed forces. It was not until October that Frederick William finally agreed to this.

Meanwhile, the British government was anxious for Austrian action. From Alsace, William Wickham, the British government's agent in Alsace and Switzerland, questioned 'the most extraordinary and unaccountable inactivity of General De Vins,' and he proposed that Austria should send from 70,000 to 80,000 'good troops across the Rhine' to assist French royalist uprisings. Vienna, however, refused.[26] Britain, having chosen to waste its regiments in the West Indies, was in no position to protest too hard.[27]

Having received Russian assurances, Austria was preparing to renew the war in September. The army covered a 400-mile cordon. Along the Lower Rhine, Clerfayt with 100,000 was deployed from the Ruhr-Lahn to the Neckar, while Wurmser with 80,000 held the front from Mannheim to Basle. Opposed were an equal number of French troops, the Army of the Meuse and Sambre under Jourdan and that of the Rhine and Moselle under Pichegru. The French crossed the Rhine in early September, but after initial successes were repulsed and forced back across the river. With Paris continuing in turmoil, with uprisings from both the Left and the Right, and the government widely accused of corruption, the French lacked their old élan and were short of manpower. Moreover their leaders had become unreliable. Pichegru had accepted money from Wickham and negotiated for a Bourbon restoration.[28] By the end of the year, the Austrians had defeated the invasion and obtained some bridgeheads across the Rhine.

Archduke Charles and the campaign of 1796-7

The campaigns of 1796 decided the outcome of the long war. Two new commanders, representing opposite systems of war, appeared. On the one side there was Napoleon Bonaparte, on the other Archduke Charles. Although overrated by dynastic historians, the archduke was a great soldier. Wellington thought him the outstanding commander on the allied side, kept from reaching his full scope by bad health. Charles was a good tactician, though as a strategist he hesitated to take risks, overestimated the strength of his enemies, and was too concerned about lines of operations and the occupation of topographical points. In strategy, as well as in matters of recruitment, he essentially remained enlightened rather than revolutionary. Still, he achieved much and his campaign in Germany in 1796 has been quoted and analyzed as much as Napoleon's in Italy that same year.

Charles was born in 1771, the fifth child of Leopold II. He was a lonely and nervous boy, suffering from mild epileptic attacks that would plague him the rest of his life. After the death of his father he went to live at the court of his aunt, the Archduchess Marie-Christine, joint governor of the Austrian Netherlands with her husband, Duke Albert of Sachsen-Teschen. There his enthusiasm for soldiering was encouraged and he received professional instruction. His chief mentor was Colonel Carl Friedrich von Lindenau, who had served as adjutant to Frederick the Great and had written several books on tactics, claiming to criticize the Frederician system, though, in fact, merely providing further 'geometric refinements.' Charles admired him and he never wholly outgrew Lindenau's influence.[29]

After the outbreak of war, Charles participated in the early campaigns under Hohenlohe and Coburg. Much of the time, however, he was absent, serving as governor of the Netherlands. In the field, Charles, a man of slight build, just over five feet tall, displayed a burning intensity and ability to inspire troops. At Fleurus, commanding the centre of Coburg's army, he reportedly urged continuation of the battle. Late in 1794, his nerves strained, he retired to devote himself to writing on military subjects.

His first work was the treatise *On War against the New Franks*, written in 1795. 'How was it possible,' he asked, 'that a well equipped, balanced, and disciplined army had been defeated by an enemy with raw troops, lacking cavalry, and with inexperienced generals?' The answer, he maintained, was that the Austrians basically conducted a defensive war, were overly concerned with lines of communications, and that the cordon system allowed the enemy to concentrate superior forces. In regard to tactics, the archduke restated several points already made by Mack. Artillery should be concentrated, and, because the enemy was poorly trained, foot and horse could be formed in two ranks. This would permit extending the battle line and provide reserves, a characteristic of Charles's style of battle. For the moment, however, he was concerned with the offensive. If properly concentrated, Charles maintained that the army could certainly defeat the French and he advised immediate and energetic pursuit, another prescription he later would fail to heed. Finally, he accused Austrian commanders of losing the war. There was too little co-operation, each general wanted to aggrandize himself and rarely was prepared to support another. 'Unfortunately,' he concluded, 'this, with few exceptions, is how our brave troops are led. Ignorance, indolence, and egotism are to blame for our misfortunes.'[30]

Convinced that he could do better, the archduke joined in an intrigue to drive Clerfayt, who had bitterly quarrelled with Wurmser, from command of the Army on the Lower Rhine. In February 1796, the general was removed and Charles named as his successor and *Reichsgeneralfeldmarschall*. But, uneasy about his ambitions, the emperor circumscribed his command authority. *Feldmarschall Leutnant* Heinrich Count Bellegarde, a sound but unenterprising general and a supporter of Thugut, was named as deputy, *Adlatus*, to Charles, and in concert with *Feldmarschall Leutnants* Lauer and Chasteler authorized to override the archduke in the obligatory council of war. On 4 April a personal letter from the emperor instructed Charles that he was to 'defeat the enemy armies one after the other if possible,' to listen to the advice of his senior generals, and above all to 'abstain from all matters not strictly military.... Experience having proved that commanders who have mixed in the former have caused nothing but mischief.'[31]

In the spring of 1796 the strategic situation was as follows: the Austrians and French confronted each other on the Rhine from Dusseldorf to Basle. Archduke Charles's army extended from near Cologne to just below Mannheim and was opposed by the Arrny of the Sambre and Meuse under Jourdan, while the Army on the Upper Rhine, commanded by Wurmser, was opposed by the Army of the Moselle under Moreau. In numbers the Austrians had an advantage, especially in cavalry. Plans were for the Austrians to take the offensive, advancing towards the Moselle, but late in May, Wurmser with 26,000 men was shifted to Italy. At the same time Charles, who had arrived at army headquarters on 11 May, was instructed to remain on the defensive. His army now numbered 90,000, while along the Upper Rhine there remained 50,000 commanded by *Feldzeugmeister* Latour. Wurmser's departure, however, had one advantage. That stubborn old warrior would not have willingly subordinated himself to Charles, but Latour agreed to do so.[32]

Reports on the condition of the army varied. From Berne, Wickham advised his government that the 'mere existence of this formidable army,' greatly contributed to the security of Britain and her empire.[33] On the other hand, Charles found his troops short of funds and rations, and with uniforms so bad as to be useless. 'In many boots the soles are made of cardboard so that they fall apart the first time they are wet, underpants and shorts poorly made, and trousers so short that I myself could not wear them.'[34]

In May, too, he drew up instructions for his generals, the *Observationspunkte*. A mixture of the old and new, the instructions gave considerable attention to skirmishing. The problem was that although on paper the Austrian service had adequate light troops, 17 *Grenz* regiments as against 60 of the line, the *Grenzer* had not been able to field their full complement and only weak battalions and some volunteer free corps were available. At that, Charles held that skirmishers were only auxiliaries to the main battle line, and that even light units should never be deployed entirely in skirmish formations. His instructions warned against the pernicious habit, adopted occasionally in the broken Flemish terrain, to disperse entire units in loose skirmish order. 'This misuse must be opposed because it weakens the impetus of the attack.' Skirmishers, he maintained, 'lacked strength ... unless they are supported by a formed body of troops giving them drive, persistence, and steadiness.' While during an attack on a village or a wood it was permissible to use a few companies of skirmishers, they always had to be backed by formed troops. 'Regular, trained, and solid infantry, courageously advancing in closed ranks at a rapid pace, supported by its artillery, cannot be impeded by scattered skirmishers ... it should close with the enemy as rapidly and in as good order as possible, overthrow him and decide the battle.'[35]

Such ideas were not new; similar methods already had been used during the Seven Years' War. New was insistence that infantry should move in column, 'the main part of the art of manoeuvring,' and a realization, that skirmishing relied directly on the soldier's motivation, discipline, and drill. In a remarkable passage, the archduke advised that training 'must not be restricted to a soldier's physical nature, but must influence his understanding and feeling. Even the most common man is receptive in some degree to this approach ... and he who acts out of conviction and on his own initiative acts with double courage and strength.'[36] These indeed were revolutionary words, though in the end the archduke lacked the time and the will to see them implemented by the lower leadership.

The campaigns of 1796 in Germany involved a series of complicated manoeuvres and marches.[37] The French opened operations in June, pressing against the outer flanks of the two Austrian armies. Their aim, apparently, was to force Charles to reinforce the wings, weaken his centre, and to prevent him from uniting his forces. The archduke's objective was to contain the French if possible, and otherwise fall back to his bases in Bohemia and on the Danube, while keeping open the option of joining with Latour. In the event, the French penetrated deep into southern Germany, but became separated. Jourdan pushed Charles's right close to the Bohemian frontier, while Moreau pushed Latour back to the Isar north of Munich. Charles had made the initial mistake of detaching too many troops to General Wartensleben, commanding his right wing, who became separated from the main body and leaving too strong garrisons in the Rhenish fortresses. He was further weakened by the defection of the German princes who hastened to make peace with the invaders. In July, Charles forcibly disarmed some south German contingents, but Baden, Bavaria, Saxony and Württemberg defected.[38] His main force was down to 24,000 foot and 11,000 horse, opposing Jourdan's 40,000 to 45,000. In August, however, Wartensleben with 26,000 joined Charles and on 24 August the archduke defeated Jourdan at Amberg, routed him again on 3 September at Würzburg, and drove him reeling across the Rhine.

The turn of the tide ended the bitter infighting among the Austrian generals. In early July, Charles had complained about intrigues to his brother Francis. Moreover, the elderly senior generals did not have the flexibility required by the fluid situation and did little to support their overall commander. Difficulties were compounded by the feuds in Vienna where factions supporting the *Hofkriegsrat*, Lacy, Francis, or Thugut, all had their own candidate for high command.[39] In August the emperor dispatched Colonel Franz Josef Count Dietrichstein, Lacy's man, to investigate. From Germany, Dietrichstein supported Charles. 'The generals,' he reported, 'are a weakness in our army. They are slow to react, refuse to obey orders, will not fight, and cannot make even simple dispositions.'[40] Conditions were no better on the Italian front. On 20 August 1796 in a letter to the British ambassador, Sir Thomas Graham, accompanying the Austrian forces in Italy, complained about the 'avarice and a curious want of subordination and the unhappy spirit of party that pervades the army.' The men, Graham reported, were quite good, but lacked leadership and provisions. 'It is not only the Commr. in Chief but the greatest number of the other Genl. Officers that need to be replaced.' Even lower-ranking officers, he wrote some weeks later, were disaffected with a service in which interest and intrigue were the main avenues of promotion.[41]

For the moment, however, Charles had outmanoeuvred the French who found themselves separated and unable to support each other. With Jourdan across the Rhine, Moreau's position became untenable. With his flank exposed and attacked by Charles, Latour, and Wartensleben, he retreated in considerable haste. Charles was widely hailed as the 'Saviour of Germany,' and Wickham reported to his government that the 'superiority of the Austrian troops when well commanded was now generally acknowledged by the Republicans.'[42] In November the French asked for a ceasefire on the Rhine front. Charles was inclined to accept, but Thugut argued that Kehl and Hüningen, the last two fortresses still in French hands, should be taken. The Foreign Minister was motivated by a sincere desire to firmly re-establish Habsburg prestige in Germany, though it would have been better, as Charles pointed out, merely to blockade the two fortresses, and transfer the bulk of the army to Italy. Kehl fell on 10 January 1797, Hüningen on 5 February. By this time there had been disaster in Italy.

In 1796 General Napoleon Bonaparte had upset all plans by turning the Italian theatre into the main one. His Army of Italy marched in April. Between 12 and 22 April, Napoleon burst through the Austro-Sardinian cordon. Sardinia asked for a truce; the Austrians retreated into Lombardy. On 10 May, Napoleon forced the Adda at Lodi and on the 20th he entered Milan. Four days later he crossed the Mincio. The bulk of the Austrian forces hastily retreated to the Tyrol and into Venetia, leaving behind 15,000 in the fortress of Mantua. Blockading this fortress Napoleon defeated four successive relief attempts. During the second attempt in September, Wurmser managed to break through to Mantua with 10,000 men, but this merely served to increase the garrison. In fact, the fortress commander, *Feldmarschall Leutnant* Canto d'Yrles, pointing out that he had neither rations nor quarters, at first refused to take in Wurmser's corps. In the end, with the alternative being Wurmser's capitulation in the field, he relented. But additional mouths did reduce supplies. Between 15 September and the end of October 1796, 4000 men died of disease and hunger. Wurmser, however, was determined to hold out as 'long as there is a horse, a dog, or a piece of bread.'[43] By January there was no bread, no horses, and very few dogs and cats, and when the last relief attempt under Alvinczy failed on 14–15 January 1797 at Rivoli, surrender became inevitable. On 2 February Mantua capitulated.

Napoleon had been impressed by Wurmser's resolve, though shutting up 25,000 men in this position later was criticized by Fieldmarshal Radetzky.[44] As it was, Austria could ill afford to lose trained troops. At the approach of the French, and with manpower low, the authorities in Vienna had raised a free corps of 1000 men, which surrendered at Rivoli after fighting well.[45] In the Tyrol the volunteer sharpshooters were alerted in July and in December 1796 the Tyrolean estates agreed to raise their number to 10,000 and provide detachments for the field army. The experiment was not an unqualified success. Senior Austrian officers had little use for semi-trained and undisciplined levies, sentiments shared by Archduke Charles.[46]

In March, with his rear secured and reinforced by 23,000 seasoned troops, Napoleon resumed the strategic offensive. Detaching a small corps to watch the Tyrol, he moved east towards the Tarvis pass and the Inner Austrian lands beyond. He still was outnumbered by the Austrians, about 44,000 regulars and some militia, with reinforcements expected from Germany, but for the moment the enemy was disorganized and incapable of offering much resistance. Napoleon

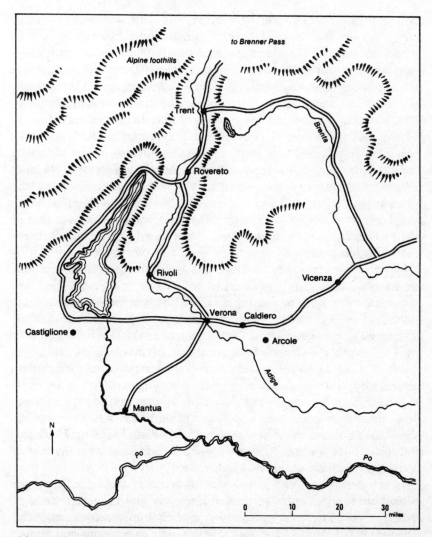

Mantua campaigns, 1796

was opposed by Archduke Charles. Although no major battles were fought, this brief campaign is worth noticing because of the shadow it cast forward to the great encounters at Aspern and Wagram.

Hoping that a decisive victory in Italy might restore Austria's fortunes, in February 1797 the archduke was sent to take command on the Italian front. 'Take with you whom you want, transfer generals and other officers from the Army of the Rhine and vice versa as you see fit,' the emperor authorized Charles.[47] The archduke was to deal with dissension among senior officers, restore troop morale, and, once reinforcements arrived, take the offensive. Sir Morton Eden, the British ambassador, hoped that the prestige and ability of the young general would 'revive the drooping spirit of the army.'[48] Charles was much less sanguine. His advice had been overruled in November and he was more concerned with saving the army than with taking new risks. Arriving at the front in early March, he spread his main forces behind the Tagliamento river to fight a delaying action. But when the French attacked on 16 March, the Austrians took to their heels. 'Neither pleas, nor rewards, nor threats,' Charles wrote to his brother, 'were of any use trying to halt the fleeing rabble.'[49] He warned that lacking artillery and cavalry, he could not hope to hold even the best positions with such 'infamous troops.' Only peace, he maintained, could save the Monarchy. 'If this army is defeated, there is no salvation.'[50]

And that was the key. Napoleon's position was by no means invulnerable. His numbers actually were inferior and his lines of communication were becoming stretched. A more adventurous general might have staked everything on one major battle, but Charles always was more concerned with preserving his army which he regarded as the guarantor of the continued existence of the dynasty. It was true, of course, that his troops were demoralized, though the bitter tone of his dispatches was perhaps a trifle excessive in its self-pity. Moreover, his dispositions were not always sound. His cordon along the Tagliamento was too thinly spread, and while he eluded Napoleon's pursuit, the Austrians invariably would take up blocking positions in the valleys to find themselves outflanked by the more agile French moving along the heights.[51]

As the French entered Inner Austria, Vienna once again experimented with popular levies. In Carinthia and Styria, closest to the French, there was little enthusiasm, and Charles discouraged such attempts.[52] In Vienna, on the other hand, citizen and academic battalions were raised in April. On 17 April the units received colours and, amid emotional scenes, left the city. But their enthusiasm waned rapidly. The Commerce Battalion, for instance, marched two miles and then decided to go home for the night, promising to return in the morning.[53] One wonders how they would have fared in combat against the hardened French veterans.

In the event, they were not put to the test. On 8 April, French elements entered Leoben in Styria, only 80 miles from Vienna, and Napoleon, anxious about an Austrian advance from the Tyrol, Austrian reinforcements from Germany, and a revolt in Verona, was eager to conclude an armistice. Finally, Vienna was now ready to oblige and on 7 April a five-day truce was agreed upon, extended on the 13th for five more days. On the 18th an armistice was signed at Leoben. While negotiations for a permanent peace continued, the two armies drew apart. The French retired to the Isonzo while the Austrians regrouped west of Vienna and in Carniola under *Feldzeugmeister* Ludwig Baron Terzy. Charles returned to the Rhine army with orders not to leave his headquarters without express permission.

The order indicated that relations between Charles and his imperial brother had deteriorated. There were malicious charges that Charles had not carried out his mission with sufficient energy and his brief trip to Vienna in February, where he had hoped to persuade the emperor to open negotiations, was held against him. As a result, the suspicious emperor had interfered with the archduke's command in Italy by sending his personal representative, Major General Count Merveldt, with authorization to communicate directly with subordinate commanders and to negotiate with the French. It was Merveldt, nor Charles, who negotiated the armstice.[54] The rationale for this extraordinary arrangement was the emperor's resolve that the archduke should never touch anything 'political.' There were, of course, sound reasons for this, but the manner in which it was done, and the fact that it came in the wake of Thugut's frequent interference with strategic designs, could not help but embitter relations between the two brothers.

Afterthoughts

After being retired from active command in 1809, Archduke Charles devoted himself to writing on military theory and strategy, including an account and analysis of the 1796 campaign in Germany. He concluded that throughout the War of the First Coalition, Austria had been at a disadvantage because in fighting the French 'who relied on a well integrated system of fortresses and a well co-ordinated strategy, it put its faith in a better organized army, bravery, and some brilliant exploits by several of its commanders.'[55] Radetzky, writing more than 40 years later, was more specific. As causes for Austria's defeat he listed continued reliance on linear tactics vulnerable to skirmishers, the cordon strategy, the lacerating feuds among commanders and the lack of an overall plan of operations, together with poor reconnaissance and communications.[56] The observations were true enough, but failed to go to the heart of the matter. Austria did lack an overall plan of operations, the quarrels among senior officers did much harm, and its tactics were outdated. But there was more. Charles, and all other Austrian commanders, were essentially old-fashioned soldiers, cautious rather than enterprising, and always concerned with the preservation of the army.[57] Their strategy was based on concepts of the eighteenth century and at best sought to defeat, not to annihilate, the enemy. Relying for the most part on fierce discipline, they rarely managed to get the last ounce of effort from their troops. A memorandum by Colonel Anton Baron Zach, submitted in April 1798, illuminated the Austrian dilemma. The French, he pointed out, had started out with a disorganized army and without supplies, yet they had been victorious because of their intense *esprit national*. Austria, he conceded, could not develop such a spirit. The army, therefore, had to rely on specific soldierly virtues – courage, fidelity, comradeship, and devotion to duty – to be shared alike by officers and men.[58] The Habsburg army was, and remained, primarily a dynastic instrument. As such it was hard put, perhaps even prevented, from making the fundamental social and political transitions that changed the nature of war. Even so, individual regiments of the Habsburg service remained very good and, though generally unsuccessful in the large battles, they often did well in smaller engagements and even after Marengo the confidence of the regimental commanders in their methods and men was very far from being shaken.[59]

1 De la Tour Dragoons (11th Dragoon Regiment) non-commissioned officer standard bearer, 1792. Note the heavy straight sabre, *Pallasch*. The regiment wore the bicorn even after 1798. (Knötel print.)

2 Members of the short-lived Vienna Volunteers, 1797. From left to right: Merchants Corps, Academy of Arts Corps, and University Corps. On extreme right a poorly armed volunteer from the suburbs. (Knötel print.)

3 Fieldmarshal Franz Sebastian Count Clerfayt de Croix, commander in the early campaigns against the French Revolution. (Oil painting from the Vienna Army Museum.)

4 Archduke Charles of Austria, about 1797. He wears a white coat, with red collar and wide gold lace, and a red waistcoat edged in gold braid. (Oil painting from the Vienna Army Museum.)

5 Cuirassier trooper, 1798. In this year the bicorn was replaced by the classical
helmet. German cavalry wore infantry style tunics with turnovers front and
back; the breeches were grey or white. Saddle furniture was red, edged in
black-yellow lace and the imperial cypher in rear corner. A sheepskin saddle
cloth covered the saddle holsters. Harness was black, fittings brass. (Plate from
the Vienna Army Museum.)

6 Dragoon trooper, 1798. Wearing the newly introduced classical helmet, the trooper is dressed in a dark green coat and carries a Dragoon carbine. (Plate from the Vienna Army Museum.)

7 Hussar trooper, 1798. Wearing the traditional Hussar costume, the trooper is shown with the peaked light shako introduced that year. (Plate from the Vienna Army Museum.)

8 Grenadier privates, 1798. A German Grenadier on the left; a Hungarian on the right. Both wear the high fronted bearskin hat and carry brass hilted sabres. Coats are single-breasted white with collars and turnbacks, front only, in the regimental colours. However, the Hungarian Grenadier is wearing light blue tight trousers and boots, while the German Grenadier wears white knee breeches and black gaiters. The pack is made of brown calf-skin and the black cartrige pouch has a brass grenade. (Plate from the Vienna Army Museum.)

9 Light Infantry privates, 1798. Raised in this year from various free corps, the battalions wore grey coats and breeches with black gaiters; the others wore long light blue trousers and half boots. Both types wore the German Fusilier helmet, but with no front plate, just brass initials 'F II'. (Plate from the Vienna Army Museum.)

III

The War of the Second Coalition, 1799–1801

THE Campo Formio settlement lasted only 18 months. While the European powers were unwilling to wage war solely to overthrow the Republic and were willing to accept limited French expansion, the Directory's policies made peace impossible. To secure its new frontiers, the Directory felt it necessary to create a 'rampart of republics.' Having organized a Batavian Republic in Holland, France subdued Switzerland in March 1798, established satellite republics in Rome and Naples, and launched an attack on Egypt. These moves threatened the security and equilibrium of Europe and by the spring of 1799 a Second Coalition had come into being, comprising Great Britain, the Ottoman Empire, Naples, Russia and Austria. Of course, only the last two states had substantial land forces and the alliance between them at best was tenuous. Vienna had justified doubts about the stability and the intent of the new Russian ruler, Paul I, and it was at odds with Great Britain, the Coalition's paymaster, over the importance of the Low Countries, vital to Britain, but a matter of relative indifference to Austria. Then too, with Russian support still far away, Austria hesitated to declare herself openly. In the end, worried by intelligence about the alliances and disturbed by Austrian and Russian troop movements, France moved first. French troops crossed the Rhine on 1 March; a formal declaration of war followed on 17 March 1799.

Austrian military reforms, 1798–9

A substantial faction in Vienna, with Thugut as its leading spirit, always had regarded the settlement with France as little more than an armistice. As early as November 1797, Sir Morton Eden, the British envoy to Vienna, reported that the government 'might find it

expedient to have again recourse to arms.'[1] General Mack, meanwhile, was preparing an ambitious, if perhaps unrealistic, plan of
operations should fighting resume.[2] Finally, on 4 February 1798,
Francis instructed Charles to bring the army as rapidly as possible to
combat readiness.[3] Charles, somewhat paradoxically, emerging as
head of a peace faction, gave a sober assessment. With finances in
ruin, the country and the army, he informed his brother, needed time
to recuperate. Above all, he warned against undertaking ambitious
reorganization schemes. 'If war does break out,' he wrote, 'before
such changes have been completed for some time, the army will be in
disarray and there will be disaster.'[4]

There already existed division and confusion in the highest
echelons. While Charles was at army headquarters in Prague, the
emperor and his military entourage were in Vienna. Despite Charles's
warnings, on 8 March 1798, Francis appointed *Feldzeugmeister*
Alvinczy to chair a *Militär-Hof-Commission* to direct the 'rebirth,
reorganization, and perfection of the troops of My Army,' with
specific attention to organization, weapons, tactics, supply, medical
services and morale. Members of the commission included Generals
Bellegarde, Unterberger, and Vincent, the emperor's adjutant general,
as well as Ferdinand Count Tige, president of the *Hofkriegsrat*, and
considered Thugut's man. Charles pointedly was excluded.[5]

In the event, the commission achieved little. During its first session
on 20 March, Alvinczy declared that the most urgent problem was to
improve 'subordination, discipline, esprit de corps and confidence,'
and called for expert testimony from officers of the fighting army.
Among the documents submitted was a lengthy memorandum by
Colonel Anton Zach, a highly decorated veteran, former instructor
at the Theresian Military Academy, then assigned as chief of staff in
Venetia. Though widely regarded as one of Thugut's confidants,
Zach deplored the growing civilian influence and feared that the
civilians 'might use the present circumstances of an unlucky war to
reach for control.' At the same time he criticized senior commanders.
It was peculiar, he noted, that the 'long war had not produced a
single great man.' Apparently, he did not consider the archduke a
great man. He also criticized the 'small mindedness, desperation, and
apathy' of the senior officers, due in part to the surfeit of regulations
adopted since the Seven Years' War which left little to individual
initiative. As for the colonels, majors and captains, he went on, they
displayed no interest in war; their conversations centred around pay
and emoluments, and on occasion drill. Only radical changes could
help. He recognized that a multinational state could not produce a

national spirit, and instead recommended the creation of an army *esprit de corps*. 'Officers and the common soldiers,' he wrote, 'are too wide apart. The officer neither knows nor values his men, and in return he is neither loved nor trusted.' He advocated that officers should live with their troops and adopt a more Spartan lifestyle. Finally, he urged that line and staff should be separated and that inexperienced young staff officers should not be given preferment over combat veterans.[6]

These radical ideas, of course, stood little chance of being adopted. Yet, the commission was by no means hidebound and it gave serious consideration to a proposal made by General Bellegarde regarding adoption of a corps system. Fifteen legions, comprised of all arms, were to constitute permanent higher tactical formations. The innovation actually was submitted to the emperor, but failed after Charles protested that 'the army should continue in its ancient organization that so often has proved victorious as long as our plans were sound.'[7]

Acting on the recommendations of *Feldmarschall Leutnant* Unterberger, the commission introduced a new musket, the Model 1798, with brass fittings, a simplified lock, and, compared to its predecessors, a slightly reduced calibre, 17.6 mm (0.69 in), the same as the French musket, and equipped with a four-edged bayonet. The piece was about one pound lighter than the current issue and could use captured ammunition.[8] Although not an exceptional design, it aroused interest abroad. In 1801 the Duke of York requested Sir Arthur Paget, the new British ambassador, to procure him a sample.[9] Adoption of the new model was opposed by Archduke Charles who pointed out that 'we have 20 million cartridges of the old calibre in stock.' The emperor overruled him, though issue of the new muskets took time. In 1799 only very few units were equipped with the weapon. Thereafter manufacture proceeded apace in the many small and middling factories and workshops, private as well as public, in Bohemia, Styria, Venetia and in and around Vienna, though issue was not completed until 1810.[10]

There was less controversy regarding other changes. To remedy the shortage of light troops, the Grenz regiments were removed from the line and designated as *National Grenz Infantrie* regiments, a cosmetic change primarily. At the same time, the various small formations of sharpshooters and free corps, except for the Tyroleans, the Le Loup and the Wurmser Free Corps, were combined into 15 battalions of light troops. A number of new regiments of the line were formed, others were retitled and their recruiting districts, in

AUSTRIAN MILITARY SHOULDER ARMS, 1792–1815

Designation	Calibre mm*	Length mm*	Weight kg*
Smoothbore muzzleloaders			
Commis – Flinte M 1754 infantry musket	18.3	1505	4.35
Trombon M 1759** Blunderbuss	46/25	1110	4.20
Commiss – Flinte M 1767	18.3	1510	4.37
Carbine – Dragoon/Cuirassier	18.3	1250	3.25
Carbine – Hussar/Chevauleger	18.3	900	3.00
Commiss – Gewehr M 1774 infantry musket	18.3	1517	4.30
Carbine – Hussar M 1779	17.0	900	3.00
Trombon M 1781	44/26	1030	4.00
Infanteriegewehr M 1784	18.3	1502	4.75
Infanteriegewehr M 1798	17.6	1506	4.20
Carbine – Dragoon M 1798	17.6	1235	3.25
Carbine – Hussar M 1798	17.6	845	2.45
Infanteriegewehr M 1807	17.6	1500	4.60
Carbine – Jäger M 1807	17.6	1230	3.55
Rifled muzzleloaders			
Jägerstutzen M 1759	14.8	1120	3.00
Kavalleriestutzen M 1788	18.3	1055	4.20
Kavalleriestutzen M 1789	17.6	690	2.50
Jägerstutzen M 1795	14.5	1050	4.00
Jägerstutzen M 1796	14.5	1025	3.80
Kavalleriestutzen M 1798	15.6	710	2.65
Jägerstutzen M 1799	14.5	1050	3.80
Jägerstutzen M 1807	13.9	1050	3.55
Miscellaneous			
Doppelstutzen M 1768 over-under rifle/shotgun	15.2	1050	5.50
Repetierwindbüchse M 1780*** repeating air rifle	11.5	1225	4.60

* Until standardization after 1866, weapons within a type had minor variations.

** Issued to 12 men in each Cuirassier squadron in 1754, modified in 1781, the weapons were withdrawn in 1798.

*** Invented by Bartholomäus Girandoni, introduced into the service in 1780, the weapon was issued to *Jäger* units 1792–7 and again in 1799. Despite its 20-shot magazine, incidence of repair and tactical problems caused the weapon to be withdrawn in 1800, though it remained on the books until 1815. About 1100 manufactured.

territory lost to France, shifted. From the fourth battalions of the Hungarian foot regiments three new units, numbers 60, 61, and 62 were formed. The Italian Infantry Regiment number 48, recruited around Mantua, became a Hungarian unit, while the six Walloon regiments retained their designation but received recruiting districts in Bohemia. In all, there now were 63 line infantry regiments.

The second combat arm – cavalry – also was augmented. The two Carabinier regiments were converted to Cuirassiers, and together with a newly organized Regiment, there now were 12 Cuirassier regiments. Differences between Dragoons and *Chevaulegers* disappeared; two new regiments were raised, for a total of 15 regiments of Light Dragoons. Two additional Hussar regiments were formed, a total of 12, including one regiment of Szekler and one of Croatian-Slavonian *Grenz* Hussars. *Uhlan* strength was raised to two regiments, while out of the mounted elements of the various free corps, a regiment of Mounted *Jäger* was found.

Together with various other new formations, including 14 companies of artillery and several pioneer units, the strength of the army on paper in 1799 had risen to 438,000 men and 102,700 horses. In fact, however, it was far less, about 300,000 men including garrison and internal security troops. Worst off, perhaps, was the *Fuhrwesen-korps* with only 695 officers and men and 616 horses.[11] Shortage of transport would hamper Austrian operations throughout the campaign.

There were only minor changes in uniforms. The bulk of the infantry continued to wear white with black gaiters; the Hungarians tight blue pantaloons. In 1798 the casquet was replaced in the infantry by a helmet with peaks in the front and back, a silk crest for officers and a wool crest for the rank and file. As usual, issues were made when available and when old items wore out, and old style uniforms and hats continued to be worn. There were no changes in the brown coats of the artillery or the hechtgrau (grey-blue) of the *Jäger*; similarly clothed the new light battalions received the infantry helmet. Dragoons, Hussars and *Uhlans* wore a variety of colours and the German cavalry received a classical helmet in 1798. Powdered hair and pigtails, a great inconvenience to troops, did not disappear until July 1805. Of course, all this was mainly regulation. In the field, troops dressed in what was available. While white coats were common, trousers, pantaloons, and overalls were seen in many colours.

Tactics and strategy

Although numerous military writers, Prussians such as Scharnhorst, Knesebeck and Bülow, and Austrians such as Archduke Charles and Zach, had pointed out that the new and more flexible tactics required to deal with the French also required a more humane approach to the common soldier, in practice little was done. Corporal punishment, both judicial and non-judicial, remained the norm and sometimes beatings were administered in full view of the French lines where such degrading practices had been abolished in 1792. Some thoughtful regimental officers were perturbed. One junior officer wondered 'whether as English commanders assert the defence of the fatherland can only be maintained with the whip and the stick?'[12] But such thinking was sternly discouraged by the *Hofkriegsrat* which in May 1798 issued a circular denouncing officers who had become attracted to such 'subversive ideas' to the detriment of good order and discipline.[13]

At the same time, despite occasional efforts to promote an effective combination of light and linear tactics, the predominance of close order fighting remained undiminished. While a noted Austrian military historian has claimed that 'by 1798 the Austrian army had learned how to fight in open order supported by closed formations,' this contention is not substantiated by the evidence.[14] On one occasion, to be sure, during the battle of Novi in November 1799, the Austrians deployed in open order, but were driven off the field in disorder.[15] Thereafter, the regulations once again stressed that skirmishing was to be employed only in a limited fashion. For instance Zach, then chief of staff to General Baron Melas in Italy, issued instructions on 1 April 1800. 'In action,' he wrote, 'troops must remember not to lose time with firing. Only a few *tirailleurs* are necessary to screen the front. If these are followed up by troops advancing courageously in closed formation, with bands playing, and keeping their formation, such an advance cannot be repulsed by an enemy fighting in open order.' Two weeks, later, on 13 April, another army order stated that 'recent actions have shown that unnecessary skirmishing can only be detrimental ... but a determined charge delivered in close order, screened by only a few skirmishers, will certainly result in victory with very few casualties.'[16] The Austrians had not abandoned linear tactics and the campaigns of 1799–1801 again revealed that they could not match the French in broken, wooded, or hilly terrain nor that their generals had overcome their concern with secure lines of communications and retreat.

The War of the Second Coalition saw the usual confusions and contradictions in allied strategy. The allies had little in common but fear of the French and among the allies Austria played by far the most important part. Accounts assigning great importance to the Russians are, in sober fact, misleading. Austria contributed over four-fifths of the allied manpower, though this fell far short of the 300,000 claimed. The British could provide at best 30,000; the two Russian corps in Switzerland and Italy numbered about 60,000 at best, and the Neapolitans had some 40,000 poor troops. The Turks contributed almost nothing. Even so, the numbers were not unfavourable for the Coalition. The French armies were depleted by casualties and desertion and their replacement situation almost desperate because of widespread resistance to the 1798 conscription law. In all, the republic mustered no more than 175,000 men to hold the line from Holland to the Adige in Italy. On the plus side of the ledger, however, was that their officers were able professionals and the available troops for the most part veterans. French staff work was excellent and their army organization provided for flexible, large, all-arms formations.

Both for the offence and defence, Switzerland was the decisive area of operations and its occupation gave France a superior strategic position. Control of the mountain passes enabled her to fight on interior lines, permitting the transfer of forces north to the Rhine and Danube and south to the Italian plains through the St Gotthard Pass. At the same time, Switzerland represented a bastion which compromised allied offensive operations both in the Danube valley and through the Zabern Gap, or through the Maritime Alps into southern France. The successful defence of Switzerland, one historian concluded, was of decisive importance in the war.[17]

Archduke Charles realized the importance of Switzerland and his two war plans, one submitted in February and a more detailed version on 9 December 1798, called for one Austrian army to clear Italy while another was to enter Switzerland from Germany to prevent the French debouching to the Danube. A third army, to be deployed in Vorarlberg and the Grisons (Graubünden) was to remain on the defensive until the other two had made considerable progress.[18] The largest force, presumably directed by Charles, was to operate in Germany. This plan, however, was changed by Thugut who, with the support of the emperor and assisted by General Bellegarde, was working on his own plans. In this war more than ever before, interference from Vienna restricted the scope of field commanders and Thugut injected his own ideas into strategy and even grand tactics.[19]

Of course, ever since the days of Maria Theresa, Austrian chancellors had exercised considerable influence on grand strategy. This had been true of Kaunitz and would remain so under Stadion and Metternich. Thugut was no exception but for the range of his activities. Also, the charge that he was motivated by hatred and spite of the archduke was not entirely true. There was bad blood between the two men, but the primary cause of the quarrel was that for Thugut political considerations overrode military plans. He perceived Austrian political interests to lie primarily in southern Germany and northern Italy and not in Switzerland. Moreover, Bellegarde, acting as his chief military advisor, feared that the French held a clear tactical advantage in the mountains. Therefore, acting through General Tige, the president of the *Hofkriegsrat*, Thugut and Bellegarde imposed a different plan. No major operations were to be undertaken until the Russian corps, then nearing the Austrian frontier, had arrived and taken their place in Germany. Archduke Charles was instructed to stand on the defensive and, in another version of cordon strategy, send a strong detachment to Würzburg to secure his right flank. Above all, a fourth army, commanded by Bellegarde, was to be assembled in the Tyrol and Vorarlberg, and Charles was ordered to detach some 20 battalions to this force.[20]

Strangely passive for several months, the archduke at long last reacted sharply. On 14 February 1799 he submitted his strategic objections, advising that though he was 'subject, general, and brother of Your Majesty,' he now had concluded that he no longer could serve under the present circumstances. The emperor's reply was angry. He accused the archduke of 'insubordination' and an 'eruption of an exaggerated sensitivity,' and hinted at 'unpleasant consequences' to come if Charles persisted. Taken aback, Charles answered in a long and somewhat abject letter, assuring the emperor of his complete devotion.[21] Yet, he was not reconciled to the situation and from his headquarters now located in Bavaria, he complained to his old mentor, General Lindenau. 'When I came here,' he wrote, 'I had hoped to concentrate my main army – some 80–90,000 – against the enemy, but I received no support and instead FML Bellegarde went to Vienna and I was ordered to detach 17 battalions and 8 squadrons to help form a reserve army of 56,000 under Bellegarde.' Charles explained that he had protested, only to be sharply reprimanded and that 'in this manner I lost 30,000 foot which are doing nothing in the Tyrol and all this so that the FML can cut a good figure without any risk.'[22] During the next months, Charles would return to this theme. He blamed the detachment of the battalions for his failure to destroy Jourdan in March and still chafed about it in July when he told Wickham about the 'false step of the Court in Vienna taking away 30,000 of his best infantry and giving it to Bellegarde.'[23]

Charles was only one of three major Austrian commanders in the forthcoming war. Following Thugut's advice, the emperor appointed

member of the imperial house, the Archduke Joseph, Palatine of Hungary. But before this could be accomplished, Charles recovered and requested to retain his position. Francis replied on 4 May, 'I have decided to keep you on as army commander.' The same letter ordered the archduke to 'abandon, for reasons that you are aware of, all enterprises which might entangle you in Switzerland,' and to make sure the order was obeyed, Charles was to have his chief of staff make an 'account of all events, troop movements, etc.' to be forwarded to Vienna daily.[28]

The reasons alluded to in this communication were military as well as political. Above all they concerned the clash of policy between Vienna and St Petersburg regarding the disposition of Italy where the allied armies had done rather well. In late March, General Scherer had crossed the Mincio into Austrian Venetia, but had been repulsed by Kray on 5 April at Magnano and retired into Lombardy. Mantua, Peschiera, and a score of other fortresses now were under siege, and the Italian population restive. Suvorov arrived with his corps in Verona on 15 April and assisted by the Austrian corps of Melas and Vukassović forced the Adda with 52,000 against 28,000 French. On 29 April he entered Milan. Moreau now relieved Scherer but, facing additional allied forces under Bellegarde bringing the total up to 120,000, and threatened by popular insurrections, he had to evacuate most of northern Italy, leaving behind garrisons in a number of fortresses and citadels.

Meanwhile, MacDonald, threatened by a general revolt in Naples supported by the Royal Navy and small British detachments ashore, was marching north, hoping to destroy the dispersed Austrian and the Russian corps piecemeal. On 17–20 June allied forces met him on the Trebbia and after three days of bloody fighting forced him to withdraw towards Reggio with extremely severe losses. In turn, this obliged Moreau, who with re-formed forces had tried to advance along the coast into the strategic rear of the allies, to retire to Genoa.

At this point there developed a clash between Austrian and Russian aims. The Tsar wanted to restore the king of Sardinia, while Austria wanted to obtain certain territorial compensations in north Italy. When on entering Sardinian territory, Suvorov issued a proclamation calling on the people to rise and restore their king, he received a sharp order from Vienna to abstain from politics, cease operations in Sardinia, and devote his main effort to the siege of Mantua still held by the French. Deeply angered, Suvorov asked the Tsar for his recall and meanwhile all cordial relations between him and his Austrian partners came to an end.

Writers often have cast Thugut as the villain in this episode, and assumed that if Suvorov had been left to pursue his plans without interference from Vienna, he might have totally evicted the French from Italy clearing the way for an invasion of France. These claims overrate Suvorov as a commander and the striking power of the Russian contingent.

Suvorov's reputation rested on his victories over the poorly disciplined and rather backward forces of the Ottoman Empire and Poland, and at that was much inflated. His strategy was primitive, calling for an attack on the enemy wherever he was found, and his tactics, based on the cult of the bayonet, were outdated and wasteful when delivered against troops relying on fire.[29] Except on the Trebbia, where the bayonet prevailed, Russian casualties usually were double that of the French. Still, on occasion he displayed extraordinary energy and his influence on his troops who adored him often produced good results in battle. Barely five feet tall, with the habits of a private in the ranks, he was considered mad by many of his contemporaries. Wickham, an eyewitness not overly fond of the Austrians whom he suspected of devious schemes, was rather taken aback when he met Suvorov in 1799. 'Had I not myself such evident proofs on the strength of his mind,' he reported, 'I should certainly have taken him for a madman.'[30] His feelings did not improve on further acquaintance. 'It really is not to be expected that an Austrian officer of rank and talents, who has any sense of his own honour and dignity, should submit without the strongest repugnance to serve under a man who conducts himself so strangely.'[31]

As for the striking power of the two Russian corps, this fluctuated widely. 'The general and field officers are, with few exceptions,' Wickham observed, 'ignorant of everything but mere regimental duty,' and in 1799, Austria had to furnish all staff and support personnel from Major General de Chasteler, acting as Suvorov's chief of staff, down to junior officers.[32] In addition, the Russian army lacked all support services, transport, engineers, and medical, and had to rely on the already overburdened Austrians. The infantry, there was but little cavalry, had no light units. Although there were *Jäger* regiments, these had little in common with their German models. They could not develop skirmish lines or act independently, and their armament consisted of poor smoothbore muskets.[33] Archduke Charles commented that in battle the 'Russian common soldier is brave and his personal courage unsurpassed,' but he also asserted that this was not good enough to fight the French because officers and men were poorly trained in tactics and deployments.[34]

Although Russian discipline was ferocious, it was applied unevenly. Suvorov himself was appalled at its slow marching pace and the numerous camp followers, mainly officers' servants and mistresses but others as well, straggling behind the marching columns. Their conduct towards civilians was atrocious. Rape and pillage was the order of the day; a British officer accompanying the force in Italy reported that the Russians 'rob, steal, and maltreat inhabitants of the country with impunity.'[35] At the same time, the Russians tended to be brash, boastful, and over-confident, and blamed all set-backs on the alleged cowardice of their Austrian allies. And with the very same Austrians furnishing not only staff and support services, but three-fourths of the army fighting under Suvorov, it can readily be seen that relations between the two allies in the field were under a considerable strain.

Given these circumstances, it was Thugut's plan to avoid a large scale Austrian involvement in Switzerland and leave operations here to the two Russian corps. Not only would this avoid further friction, but leave Austria free to pursue its designs in northern Italy. What Thugut forgot was that the Russians were neither equipped nor trained to operate in the mountains and that success in Switzerland was vital to a successful prosecution of the war.

By the time the long drawn-out negotiations were completed, Charles, in a rare defiance of orders, had crossed the Rhine into Switzerland and, in a well-planned battle in which elements from Hotze and Bellegarde participated, fought the first Battle of Zurich on 4 June 1799. Although the Austrians had a numerical edge, 55,000 to 45,000, Massena made an able defence and managed to evacuate the city and retire in good order to positions on the Limmat. Charles, having suffered 3400 casualties against 1600 French, hesitated to press on, having exceeded his orders and fearing that he would be blamed for heavy losses.[36] Wickham reported that Charles had entered Switzerland 'without any authority from Vienna,' and that his 'HRH not only has never been able to obtain the slightest mark of approbation from his court' and 'is, or affects to be, extremely uneasy on that account.'[37]

In fact, the emperor was annoyed and on 10 July Charles finally received a cool letter ordering him to remain passive until relieved by Suvorov's corps from Italy and the Russian auxiliary corps from Germany under the arrogant and incompetent Korsakov. Three weeks later, formal instructions confirmed this arrangement. After the Russian arrival, Charles was to command the imperial army between the Neckar and Switzerland. He was to cross the Rhine near

Mannheim, though only as a demonstration, while in reality he was to prepare going into winter quarters.[38] Charles's objections that this was the end of any prospect for taking Switzerland, the key position in Europe, were overruled. On 12 August the first elements of Korsakov's corps arrived at Charles's headquarters in Kloten, but, as the archduke had suspected, were in no state to carry out operations independently. Ten days later Wickham wrote a somewhat ill-advised letter to Suvorov, who still had received no movement orders, that 'you cannot be ignorant that since the 6th of June to the 15th of this month, one of the finest armies that the House of Austria ever equipped for the field ... has remained within its lines ... without undertaking anything against the enemy's position.' And, he continued, 'your Excellency must even hear with distress, if not surprise ... that the enemy has detached a very considerable force on our left, ... cut off communications with Italy ... and has made himself master of the important and almost impregnable position of Mount St Gotthard.' He added that he had implored the archduke to act offensively but to no avail.[39] This communication did not aid future co-operation between the allies.

The collapse of the Coalition, August–December 1799

In Italy, the French had assembled another force, combining Moreau's and MacDonald's armies, in July and entrusted it to Joubert. Joubert's orders were to bring the Austro-Russian force under Suvorov to battle before it had received reinforcements. On 15 August Joubert attacked at Novi, some 30 miles north of Genoa, but was defeated when General Melas, marching to the sound of the guns, fell on his flank. Joubert fell in action; Moreau led the army back to Genoa.

On 27 August Suvorov finally received orders to march to Switzerland; Melas, a sound soldier, was to remain in Italy with 60,000 Austrians, while Charles was to create a diversion on the Rhine in support of a planned Anglo-Russian landing in Holland. By this time affairs had deteriorated in Switzerland. Massena, in support of Joubert, had become active again. This placed Charles in a dilemma. His orders were to quit Switzerland forthwith, but now Massena's offensive threatened his rear. To disengage himself safely, he combined with Korsakov in an attack against the French positions on 16–17 August which, due to poor staff work, failed miserably. Having acted against orders, Charles had little choice but to remove his troops to Germany, leaving behind a small corps under Hotze to support Korsakov. On 25–26 September, Massena attacked this poorly led force and drove it towards Schaffhausen.

Meanwhile Suvorov was making his way north through the Alpine passes, supported in his passage of the St Gotthard Pass by Austrian troops under Auffenberg. He planned to stage a concentric attack on Massena, requiring a concentration in striking range of a bold and mobile enemy. But Suvorov moved far too slowly and the terrain forced him to direct his artillery by a longer route. When he finally arrived at Wagen in October, Massena already had spoiled his plan and, as Wickham now discovered, the Russian force was 'not in a state to act by itself as an army.'[40] His suggestions that something still might be accomplished if the Russians would co-operate with Charles was met by an outburst of rage by Suvorov and a meeting between the two commanders did nothing to improve matters. By the end of October, Suvorov used his authority to remove his army from Switzerland into winter quarters near Augsburg, from where a very disappointed Wickham reported that the Russians were totally demoralized. Their withdrawal, he noted, was due to the 'almost unanimous desire of the army to return to Russia and to an evident dread of meeting the French.' Future co-operation with the Austrians was highly unlikely and the blame rested with Suvorov. 'It is impossible,' he concluded, 'that this man should be employed again.'[41]

Also in October, the Anglo-Russian expedition to northern Holland had failed despite initial success that included seizure of a good part of the Dutch fleet. There were acrimonious quarrels between the Duke of York and the Russian commanders and in the end the enterprise resulted in defeat and a hasty evacuation. The volatile Tsar already had broken relations with Austria; now he ordered his northern contingent home and by the turn of the year the alliance came to an end.

If London was less concerned with the loss of the Russian ally this was due to the glowing accounts about the Austrian army reaching London from Wickham and other sources. Already in June, Wickham had noted that 'it is impossible for those who had seen the Austrians at the former period [i.e. 1797] not to observe and be struck by the difference.'[42] In October he became much more specific. 'The Austrian army is certainly very superior to what it was.' Men as well as officers had improved. 'The troops are unquestionably better and animated by a very different spirit.' As for the officers, he admitted that the army was 'still miserable defective in generals,' but that the field grade and staff officers had much improved compared to their predecessors. 'In point of activity, real courage, and the desire of distinguishing themselves there is certainly no comparison.' While the previous set was super-cautious, 'approaching timidity,' the new men 'seem disposed on every occasion to hazard everything rather than to remain on the defensive.'[43] Perhaps this overrated the fighting quality of the Austrians, but London was impressed and Grenville, the Foreign Secretary, concluded that Austria 'alone continues to act offensively and vigorously against the irreconcilable Enemies of His Majesty & of the General tranquility of Europe.'[44]

Actually, in the latter half of 1799 the Austrians on the Rhine had gained only minor successes. In September, Charles had taken Mannheim, though he had then pulled back in order to be able to aid Suvorov and the French to the Middle Rhine. By October, the French held Mannheim and a number of other positions, while the bulk of the Austrian army remained concentrated at Donaueschingen. Fighting now tapered off and Charles, once again at the end of his nervous energy, requested the emperor to relieve him. He claimed that he was in failing health and 'shall be sick if I am forced to continue soldiering. There are hours, even days, when I no longer can mount a horse.'[45] But Vienna delayed relieving him until 2 February when Kray finally was named to succeed him and the general did not arrive to take over command until 17 March 1800.

In October 1799 the situation had changed drastically. Napoleon returned from Egypt and within a month had overthrown the Directory and made himself master of the republic with the title of First Consul. He immediately set to reorganize the French armies, though progress was slow. The French situation became more complicated when, in early November, the Austrians launched an offensive, striking against the French army in Italy. Decimated by sickness, disease, and desertion, the army was defeated and split. One part under Massena was driven into Genoa; the other under Suchet retreated to Nice. On the other hand, the Austrians also were weary and short of supplies. Operations ended in December when both sides went into winter quarters. While the fronts were quiet, Charles tried to raise additional troops from the militia of the Austrian territories in southern Germany. To be sure, their goal was not an unformed popular levy, but volunteers for new *Jäger* and mobile battalions. Major General Josef Baron Simbschen, a Military Border officer, was to supervise the effort and Vienna was to provide the necessary funds.[46] In the end, little came of this. As in France, the population of the Rhineland, and for that matter even in the interior provinces, was thoroughly tired of war and there was little enthusiasm for service in a regular or semi-regular force.

The campaigns of 1800

On assuming office as First Consul and aware of the sorry state of the French armies, Napoleon opened peace negotiations with Vienna. The Austrians, however, considering themselves in an excellent strategic position, and perhaps misled by promises of more British support than would be forthcoming, rejected the feeler. Faced with the prospect of renewed war, Napoleon gave priority to building up Moreau's Army of the Rhine to 100,000, and also began to collect a Reserve Army of 60,000, a figure never reached, around Dijon. Massena's Army of Italy, 36,000 at best, was left to fend for itself, though Napoleon hoped to relieve it by a manoeuvre on the rear of Melas's army that would decide the campaign in Italy.

On the Austrian side, and in consultation with the British government, the *Hofkriegsrat* had devised an ambitious campaign plan. While Kray was to advance across the Belfort Gap, Melas (about 90,000 strong) was to penetrate through the Maritime Alps to Lyon and some distance beyond unite with Kray's army for a march on Paris. Melas was to be supported by the British Mediterranean fleet and there also was talk of a British landing force to be collected at Minorca to strike at the rear and the flank of the French while the Austrians operated against their front. The existence of the Reserve Army was discounted.

In the event, Melas began operations in early April. Leaving behind 20,000 men to watch the Alpine passes north, and 10,000 men under Ott to blockade Genoa, he pushed Suchet's remaining force back behind the Var. At Nice, Melas halted to await the fall of Genoa before proceeding through the mountains. Besieged by land and sea by the Austrians and British, Massena grimly held on as his supplies ran out and capitulated only on 4 June 1800. By this time Napoleon's Reserve Army, with such reinforcements as he could scrape up, had moved through the Great St Bernard Pass, with auxiliary advances and feints in the Little St Bernard and Simplon passes. Surpassing considerable obstacles the First Consul debouched into the Lombard plain, threatened the Austrian lines of communication and occupied Milan on 2 June. Melas, finally convinced that the Reserve Army really existed, had begun to move north on 19 May, leaving behind a small detachment at Nice to contain Suchet as well as Ott to blockade Genoa. He first concentrated near Turin and then, having received intelligence, moved east. On 14 June the two armies met on the plain of Marengo some six miles east of the fortress of Allessandria.

With both sides having detached forces, the numbers in action were small. The Austrians numbered 32,000 with 7000 cavalry and 100 guns; the French initially had 18,000 and 40 guns. The Austrians attacked first and though Melas had made poor dispositions, including too few bridges across Fontanone Creek which cut across the battlefield, superior numbers counted and after heavy fighting the French were driven back. Convinced that the day was won, Melas ordered pursuit and left the field. But the French were not routed and the arrival of a fresh division turned near-defeat into victory. Napoleon ordered a counterattack, surprised the Austrian columns forming up for the pursuit and in turn drove them back in disorder. Some units managed to form lines and cover the retreat, but in the late afternoon rout became general.[47] The next night a shaken Melas signed the Armistice of Allessandria, evacuating all of Lombardy as far as the Mincio and halting all fighting until Vienna had replied to another French peace offer. Napoleon was well pleased and a few days later he sent Melas the sabre he had captured in Egypt, asking him to accept the weapon as a 'symbol of the high esteem for the conduct of your army on the field of Marengo.'[48] The First Consul added that he hoped that peace would soon be restored between their two countries and that war was due only to British machinations.

Contributing to Napoleon's generosity was that he had just received news that Moreau had driven back Kray almost all the way to Austria. Since Charles had left, the Austrian army in Germany had declined fast. Constant feuds among a disunited and scrapping staff had disrupted the higher echelons and played havoc with the already shaky morale of the rank and file. The supply system was not working well and desertions increased alarmingly.[49] Moreover, the army once again was deployed in cordon. While the main force stood at Donaueschingen, there were detachments at Rastatt, Basle and Schaffhausen, a front of nearly 169 miles covered by 60,000 men. Another strong detachment, 20,000, was even further away in Vorarlberg. Moreau had been reinforced to 120,000 men, organized in four corps. At the end of April he advanced, easily piercing the cordon and defeating Kray at Stockach on 3 May and two days later at Möskirch. Kray hastily withdrew into a fortified camp at Ulm and when he received news of the Armistice of Allessandria he concluded a similar arrangement, the Armistice of Parsdorf, which ended fighting, subject to 15 days' notice. In the event, the armistice ran until 13 November 1800.

By the end of June, it had become clear that Kray could no longer be kept in command. The emperor wanted to recall Charles, but Thugut objected. The archduke once again was pressing for an immediate peace while Austria still had an army.[50] He was not alone in this. On 22 July *Feldmarschall Leutnant* Schmitt, who had served both Charles and Kray as chief of staff, submitted a memorandum concerning the 'possible outcome of a campaign in Germany.'[51] The enemy, he asserted, was growing in power and numbers. Should hostilities be resumed, Napoleon could push into the Tyrol and cut communications between Germany and Italy. No troops were available to reinforce the Tyrol and there was really no other option but to make peace. Thugut, however, had just concluded a new subsidy treaty with Great Britain in June and also was motivated by a genuine hatred of the French. But during the summer and autumn his policies had become widely unpopular in Austria, and in September the Minister resigned to be succeeded by Count Cobenzl.

Even so, he retained influence and when during the summer new recruits as well as some 30,000 auxiliaries from Bavaria, Swabia, and Wurttemberg were hired to serve with the Austrian army at British expense, the emperor decided to resume the war.[52] This, however, required a more popular commander than Kray's immediate successor, *Feldzeugmeister* Baron Lauer, a fierce disciplinarian and an experienced engineer, but lacking experience in handling an army. Dynastic considerations made it desirable for a member of the imperial house to hold the position. Thugut, still in office, approached both Archduke Ferdinand and Joseph, but the first refused to serve while the second claimed that as Palatine of Hungary he was indispensable in raising the noble *insurrectio*. After Thugut's fall, the emperor offered command to Charles. The archduke, claiming to be too sick for active duty, turned him down. There was nothing left but to place the army in Germany under the titular command of Archduke John, 18 years of age, innocent of all but the most elementary military training and without experience. While Lauer continued as second in command, assisted by Colonel Weyrother as chief of staff, and held the real authority, John nevertheless could not wholly deny responsibility. He anxiously wrote to Charles who replied with a long series of letters crammed with advice.[53]

In November 1800, the emperor decided to reopen the war. Austrian plans called for an advance from the Inn to the Isar, a crossing of the river at Landshut and then a swing south to crush Moreau's left flank and cut French lines of communications just west of Munich. For his part, Moreau planned to concentrate his left wing near Munich, while his right and centre advanced towards Salzburg.[54] As was true of most Austrian staff planning then or later, the scheme showed a tolerable appreciation of the terrain, but little regard for the mobility of the enemy, though by Napoleonic standards Moreau was slow moving. In the event, the Austrians found themselves unable to commence operations when the armistice ended and were delayed until 29 November by lack of supplies, low morale and poor weather. By the time they moved, Moreau's left had advanced and John now abandoned the idea of a wide out-flanking manoeuvre in favour of a direct advance southwest to Munich, following the major road through the Hohenlinden forest, some 18 miles east of the city. Here, on 2 December, the Austrian columns ran head on into French positions hidden in the woods and bushes, terrain ideally suited to light infantry tactics. Trying to break through, one Austrian Cuirassier subaltern remembered that 'the troopers were suddenly fired upon by enemy *chausseurs* stationed in the tree tops,' and driven back with heavy casualties.[55] The Austrians' discomfiture was completed by a largely unplanned, though effective, French advance on their left and at this point John's army disintegrated. It was not a retreat but a rout. Attempts to form a line of resistance covering Salzburg failed. The army was totally demoralized and there were mass desertions. Nothing was left between Moreau and Vienna.

In this dire emergency the emperor once again appealed to Charles who after some hesitation declared that he 'was willing to sacrifice himself for the state,' and, on condition that he be given a free hand, assumed command on 17 December.[56] It was far too late. The troops no longer had combat cohesion, they only wanted peace. Austrian militia volunteer battalions refused to march, and the Hungarian Insurrectio refused to muster. In Vienna, Francis told the burghers that there was a threat of siege which induced many to flee, while the court made arrangements to evacuate the capital. Resistance no longer was possible and with the French already in Upper Austria, an armistice was signed at Steyr on 25 December, followed on 9 February 1801 by the Peace of Luneville which reconfirmed the arrangements of Campo Formio.

Conclusion

The defeat of the Second Coalition was rooted in large part in the inability of the ill-assorted allies to agree on common strategy and war aims. The lack of an effective land force reduced Great Britain to strike some questionable diplomatic bargains; the instability of the Tsar aggravated relations between major allied commanders. As for the Austrians, the campaigns of the Second Coalition reconfirmed the tenacity of their soldiers and the shortcomings of their commanders.

Even Archduke Charles had been far from his best and whether his presence in November 1800 would have made any difference is questionable. Given his mood at that time, it would appear just as well that his reputation was not put on the line. Now, with his reputation intact, he became the only possible choice as the man to reform the Austrian military system.

IV

Archduke Charles and the First Reform Period, 1801–5

DEFEAT once again demonstrated the need for reform of the Austrian military system and for the next three years. Archduke Charles, endowed with extensive powers, sought to implement change despite the opposition of entrenched interests and the suspicions of his imperial brother. In the end, little had been accomplished. When, against the archduke's express desires, Austria challenged Napoleon in 1805, the army still was understrength, ill-equipped, poorly trained, and with indifferent leadership. Much of the blame for this has been attributed to the reactionaries at court and in the army, especially the ambitious and vain Mack who collaborated with these elements. This, of course, was true, but Charles was not blameless. He believed that more than military reforms were needed. There was a crisis of public confidence in the government, near chaos in the administration, and the economy was in worse shape than that of France on the eve of revolution. An overhaul of the civil as well as military administration, in his opinion, was imperative, and to carry this out, Austria needed an extended period of peace, secured, if necessary, by an accommodation with France. The archduke's plans were political as well as military, and this precisely was what the emperor and his advisors had long sought to prevent. From the outset, therefore, opposition was inevitable.

Moreover, the archduke's personality, and his choice of associates, tended to harden existing sentiments. Charles never took criticism well and, suffering frequent spells of introversion and insecurity, he alienated old friends and supporters. Finally, during this first reform period, Charles was preoccupied with administration and gave little attention to improving the combat readiness of the army. Perhaps subconsciously he hoped that a low state of preparedness would prevent the statesmen from plunging the Monarchy into a war she was bound to lose.

Ministerial reorganization

During the dark days after Hohenlinden and Luneville, Archduke Charles had become a patriotic myth. In his person, Princess Elonore Liechtenstein proclaimed, 'reside all the honour and good reputation remaining to us,' while the poet August Iffland wrote that 'only one bond held the Monarchy together ... Archduke Charles.' He no longer could be denied. Before he accepted command of the army in December, Charles had been able to impose a number of conditions, including the appointment of General Baron Duka as his chief of staff and the transfer of Matthias von Fassbender, a trusted civilian associate, into the Austrian civil service with the rank and title of a supernumerary *Hofrat*.[1] On 9 January 1801, that is before the Treaty of Lunéville had been signed, the emperor promoted Charles to fieldmarshal and appointed him president of the *Hofkriegsrat* with instructions to 'submit a detailed plan for the regulation of the military establishment of the entire Monarchy.'[2]

Charles immediately proposed no less than a restructuring of the governing system of the empire. Acting apparently on Fassbender's advice, he persuaded his brother to abolish the *Staatsrat*, a body which had failed to co-ordinate internal affairs and was without influence in foreign affairs, and to replace it with a *Staats und Konferenz Ministerium* representing three major ministries – those of the Interior, Foreign Affairs, and War and Navy. The Interior Ministry was entrusted to Count F. Kolowrat-Krakowski, Foreign Affairs were handled jointly by Counts Colloredo and Cobenzl, the first an old tutor of the emperor and friendly with Thugut, while Charles with the title of *Kriegs und Marine Minister*, directed all military and naval concerns. It was planned that the ministers would meet frequently to discuss common problems, and report directly to the emperor in matters concerning their separate departments alone. The emperor, an absolute ruler, then would be in a position to take immediate decisions. Charles participated in the ministerial conferences and reported on matters concerning peace and war as well as the budget. He had direct access to the monarch in regard to senior promotions, major operations, and war plans, and had the authority to make independent decisions regarding organization, recruiting, remounts, uniforms, and generally all the day-to-day affairs of the military establishment.[3]

Soon after the *Staats und Konferenz Ministerium* began its work on 1 September 1801, Charles received further powers. On 10 September, Fassbender suggested to him that the *Hofkriegsrat* had become redundant as an independent agency and that it should be reduced to an executive branch of the War Ministry handling a number of clearly defined duties such as recruiting, pay and pensions, equipment, observance of regulations and the like.[4] This was done with surprising speed. On 29 September the *Hofkriegsrat* became subordinated to the War Ministry, losing its right of direct access to the emperor. Not since the days of Prince Eugene of Savoy had any general held so much power in the Habsburg realm. As Lord Paget, the newly arrived British ambassador at the Viennese court, remarked, these arrangements meant the eclipse of Thugut and his faction, and that the 'Archduke may certainly be considered at this moment as the leading man in this empire.'[5]

Yet Thugut's influence still was far from totally eliminated and moreover, some believed that Fassbender rather than Charles was the moving force behind the events. This certainly was the opinion of Fieldmarshal Prince Schwarzenberg who noted in his private diary that Fassbender pushed Charles to assume a role far beyond his actual ability. 'Fassbender imagined a weak man to have the powers of a giant, yet, though this man [i.e. the archduke] was able to look like such for brief periods, he lacked the energy for a sustained effort.'[6] Schwarzenberg perhaps underrated the archduke and over-rated Fassbender. Other observers were more circumspect. Radetzky, later a fieldmarshal and one of Austria's greatest soldiers, wrote that Fassbender was a 'hard working intelligent man,' while Archduke John agreed that he was hard working and intelligent, but also noted that his rapid rise had 'caused him to lose perspective.'[7] Fassbender was a complex and not wholly admirable figure, given to machinations, insecure, easily swayed, and like so many weak men, overbearing when he thought he had the upper hand. As John feared, his manners as much as his restless activity created enemies among senior generals and officials and contributed to the backlash against his patron, the archduke.

Although there are many other opinions of Fassbender, few flattering, he has remained a figure of mystery. For a few years, however, this minor Rhenish nobleman from Trier, one of the many German refugees and exiles from the French Revolution in Vienna played a major, some would say decisive, role in the Austrian military establishment. Born in 1764, he studied at Mainz and Göttingen, taught constitutional law in his hometown, and after the French occupied Trier he became an official in the *Reichskriegskanzlei* of the Holy Roman Empire. In 1796 he organized intelligence activities in the Rhineland for Charles, and in recognition of his services rose to head of that chancery and in 1799 was appointed confidential advisor to the archduke. He shared the archduke's dislike of Thugut and when Charles became the leader of the Austrian military establishment he carried Fassbender with him. In April 1801, Fassbender received a regular appointment as *Presidial Hofrat* and on 3 September he was named *Staats und Konferenzrat*.[8]

Fassbender's influence and authority far exceeded those normally held by a senior civil servant in the military establishment. Despite his lack of actual military experience, he soon became far more important than General Duka, the archduke's chief of staff. On 12 April 1801, Charles informed Fassbender that he intended to 'return the army to a respectable posture so as to enable the emperor to assert his position among the powers of Europe.' As a first step, the archduke proposed a complete overhaul of office procedures in the central military administration, to reduce the number of officials, eliminate unnecessary paperwork, 'avoid extravagances in order to save time and money.' He instructed Fassbender that the 'responsibilities which I in my capacity of president of the *Hofkriegsrat* shall assign you involve the elaboration of plans for a complete reorganization of the military establishment, restructuring the *Hofkriegsrat*, and determining the proper relationships between the various military departments. . . . To deal with these very important responsibilities, and with such confidential assignments as I shall entrust to you, you will be excused from all routine duties.'[9] Apparently satisfied with Fassbender's application and progress, on 23 August Charles went one step further and named the civilian as his deputy whenever the archduke found it necessary to leave the capital.[10] Such rapid promotion and wide powers could not fail to arouse animosities and to reassure Fassbender, Charles promised him on 25 August that he was well aware that his actions would create enmity, calumny, and intrigues, and that everything would be tried to turn the monarch against him, but he promised 'you can count on my support as well as that of His Majesty who has promised this in a personal letter.'[11]

Thus armed, Fassbender did not restrict himself to administrative matters, but took an interest in fortifications, officer training, and even the preparation of new drill manuals. Such intrusions into purely technical matters might have been tolerated in Britain, and were commonplace in republican France, but they were very unique in Austria, and senior officers bitterly resented the intrusions of this presumptuous civilian.

Reforms of the central military administration

The newly created War Ministry functioned between 1801 and 1806, though from late 1804 on it functioned merely on paper. In any case, it always used the reorganized *Hofkriegsrat* as its executive organ. It did provide a separate chancery for Archduke Charles who directed major army policies, reorganization schemes, strategic planning, and senior appointments. For personnel matters he relied on the adjutant general, Colonel, later General Count Bubna, while strategic and operational plans were entrusted to General Duka, the Chief of the General Staff. In addition, the Directors of Artillery and Engineering, Fieldmarshal Count Joseph Colloredo and Archduke John, also reported directly to Charles though their directorates remained part of the *Hofkriegsrat* organization.

Actual army administration was handled through the *Hofkriegsrat* which on 1 September 1801 assumed a new structure. The basic division into three major departments, each with a number of subordinate directorates and sections, was kept. Department I, the military department, was responsible for general administration, engineering, artillery, and the Military Border; Department II, the political-administrative department, dealt with recruiting, remounts, equipment, supply, pay, and medical arrangements, while Department III continued to administer courts martial and other disciplinary measures. Superficially, there really was but little difference between the old and the new *Hofkriegsrat*. The number of officials had been reduced from 210 to 160, a number of senior bureaucrats were replaced with generals, and overall outward appearance militarized, even the civilians had to wear uniforms.

There was, however, a decided improvement in administrative efficiency. On taking office Charles found sacks of invoices, reports, and correspondence, a total of 154,000 unpaid bills and 33,000 unsettled claims for pensions and supplies. Some officials declared that it would take 40 years to settle all these accounts. Fassbender was able to speed up procedures and within two years a document in *Hofkriegsrat* channels passed through only 23 instead of 48 hands and the total number of separate documents issued by this agency in 1804 had declined by 55,000 pieces from the previous year. When he resigned as war minister, Charles reported with pride that 'I can look with sincere satisfaction on the exemplary order in which I hand over the accounts to my successor ... and to contemplate the very real advantages this provides for Your Majesty's state, the army, all those concerned, and above all the widows and orphans.'[12]

Charles has been faulted for his emphasis on administration and bookkeeping, but this must be considered in the overall context of state finances. With the Monarchy bankrupt, the military budget had been cut from 87 million florins in 1801 to 34½ million in 1804. It still was larger than the military budgets of 1792–6 and there were those who blamed Charles for increasing military expenditures in peacetime. In defence, Charles pointed out to the emperor that prices for raw materials and finished goods had risen by over 100 percent since 1790, and that there were heavy new pension obligations. Finally, it no longer was desirable to station troops in the interior of the Monarchy and in locations where their upkeep was cheap. Austria now faced major potential enemies across her frontiers – France, Prussia, and also Russia – and it was necessary to keep troops deployed at all time. Cantonments, barracks, new fortifications, and material were required.[13] And under conditions of financial stringency, Charles was trying to squeeze extra money out of available funds. To be sure, in 1793, with circumstances much more desperate, France had improvised great armies, but Austria was not, and never could be, a revolutionary country, and Charles himself would never have used the aroused energy of a people. He was, and remained, a typical enlightened conservative.

He could take some credit for improving the position of the General Staff. In March 1801 he requested the emperor that this organization should not be disbanded or reduced at the end of each war and that a permanent cadre of 21 staff officers – the term 'staff officer' denoted a rank above major – be retained together with 16 captains and 12 subalterns. On 23 March, Francis appointed General Duka as 'Quartermaster General even in peacetime' and generally approved the archduke's proposals. In his first instructions to Duka, Charles instructed him that his staff was to be engaged in making plans 'covering long periods and entire campaigns,' and that the Chief of the Quartermaster General Staff would not merely implement the commander's ideas into practice, but act as his 'proper and well prepared advisor to examine intelligence and projects of all kinds.' At the same time, however, Charles indicated that the commander retained ultimate decision-making powers.[14]

The new arrangements remained largely on paper until 1805. Duka did work out plans for the archduke and generally supervised the operations of the staffs with the armies in Italy and Germany, but a real operational General Staff did not function until late in 1809.[15]

Officers and men, 1801–5

Charles frequently had complained about the quality of officers and he made efforts to improve the training of junior officers and to raise the morale and status of the corps as a whole. Little could be done to improve the financial picture. While senior officers were well paid and often had private incomes, most junior officers had to live on their pay, with scales unchanged since 1748, despite the rampaging inflation. The officers, complained the archduke, 'compare their lot with the better compensated civil servants and lose all interest and enthusiasm for their calling.'[16] Under these circumstances there was a marked decline in officer entries. The old nobility never had been as prominent in the Austrian service as it was in Prussia. Indeed, in 1806, Archduke Charles wrote to his brother Francis that the 'nobility no longer feels honoured in fulfilling its obligations to serve. It does not serve any longer and if it serves it does not serve well!'[17] And because the losses of the long wars and the declining number of well-born aspirants could not be made good by the handful of graduates from the military academies, subsidiary cadet schools, admitting pupils from the middle and lower middle classes, were founded in the provinces. At the same time there was an increase in the number of regimental cadets and some promotion from the ranks. With poor training and limited prospects, these new officers further depressed the level of professional competence. An illustration of their low educational qualifications was provided in 1802 by *Feldmarschall Leutnant* Unterberger who, as already mentioned, found it necessary to issue a detailed plan of instructions, including basic additions, subtractions, and divisions, for his junior officers because, as he wrote, only a few had graduated from the academies while the rest were totally ignorant.[18]

To improve the professional level of the officers, orders were issued to modernize the training of cadets, ensigns, and lieutenants with less emphasis on formal drill and more attention to practical manoeuvres. Moreover, Charles attempted to raise morale by improving relations within the regiments. 'Too much harsh discipline is as damaging for the service as too great laxity; only just and equitable treatment can maintain the esprit de corps in the officer corps.'[19] In 1802 he attempted to outlaw the morale destroying purchase of rank, even the long tolerated 'conventions,' though with the shortage of junior officers he could not make this stick and in the end reversed himself arguing that the 'army lost little if an officer quit who was prepared to sell his commission.' Nothing also could be done about the abuses inherent in the system of *Regimentsinhaber*, the regimental proprietors, especially nepotism, though in the worst instances the archduke tried to dismiss officers who were unable to 'give effective assistance in the rehabilitation of their regiments.'[20]

Charles encountered mixed results in his efforts to modify recruitment and conditions of service for the enlisted ranks by extending conscription to Hungary, systematizing the exemptions in the 'conscripted' lands, and by shortening the periods of service.

In 1796, the Hungarian Diet had voted a cash contribution of 4,400,000 florins and substantial quantities of supply in kind. Also, though denying that this constituted a binding precedent, the Diet had raised the strength of the standing army recruited in the kingdom to 52,000, enough to provide for the additional regiments raised in 1798. But in 1802 the Diet balked. The French threat seemed to have disappeared while the new central governmental structure was perceived as dangerous to Hungary's special interests. Charles had requested a regular contingent of 64,000 men, the introduction of conscription, and a cash contribution of 1,200,000 florins. The Hungarians countered with a long list of demands which Charles characterized as nothing less than an attempt to gain control over military affairs and advised the emperor to reject for reasons of state.[21] In the end, after two years of wrangling, there was a compromise. The Hungarian contingent in the standing army was raised to 63,264 with 6034 annual replacements and another 12,000 recruits in case of a general mobilization. But this arrangement was to run for three years only and the Diet flatly refused to consider conscription. It also voted only half of the cash requested.[22]

Clearly, as Charles bitterly observed, Hungary was pursuing a particularist course, though this time it appeared that it was not just the 'ruling nation' but a much wider cross-section which supported the Diet. Moreover, and particularly worrisome to the archduke was that in 1799–1800, Hungarian infantry regiments, renowned for their fierce fighting spirit, had suffered an extraordinarily large incidence of desertions.

To make military service more acceptable, if not popular, Charles wanted to limit the terms of enlistment for the rank and file. One report estimated that in the conscripted provinces no fewer than 27,000 potential recruits had fled their home to escape the army.[23] 'Life long service,' he wrote, 'creates an army which at the outbreak of war is already superannuated, consisting of decrepit soldiers who either will be invalided out after a few months campaigning, or who are disaffected and ready to desert or even to enlist with the enemy when captured.'[24] His efforts to reduce the term of service to a uniform eight years in all the branches failed. Discharged soldiers, he was told, might contribute expert leadership for popular revolt. He settled for reducing the term to ten years in the infantry, 12 years in the cavalry, and 14 years in the artillery and the technical troops. On 4 May 1802 there appeared a new service law implementing these changes which also were to apply to serving soldiers in gradual stages. In addition, the law provided amnesty for all those who had fled the country because of fear of lifelong service.[25]

There still remained the problem that the basic conscription law was capricious in application and provided all too many exemptions. Of course, in contrast with some officers such as Colonel Zach who already in 1796 had urged universal military service with no exemptions, Charles merely wanted to improve the existing system. As he pointed out in March 1804, Austria could raise a very large army if it was willing, like France in 1793, to have the 'whole nation become an army, the whole state an encampment, where every able bodied man would be made a soldier and all supplies directed to provide for the army. Such a mobilization, of course, would ruin industry and national prosperity and be destructive of the entire established order.'[26] The new conscription law, promulgated on 25 October 1804, regulated the enrolment of men as well as draft and pack animals. Conscription was to be handled by permanently appointed officers in each district, but exemptions still remained numerous. Among others, it exempted nobles and their sons, the clergy, students at higher schools, the only sons of independent peasants, teachers and their assistants, postal clerks, lawyers, merchants and their bookkeepers, apothecaries, managers of industrial enterprises, foremen of salt, saltpeter, powder, and iron works, barge captains and sailing masters, and many other agricultural, craft, and industrial occupations.[27] Clearly, the law was above all concerned with preserving the economy; it applied only to the Austrian lands, except the Tyrol, to Bohemia/Moravia and Galicia and did little to widen the recruitment base.

Concern with economy also permeated efforts to reorganize the Military Borders, though in this case, with the *Grenzer* expected to support themselves by agriculture, the emphasis was understandable. For some time now administrative and economic conditions on the Military Borders had been deteriorating.[28] Since the early eighteenth century no less than 30 different schemes, systems, and reorganizations had been tried. Each time the primary purpose of these reforms was to raise the fighting strength of the Border, but ultimately the continuous drain on manpower had made conditions almost unbearable. At the outset of the War of the First Coalition only a few composite battalions had been provided; by 1794–5, however, over 13,000 *Grenzer* were in the field, while others manned the military cordon against the Ottoman Empire. During the War of the Second Coalition the Military Borders mobilized 36 battalions as well as a Hussar regiment and sharpshooter detachments, while again maintaining the cordon. Although the *Grenzer* fought with credit in Italy, Switzerland, and Germany, replacements became a problem and *Grenzer* morale was hard hit by reports about conditions at home. In June 1800, several units mutinied and after this the view that the *Grenzer* were 'shiftless, false, and totally undisciplined' attained currency among many Austrian senior officers. There now was sentiment to disband the institution.

In 1802, Charles appointed Archduke Ludwig as director general of the Border and charged a commission, headed by Major General Klein of the Military Border Section in the *Hofkriegsrat*, to make an investigation, submit a comprehensive report on conditions, and make recommendations. Commission members travelled the extent of the frontier districts, reports were collected in Vienna, and in the end Klein opposed the dissolution of the *Grenzer* regiments and instead argued for a basic reappraisal of their military role. He maintained that attempts to make the *Grenzer* into regular infantry were futile. This was contrary to their national custom and temperament, and because they also had to look after their farms in order to live, they had 'very little time to learn complicated drill and evolutions.' He suggested a reorganization which would take into account that they could 'not be effectively trained or employed as troops of the line, but that their natural aptitudes make them highly suitable as scouts, vedettes, and skirmishers.' Before Charles would implement these recommendations, he ordered another spot survey of economic conditions and the commission again recommended an entirely new code of basic laws for the Border. Charles agreed and the commission set itself to devise a new code to supersede all previous legislation. Before this could be drawn up, however, Charles resigned and most of his schemes were suspended.

Finally, during this first reform period, a number of officers close to Charles investigated the potential of popular levies. The Tyrolean sharpshooter levies had turned out in 1797 and 1799, but their enthusiasm had been short lived. In general, as Colonel Mayer von

Heldenfeld, one of the archduke's close collaborators for some years, wrote, no hastily mustered armed mass, whether called 'militia, *Landsturm*, volunteers, *Cerniden, insurrectio*, or fencibles – in fact any armed force if it is not composed of trained troops – has any more hope of standing against our enemy than the papal soldiers or those of Cardinal Buffo – even if it was commanded by a Xenophon, Alexander, Turenne, Eugene, Montecuccoli, Condé, Frederick, or Bonaparte.' Moreover, to commission its officers would destroy 'all military concepts of honour, and esprit de corps and thus become the grave of the regular army.'[29] These rather flowery words reflected the archduke's sentiments and, against the advice of his rather more romantic brother John, the militia institutions of the Tyrol were curbed. Instead of the general levies, four militia regiments were projected, but only partially organized, and in 1805 these regiments did not do too well.[30]

Army reorganization and training, 1801–4

There was little change in the composition of the army in this period. Perhaps revealing a continued lack of appreciation for light infantry tactics, the 15 light battalions created in 1798 were disbanded in 1801. To take their place a regular *Jäger* regiment was formed, designated as the *Tyroler Jäger Regiment*, comprising of three battalions with six companies each, armed, at least in part with the rifled M 1796/9 *Jägerstutzen* and the distinctive Austrian broad-bladed sword bayonet. Cadres for the new unit were found from Tyroleans serving in the Le Loup Free Corps and in the 46th Infantry Regiment recruited in the land. The Tyrolean *Jäger* would make an excellent record for themselves, but even so the fact was that, apart from the *Grenzer*, instead of 15 there now existed only three light battalions.

Because a major portion of the likely theatres of operations against France, Switzerland, Italy, and the Tyrol offered little scope for major cavalry actions, horse regiments were reduced from 42 in 1799 to 35, though curiously the *Chevauleger* regiments were revived. By 1804 there were eight Cuirassier, six Dragoon, six *Chevaulegers*, 12 Hussar, and three *Uhlan* regiments, a total of 280 squadrons. The artillery branch was augmented. From personnel of the disbanded Artillery Fusilier Battalion as well as from various independent companies, a fourth artillery regiment was formed. In rough numbers, Austria now had 1800 pieces of artillery, with the majority of guns still distributed in the line artillery of the foot regiments. As for the foot, there were no further changes up to the summer of 1805.

Standards of training in the army varied. Because of the financial stringency, troops still remained widely scattered and, though this was undesirable for rapid mobilization, many regiments were stationed in the eastern provinces where their upkeep was cheaper. Moreover, training was impeded by the unfortunate practice of sending a substantial proportion of enlisted men on unpaid furlough to save money. Cobenzl, no friend of the archduke, complained to Colloredo that this distribution of troops, 'undertaken by the military without any consultation about the requirements of foreign policy,' left Austria open to the threat of a sudden military strike by France. 'We pay,' he wrote, 'to keep up three hundred thousand men and yet must tremble before a surprise attack. This is an outrage which is hard to comprehend.'[31]

Colloredo was equally critical of Archduke Charles's military administration. On 25 October 1803, he complained to his friend Thugut that the great camps of instruction held at Laxenburg and in Moravia revealed the 'capabilities of the rank and file and the total ineptitude of the officers.'[32] Even Fieldmarshal Schwarzenberg expressed the opinion that the exercises conducted at the camps of instruction were useless, outdated, and poorly planned. He blamed Duka whom he characterized as an officer lacking fighting experience.[33] Overall, the thrust of these critics was that Archduke Charles had wasted too much time, money, and effort on administrative reforms and that he had not prepared the army for war.

These charges, albeit pressed for political reasons by politicians and officers eager to remove the archduke, seen as an obstacle to their war policy, were not entirely without foundation. The number of troops available for service was inadequate even within budgetary restrictions, and the training of troops was conducted largely according to models dating back to the period of the Seven Years' War. While there were exceptional regiments, such as the Cuirassiers at Sopron (Ödenburg) commanded by Radetzky, for the most part the suggestions offered by Archduke Charles revealed an almost obsessive concern with trivia, whether the bands played at proper intervals, or whether alignments were correct.[34] For all that, the field days in the camps of instruction sometimes took a violent turn. A veteran remembered that at Minkendorf in Lower Austria, where 36,000 men were assembled for training, the officers spent a great deal of time banqueting, but little on training. During the one major field day, staged for visiting Emperor Francis, the plan called for several cavalry regiments to simulate an attack against two Grenadier battalions. The exercises ended hastily when, contrary to the script, the foot did not break when charged, but formed squares, several Grenadiers discharging small stones from their blank loaded muskets. The enraged cavalry, having suffered several casualties, now used its sabres and before order could be restored there were three dead and some 60 wounded.[35]

The Russian alliance and court intrigues, 1803–5

Following the break-up of the Second Coalition, Britain, too, had made peace at Amiens in March 1802. This makeshift arrangement, however, was short lived. While Napoleon consolidated his power at home, voted Consul for Life in 1802 and on 2 December 1804 crowned himself Emperor of the French, his actions abroad affronted the former partners of the Second Coalition in almost every way. The uneasy peace with Britain broke down in the spring of 1803. In May, hostilities resumed. The Royal Navy blockaded the French coast, while Napoleon went forward with preparations to invade England, already begun before Amiens. Shipping was collected and seven army corps, the Army of the Ocean Coast with headquarters at Boulogne, assembled in camps from Brest to Hamburg. Hanover was occupied and the Adriatic ports of Ancona, Brindisi and Otranto seized. In southern Germany, Napoleon pressed his advantage and made a number of secondary states such as Bavaria and Württemberg into clients and potential allies. In Italy he extended his control. Most of the north passed under French control, either annexed or ruled by relatives of Napoleon, with Lombardy constituted as the Kingdom of Italy ruled by a viceroy, his stepson Eugene de Beauharnais. Even Russia, now ruled by Tsar Alexander I, a liberal minded, if somewhat unstable, young man who had succeeded to the throne following the assassination of his father Paul, was alienated. Originally favouring an accommodation with Napoleon, Alexander turned against him following the wanton kidnapping and execution of the Duc d'Enghien in March 1804. British diplomacy and gold contributed to forging a new coalition, but Napoleon's provocations provided much of the impetus.

In Austria sentiment was divided on the wisdom of renewing the alliance. While Cobenzl and Colloredo, joined by certain other personages at court, were convinced by 1803 that only a new alliance with Russia could save Austria from Napoleon's boundless ambitions, the emperor was reluctant and Archduke Charles completely opposed to such designs. For the moment, what may be called the ministerial and the archducal factions in Vienna were in balance and therefore when in 1803, Colonel Carl Baron Stutterheim was sent to St Petersburg as military plenipotentiary, his mission assumed a dual aspect. Cobenzl wished to open a military relationship with Russia; Charles hoped to obtain data on the Russian army showing that force lacking in combat strength so that he could counter any bellicose schemes.[36]

Matters became more acute in 1804 when Tsar Alexander approached Britain and Austria about the prospects of renewing the anti-French alliance. In March, Charles submitted a memorandum to the emperor in which he warned against any military undertaking. France had more manpower, 421 infantry battalions compared to $240\frac{1}{2}$ Austrian; 78 mounted regiments against 35 Austrian. No real help could be expected from Russia in the main theatre of operations – northern Italy. Even if the Tsar provided 150,000 men, there was the question whether 'some trivial quarrel among generals or other such pretext will once again give them a reason to leave Austria to continue the war alone.' In any case, Austria would be on its own during the opening stages of a conflict; one no longer could count on Bavarian or Württemberg troops, and hope for an Italian revolt was futile. Russia was an untrustworthy ally with interests in the Balkans opposed to those of Austria, and Britain was unlikely to risk a powerful land force on the continent. British preoccupations with Flanders had ruined previous campaigns and 'apart from Marlborough, no Englishman has ever believed that control of the seas could be achieved by fighting on the Danube.' Charles concluded that, even if the military operations were successful, the country's economy and prosperity would be ruined. Only peace could provide real advantages.[37] The memorandum, remarkable for its determined advocacy of peace, put Charles in direct opposition to Cobenzl and Colloredo who now realized that he was the main obstacle to their plans.

However, with his immense prestige and popularity, Charles could not be attacked that easily. Therefore, the two now embarked on a truly Byzantine intrigue, determined to undermine his influence by suborning Fassbender, discrediting Duka, and challenging the archduke's military expertise by calling on another renowned soldier. As Cobenzl wrote to Colloredo on 9 March, Charles had not really explained what resources the Monarchy would have available in a conflict, especially in case of France being the aggressor. It just was not enough to wish to stay out of a war. Moreover, he claimed that Charles had painted far too black a picture. 'Would a lost battle on the Adige, for instance, necessarily place Vienna and Austria in imminent danger?' He answered this question negatively, asserting that it looked as if 'Messrs Duka and Fassbender' had really written the memorandum. Perhaps, he concluded, a well-known military expert should be consulted. Both Bellegarde and Mack were suitable, but because Bellegarde was too dependent on the war ministry 'it appears to me that Mack would be better qualified to comment on the points I have raised.'[38]

At this point Mack seemed destined for obscurity. After serving in various senior capacities on the staff of the armies on the Rhine, Mack had resigned in 1795. Recalled in 1797 and promoted to *Feldmarschall Leutnant*, he again served as a staff officer and in 1799 had been named commander of the Neapolitan army. Following a disastrous campaign, in which his troops turned against him, he had to flee, surrendering himself to the French. In the following year, breaking his parole, he slipped out of France and since then had lived in semi-retirement on his Bohemian estates. It speaks volumes about the atmosphere at the Viennese court that such a man, grandiose in his plans, presumptuous and vain, incapable in execution and unlucky for good measure, should have been seriously regarded as an authority for the conduct of a war against Napoleon.

Francis, however, was tired of hearing bad news and increasingly looked to Cobenzl, an accomplished courtier if little else, and to Colloredo, his old tutor and confidant, for direction. Under their influence he sent the Tsar a letter on 1 April, 1804, inquiring about the assistance 150,000 Russian troops would give Austria in the case of a hypothetical conflict with France. At the same time he also asked about Russian intentions towards Prussia and the Tsar's political and territorial objectives. Leaking out, compounded by reports about an intended Austrian concentration against Bavaria, the letter caused concern in France and nearly precipitated the feared French attack. Sir Arthur Paget reported that the French ambassador had told Cobenzl that he would be wrong to assume that Napoleon was 'entirely taken up with his preparations against England, for that the event might prove that he had 60,000 French who could be at Munich before the Austrians.'[39] It was a prophetic warning, though it went unheeded. Only Charles remained cautious and after the Senate in Paris had 'entrusted' Napoleon with the hereditary title of emperor, counselled his brother to recognize the new dignity at once. 'Here is an opportunity,' he wrote, 'that perhaps will never return to improve relations with France and thus to regain a decisive role in European affairs.'[40] This was grist to the mills of the war party which alleged that Charles was too sick to be a competent judge of military affairs and that he was too francophile. Moreover, the archduke was surrounded by incompetent, perhaps even treacherous men. And with the Emperor Francis' always latent suspicions of his brother aroused, Cobenzl and Colloredo unfolded the next step in their campaign to isolate Charles.

On 29 July, Cobenzl informed Colloredo that 'two men are primarily responsible for the deplorable state of our army: Duka and Fassbender.' He continued that a new chief of the Quartermaster General Staff was absolutely necessary and that Fassbender should be forced 'to make good his promise ... [to influence Charles] to replace Duka with Mack.' Fassbender, Cobenzl pointed out, was a vain and ambitious man who had committed some serious indiscretions, but he was a useful tool. 'I am only recommending using Fassbender because I know of no other way.'[41] Fassbender now changed his allegiance and behind the archduke's back he began to co-operate with the war party, providing information and documents to Mack and Cobenzl. Nothing much remained secret in Vienna and by September the British government was concerned about the various intrigues which 'would only lead to a repetition of those dangerous and calamitous conclusions of the last war.'[42] But Britain influence in Vienna was not great – no subsidies were provided at this time – while, as so often in periods of stress, Charles retreated into inactivity.

Meanwhile, with the emperor's tacit consent, negotiations with Russia proceeded and on 6 November 1804 a preliminary Austro-Russian treaty was signed in St Petersburg. The document was somewhat vague. It envisaged a combined army, 235,000 Austrians and 115,000 Russians to engage in operations according to a joint war plan not yet determined. Both partners agreed to sign no separate peace and the Tsar promised his good offices to obtain British subsidies for Austria. Although the treaty touched on basic military issues, Charles had not been informed and when Cobenzl disclosed the terms to him on 7 December, a rather stunned war minister warned that the Russians could not be relied upon and that the Austrian army was in no condition to undertake any operations. With the peace establishment much under strength, only 40,000 men at best could be considered combat ready. Moreover, this was an unbalanced infantry force. The horse regiments were short of mounts and not a single artillery battery had its full complement of draft animals. According to Duka, Charles informed Cobenzl, a minimum of six months would be required to bring the army up to a state of preparedness for war.[43]

The fall of Archduke Charles and the rise of General Mack

Charles had told the unvarnished truth, but at this point the emperor and his hawkish ministers preferred to remain in almost wilful ignorance of the limitations of their army and the power of the adversary. They did not heed Charles's warnings and instead listened to the comforting words of Mack who asserted that everything – the army, its equipment, and even finances – all were in much better shape than reported by the archduke. Mack assured the emperor that he not only could mobilize the army in a very short time, but also that he would introduce tactical and logistic reforms making it more than equal to the French. Francis now decided that Charles would have to comply and under the pretext that the archduke had been earmarked for command of the main army in Italy in the coming war and that the *Hofkriegsrat* could not be left without a responsible head in his absence, he began to press Charles for restoring the agency to its former independent position. 'When you and John will have to depart for the armies,' he wrote on 10 January 1805, 'how would I or anyone else be able to conduct the machinery of war? You would not be able to direct it from the field.' The emperor continued that he could order the change, but preferred to appeal to the archduke's conscience so that 'you yourself will undertake the measures required for the welfare of the state.'[44] Charles at first tried to temporize, but two weeks later a peremptory personal letter from his brother informed him that the decision had been made and that the *Hofkriegsrat* would be separated from the war ministry. However, Francis assured Charles that as 'war minister you will remain my chief military advisor and continue at the centre of military affairs relieved of the burdens of routine administration. I place my confidence in you and assure you of my love.'[45]

But these soothing words merely tried to hide the fact that the emperor had decided to elevate Mack to a decision-making position. When, trying to salvage his influence, the archduke suggested that Archduke John should be appointed president of the *Hofkriegsrat* with Fieldmarshal Liechtenstein as vice-president, the emperor bluntly informed him on 7 March that 'you should not presume that you are to retain any authority over this agency, or that any part of the military administrative business will be referred to the war ministry . . . in the future, all reports, memoranda and protocols from the *Hofkriegsrat* will be submitted to me.'[46] Aghast at these developments, Paget commented that the objective of this 'conspiracy, for I can call it by no other name,' was to remove Charles and perhaps even to reduce the army. Above all, there was an attempt to restore the old *Hofkriegsrat* to power. The most likely candidates for presidency of this body included 'Prince Leopold of Auersperg, one of the worthiest but most stupid of men, General Kolowrat, who now commands in Bohemia, and of whom I know no one of quality to recommend him, the Generals Latour and Alvinzi, who are remarkable for having always been beaten by the Enemy, and the Prince Charles Schwarzenberg, who from his fitness for the Situation ... will not receive the appointment.'[47] For once Paget was correct. On 18 March 1805, the emperor appointed *Feldzeugmeister* Baillet de Latour as president of the *Hofkriegsrat*, though Schwarzenberg was named vice president.

Charles retained the nominal title of war minister and the ministry itself continued until 1806. As he said himself, however, he no longer had any real power but had become a rubber stamp. Even so, Fassbender managed to convince him not to resign from the service entirely. Moreover, Fassbender also told the archduke that Duka had to go and that he had to accept Mack as chief of the Quartermaster General Staff, explaining that if this was not done the emperor would retain Mack as his personal chief of staff.[48] After some hesitation, the archduke accepted the inevitable. On 22 April 1805 he wrote to Francis that although he had repeatedly explained why he 'considered it morally impossible to achieve those objectives for the good of the service which HM hopes to achieve by the appointment of FML Mack ... I am used to obey ... though I request that your instructions to Mack will make it clear that he is to work under my direction.'[49] Duka now was banished to Temesvar in the distant Banat, and Fassbender, too, his usefulness exhausted, was pressured by Cobenzl to resign.[50] By this time Paget had mixed feelings about the changes. While he rejoiced at Duka's removal and recognized that Charles was the strongest opponent of Austria joining the coalition, he conceded that the archduke had brought the army to a 'degree of perfection hitherto unknown in this country.' The ambassador was especially sorry about the removal of 'M. de Fassbender ... for whom I entertain the highest opinion.' Overall, he concluded that it now was likely that the new order would result in the 'acquisition of greater Imbecility and Supineness.'[51]

In fact, there developed a curious situation. The conduct of high policy of the Monarchy reverted back to the old system of personal decisions by Emperor Francis, taken after consultation with whatever person within an inner ring of confidants he thought best. While Charles was told to prepare plans for mobilization and the coming campaign, Mack was quietly told to do the same and throughout the summer, Austria did not formally join the Third Coalition until August; the two men worked at cross purposes. The archduke continued to issue cautious, even despondent, reports about the state of the army and insisted that the main threat was in Italy; Mack threw himself into a reform of the tactical system and pushed for a major effort along the Danube into Bavaria. It was clear, however, that Mack had gained ascendancy over the cautious archduke. In this confused and half-hearted fashion Austria drifted towards the disasters of Ulm and Austerlitz.

V

Ulm, Caldiero and Austerlitz: the Campaigns of 1805

THE war of 1805 occupies an unhappy place in Austrian military history. Undertaken with inadequate preparations, conducted without much skill by a bitterly factionalized high command, and lacking popular support, the fighting lasted only two months. In Germany General Mack, facing the foremost military genius of the times, Napoleon, led the army to surrender, while in Italy Archduke Charles gained a defensive victory but then moved too slowly to affect the final outcome in Moravia. With dissension and bickering at the highest levels, troop performance was uneven and overall, Colonel Angeli, an eminent Habsburg military historian, observed that both the preparation and the conduct of this war were so erratic that a psychological rather than a strategic assessment seems indicated.[1]

Planning and preparation for war, 1805

Throughout the spring and summer of 1805 differences between statesmen and soldiers, and quarrels among generals interfered with planning and preparations. As a result, Austrian preparations for war displayed a 'curious transition from half-measures and prevarication to an almost panic-stricken scramble.'[2] In April the emperor had removed Archduke Charles from his central decision-making position by re-establishing the *Hofkriegsrat* as a separate agency and had further undercut his authority by appointing General Mack as his chief of the Quartermaster General Staff and granting the general direct access to his own person. A permanent conflict between the two leading soldiers was created, that in the final analysis could only be resolved by the Crown. Emperor Francis, however, could not decide between supporting either Charles or Mack and he lacked the ability to force a compromise. As a result, the war plans adopted were neither a clear victory for the archduke or the general, nor a combination of their plans, but a collection of conflicting viewpoints perpetuating indecision and lack of direction.

Although the Austro-Russian treaty of November 1804 obliged the Habsburg Empire to furnish 275,000 men against Napoleon, neither the emperor nor his state vice-chancellor, Count Cobenzl, really had a clear picture of the military resources of the Monarchy. Moreover, they believed that they still had a choice. As late as April 1805 Cobenzl assured an anxious Charles that as of 'this time our obligations are purely defensive.'[3] This did little to reassure the archduke who the very next day submitted a memorandum to the emperor reiterating that if it came to war, Italy would be the decisive theatre and that all available forces should be concentrated for an advance into Lombardy.[4] The fact that since 1803 the French army had been assembling in an arc from Hanover to Brest in preparation for a landing in England, making a rapid shift to southern Europe unlikely, does not appear to have bothered Charles. But then, he really did not want war and he had instructed Duka, then still Chief of the Quartermaster General Staff, to prepare an elaboration on the state of the army. On 22 April, Duka gave as his 'most humble and obedient opinion' that the army was not prepared for war. The war footing stood at 300,000, but over 33,000 men were lacking in the active infantry and cavalry regiments. Moreover, this included 11,455 semi-invalids carried on the muster rolls. The remount situation, the general reported, was unsatisfactory; only 23,000 remounts were available. Altogether, even after mobilization, the Austrian army would number 60,000 foot and 20,000 horse less than at the outbreak of the last war.[5] Of course, Duka's opinion no longer counted. The emperor, pressed by Cobenzl and Mack, already had decided to dismiss the general and appoint Mack in his place.

Charles did not give up the fight. On 2 May he submitted his own estimates on combat readiness, supported by opinions from Generals Archduke John, Schmitt, Lindenau, and Duka. He noted snidely that 'General Mack was asked to contribute but had stated that he would report to His Majesty personally.'[6] The archduke argued that hostilities should be avoided, though he conceded that 'it now is possible that Napoleon will force us into war.' Therefore, he urged that preparations should be undertaken at once. Austria had lost both 'the Turkish and the French Wars because we were poorly prepared and entered into conflict with only half of our means.' Units should be brought up to full strength and sent to their war stations, and, with an early offensive in Italy in mind, he called for magazines to be established in Venetia, the Tyrol, and Inner Austria. For troop distribution, he suggested 116 battalions and 16 squadrons for Italy, 40 battalions and two squadrons for the Tyrol, and 50 battalions and 21 squadrons in Germany. He asked that 15 new light battalions be raised.[7]

The comments by John, Schmitt, Lindenau, and Duka supported Charles. Schmitt and Duka warned that the exhausted Military Border could not furnish sufficient light troops, while John doubted that the Russian auxiliary armies in Germany would really comprise 100,000 men. He agreed with Charles that in any case, the Russians would require substantial logistic and staff support. All contributors agreed that preparations to place the army on a war footing should start at once because, contrary to Mack's opinion, this could not be done in a few weeks.

Mack, on the other hand, claimed that a very substantial force could be rapidly assembled. He was supported by Cobenzl who, according to Sir Arthur Paget, spoke in a 'vague and mysterious way of augmenting the Austrian army in Italy to Sixty Thousand men.' Apparently Cobenzl was referring to the fact that for some time now there had been a surreptitious build-up of forces in Italy and the Tyrol. Already in October 1804, under the pretext of containing the spread of a yellow fever epidemic in Spain, Austria had reinforced her frontiers in Italy and the Tyrol and organized a sanitary cordon. Then, when in preparation for his coronation as king of Italy in May 1805, Napoleon assembled 40,000 men at Marengo, General Belle-garde, commanding in Italy, was ordered to concentrate 12 battalions and six squadrons near Udine and to take command of all troops in Venetia, Carinthia, and south Tyrol, a total of 49 battalions and 22 squadrons.[8] This build-up was largely cosmetic, but Mack considered it sufficient for Bellegarde to take the offensive, while Charles favoured instructing the general to withdraw if attacked.

In early May, the controversy was brought before the emperor in a military council. On this occasion, Paget reported to London, Arch-duke Charles more strongly than ever spoke against war and while the ambassador was 'happy to say that General Duka has quitted at last,' he was worried about the archduke's military secretary (head of military chancery), *Feldmarschall Lieutenant* Count Grünne, a former tutor of the archduke, whose 'pacifist disposition and admir-ation of Bonaparte have probably procured him that distinction.' And such was the Byzantine atmosphere at court in Vienna that unproved rumours and allegations against Charles and his closest advisors circulated freely, were repeated, and sometimes given credence.

Paget's allegations also mirrored his frustrations with Austrian hesitation to adhere to the Anglo-Russian alliance concluded after long negotiations on 11 April 1805. Although the Tsar promised to produce a large allied army, half a million men were mentioned, he clearly could not do so unless Austria, and if possible Prussia, could be induced to join the coalition. And Austria hesitated until late May when Napoleon accepted the Italian Crown and in early June annexed Genoa, the last nominally independent state in the region, to his new Kingdom of Italy. Vienna now instructed its ambassador in London to accede to the coalition. After some bargaining over subsidies, Austria, claiming to be ready to field 320,000 men, asked for £400,000 annually as well as an immediate cash advance to help defray mobilization costs, the agreement was signed on 9 August. In the event, Austria received but little cash. At first the British government could not decide how and when to pay such a large sum and by the time a British military mission had arrived to check on Austrian troop strength, Mack already had been destroyed in Bavaria.[9] Shortage of specie contributed to Austrian troubles in 1805.

Meanwhile Tsar Alexander continued with his grandiose, if totally unrealistic plans. In July he sent his adjutant general, Major General Baron Ferdinand Wintzingerode to Vienna where on 16 July an Austrian military committee composed of Charles, Mack, and General Schwarzenberg agreed to a grand strategic outline, envisaging an offensive from the Baltic to the Adriatic. In the north a Russo-Swedish force of 36,000 was to push west from Swedish Pomerania. On their left 40,000 Russians under Bennigsen were to support the Prussian army moving towards Hanover and Holland. An Austrian army, 89,000 strong, would enter Bavaria and there wait for the arrival of a Russian army under Kutusov, 55,000 strong, which, moving in six equal columns through Galicia, Moravia, and Austria, would arrive at Braunau on the Inn on 20 October. A third Russian army under Buxhowden, another 50,000, would follow later, ready either to support the Prussians or to join the Austrians by way of Bohemia. Austria's main army, 142,000 men, was to assemble in Italy, its communications with the army in the valley of the Danube safeguarded by 53,000 Austrians in Vorarlberg and the Tyrol.[10]

Once concentrations had been completed, the army in Italy would break into Lombardy, reduce the strong fortresses there, and then swing northwest into Switzerland to unite with the combined Austro-Russian armies in Bavaria for a push into France through the Belfort-

Hüningen region. To assist operations in Italy, the Russians proposed that 25,000 Russians and 9000 British be landed at Naples where they would be joined by the Neapolitan troops for an advance north. In addition, the Tsar expected troops from Denmark, Mecklenburg, Saxony and other north German states to eventually join this great offensive against Napoleon.

From the outset, these were castles in the air. Prussia had not joined the coalition and in the end failed to do so. In fact, the king of Prussia preferred to accept Hanover as a bribe from Napoleon rather than risk the uncertain results of war, prepared to safeguard his neutrality by mobilizing a strong army of observation. The master-plan therefore was restricted to the advance on the Danube and the offensive in Italy. And here there was no chance of assembling the large armies projected. Nevertheless, Mack, an incurable dreamer, pressed for an early advance into Bavaria designed to force the elector of Bavaria into the coalition. He persisted in this plan despite a warning from Wintzingerode on 6 August that there was no hope of speeding up the arrival of the Russian columns or of providing substantial reinforcements. There would be 16 regiments, a total of 56 battalions, with Kutusov but no more, and he could not give any definite promises on the movements of Buxhowden's army.[11]

In August, Charles who had been optimistic in July, returned to reality and when a conference met on 29 August at Hetzendorf to outline strategy in Germany he argued that while the army in Italy should take the offensive, the forces in Germany should hold back until the actual arrival of the Russians.[12] This was sound advice and at first the emperor was inclined to agree. Cobenzl and Colloredo, however, supported Mack's plan. On 2 August already, Cobenzl had informed Colloredo that 'everything has been calculated so that Napoleon ... cannot appear before we have been joined by our allies ... there is no need to worry on this account.'[13] Mack, in fact, had calculated that the emperor could not appear in strength in Bavaria sooner than in 69 days, while the Russians would be fully concentrated at Braunau 64 days after leaving their base at Brody.[14] Therefore, the emperor permitted Mack to enter Bavaria, occupy Munich, and advance to the line of the Lech.

The conference also settled command arrangements, though the lines of authority were muddled at best. Because the Russians insisted on a supreme commander of high rank, Emperor Francis assumed this position, naming the 24 year-old Archduke Ferdinand d'Este as nominal commander in Germany. Mack, with secret powers to override Ferdinand, was appointed the emperor's personal representative endowed with the army and General Mayer was designated as his chief of staff. Command in Italy was entrusted to Charles with General Zach as his chief of staff.[15]

Even at this late date there existed no detailed plan of operations. Francis requested Charles to elaborate such a plan, and though the archduke objected at first, asserting that Mack might as well be responsible for this, he eventually complied. The final strategic plan, worked out by Charles, Lindenau, and Mayer, was hastily adopted on 5 September, two days before the advance guard crossed the Bavarian frontier. It confirmed earlier strategic objectives, though it revised the order of battle. By drawing on all available reserves, the army in Italy was raised to 171 battalions and 96 squadrons, 95,000 men. Also at Mayer's insistence, forces in Germany were strengthened by 30,000 men originally destined for Italy, and until these reinforcements arrived they were set at 88 battalions and 148 squadrons. In addition, with Switzerland having declared its neutrality in late August, forces in the Tyrol were split. Those in the northern sector, 44 battalions and ten squadrons, were placed at Mack's disposal, while Charles was authorized to call on the 21 battalions and six squadrons in the south. All this left only 35 battalions and 18 squadrons for internal security duties in the interior of the Monarchy.[16]

Writing after the Austrian army in Germany already had been destroyed, Paget perceived two major mistakes in grand strategy. The major fault was 'to have taken the field [in Bavaria] with too small a force,' especially when it already was clear by July that Napoleon had abandoned his projected invasion of Britain and that it was likely that he would strike in Germany rather than in distant Italy. An explanation for all this, Paget wrote, was the friction within the Austrian high command. Mack, aware of the archduke's enmity, 'was unwilling to inflame that animosity by a proposal to withdraw from Italy any considerable number of troops' and 'to this false and misplaced delicacy therefore are in great measure owing the present misfortunes.' The second mistake was the headlong advance into Bavaria, which relied on more rapid support from the Russians than was actually available, 'from whence ... the Austrians voluntarily and with their eyes open chose to commence hostilities singlehanded against the French.'[17]

Paget certainly was right on the first point, though his explanation was wrong. The record does not show that Mack was 'delicate' and, his army in Germany received substantial reinforcements both from Italy and the Tyrol. To be sure, these arrived piecemeal and in many cases too late, though there is no indication that Mack ever was deterred by this prospect. His rash advance beyond the Lech was made on the basis of false assumptions and against the advice of his chief of staff. Finally, even if all reinforcements had arrived and even if the Russians had been able to move faster, it remains doubtful whether Mack and Kutusov combined, a total of some 100,000 men at best, would have been able to meet the onslaught of Napoleon's *Grand Armée*, almost 180,000 well trained and superbly led troops.

There certainly were tensions in the divided Austrian high command. Archduke Charles, naturally, had come to despise Mack and his intrigues and was cool to the war. By September, as will be seen, he was alarmed by the progress of affairs in Germany and had abandoned his idea of an early offensive in Italy. His main concerns now were defensive, to preserve his army. The key figure, however, was Mack whose personality and actions puzzled contemporaries and have remained an enigma. A romantic and a pedant at the same time, he fluctuated between extreme rashness and curious irresolution. He liked grandiose projects, full of exact and complicated manoeuvres, though he often forgot that he did not have the instruments to execute them. For that matter, he conveniently tended to mistake a good plan for action.[18] In short, Mack was the wrong man to be entrusted with army command and the emperor together with Colloredo and Cobenzl must bear responsibility for that. Yet, in September Count Cobenzl who had been the main person responsible for propelling Mack to his position, was well pleased. He wrote 'what a difference one man can make in affairs when he is capable and understands his business.' In contrast with Duka, he continued, 'who always was sure that a war would end badly' and who had claimed that six months were required to mobilize and deploy the army, 'Mack has done everything in two months.'[19] But the minister was wrong, mistaking heedless motion and a furious last minute scramble of new regulations for genuine achievement. The truth was that in early September the Habsburg army was not ready for major combat operations.

Military reforms, 1805

This lack of combat readiness was in large part due to Mack's determination to delay mobilization in order not to provoke Napoleon. Mobilization and concentration of troops had begun only in July and was accelerated in August, yet these leisurely proceedings were inadequate to bring units up to strength. By late August, battalions, supposed to number 800 had 500 at best, while the strength of cavalry squadrons, set at 131 troopers for heavy and 150 for light horse, rarely reached above 100 troopers. Artillery batteries lacked draft teams and had to be moved by hastily requisitioned horses.[20] There existed no fixed order for higher tactical formations; regiments, battalions or squadrons were assigned to a field commander who arranged them into semi-permanent brigades or divisions. Normally two regiments made up a brigade accompanied by some artillery, and two brigades formed a temporary division. Advance guard divisions were formed from light troops, horse as well as foot, while grenadiers and heavy cavalry made up the reserve divisions. Corps, or as they often were called, army detachments, also were composed in an *ad hoc* manner and altogether Austrian higher formations lacked the habit of working together as a cohesive whole.

Contributing to the confusion in the army were a number of hasty reforms pushed through by Mack in the summer of 1805. For some time now, a commission chaired by Grünne had deliberated on reorganizing the cavalry, now reduced to 35 regiments. Reforms took effect in April 1805. All units, light and heavy, were formed with eight squadrons, with 131 men in the heavy and 151 in the light regiments. Also confirmed was the practice of forming up for combat two instead of three deep.[21]

Changes in the organization and tactics of the infantry, the most numerous arm, were more important. Their origins can be traced back to Mack's army instructions of 1794 and to various commissions deliberating in the years 1801–4. In 1804, Mack had produced a draft for a revised infantry manual. He favoured retention of the linear order, though, as he already had done in 1794, he suggested that the third rank might be used to extend the frontage or to provide skirmishers. Perhaps his most perceptive observation recognized of the special problems posed by a multinational army. 'No other army in Europe,' he wrote, 'has the problem of a rank and file differing totally not only in language but also in custom from its officers.' Therefore, Austrian troops required both a longer training period as well as a larger complement of officers and non-commissioned officers than the French. The latter could train a soldier in eight days and a non-commissioned officer in four weeks and still had only 17 officers and non-commissioned officers in each company. By contrast the larger Austrian companies had only half this number of leaders and this was inadequate.[22]

Such considerations should have made Mack cautious in introducing major reforms in organization and tactics. But this was not his style. During the meeting of 29 August, he pressed for continued implementation of tactical, organizational, and logistic reforms even though the army was to march within a week. And when Charles objected that the outset of a campaign was hardly the proper time for such changes, Mack bluntly replied that 'one already had deliberated on these matters for four years and nothing had been done.'[23] As a result, implementation of new infantry regulations already sanctioned by the emperor on 20 June was continued, though these changes were never completely implemented in Germany and do not appear to have been applied in Archduke Charles's army in Italy.

The modified regulations simplified individual arms drill by eliminating a number of ceremonial movements, abolished firing by the third rank and by platoons, reduced the occasions for half-company volleys, and placed fire-control in the hands of the battalion commanders. The pace of 75 steps per minute was retained, though a 'double step' of 120 steps a minute was permitted for certain evolutions. In combat, the two-company division became the main movement element.[24] Many of these changes were sound and were incorporated in the famous manual of 1807. The timing, however, was poor and created complications.

Adding even more complications was a reorganization of the foot regiments into four Fusilier and one Grenadier battalions, each battalion with four companies and nominal company strength of 160 muskets. *Grenzer* regiments were on a smaller establishment with three battalions of four companies each. All units contained substantial numbers of ill-trained and poorly equipped recruits, none more than the *Grenzer*. Mobilized in very substantial numbers, 48,000 in all, their performance in this war was uneven. While Duffy described them as 'probably the most enthusiastic troops,' General Schönhals, a contemporary, claimed that they had been mustered too hastily, lacked training, boots, uniforms, and even serviceable muskets. This, he thought, might have affected their performance, which, he noted, did not justify their reputation. On the contrary, he wrote, 'every report complained about their unreliability and lack of courage in battle.'[25] Reorganization in general did not improve morale. As one infantry captain complained, the reshuffling necessary created confusion so that the 'common soldiers no longer knew their officers and the officers did not know their men.'[26]

There was little change in the organization and tactics of artillery. The establishment remained inadequate, four field regiments with 16 companies apiece. With a total of only 11,260 gunners, labour still had to be provided by untrained infantrymen. Batteries lacked permanent draft teams and drivers, and last minute requisitioning proved difficult. As a result, the artillery embarked on the campaigns of 1805 with only slightly more than half of its field establishment.

Tactical dispositions remained antiquated. Austrian artillery remained divided into two different types, line guns to furnish close support and reserve guns to be employed under central control. Most of the infantry brigades received a 3-pounder battery, but cavalry brigades lost their guns. The great majority of light guns were distributed among the battalions and the Austrians rarely managed to achieve concentration of fire. The capabilities of the artillery reserve were improved slightly by additional ammunition carts for its park.[27]

For all his shortcomings, Mack understood that one of the main elements of Napoleonic warfare was moving fast and during the advance into Bavaria he issued an army order sharply curtailing regimental and individual transport. Tents were to be provided for only one half of the troops, the remainder were to bivouac, and army transport was to carry only enough flour and fodder for three to four days. 'The enemy,' Mack wrote, 'has conducted all his campaigns without transport columns and his infantry officers marched on foot.'[28] Mack did not go so far, every officer still had a horse, but his baggage allowance was to be sharply reduced. It was Mack's intention that the army live off the land in order to move more rapidly.

As it turned out, the Austrians were unable to operate like the French. Troops could not suddenly acquire a knack for foraging and soon suffered extreme want. Moreover, movement did not speed up very much. Contemporaries and historians often have blamed the still excessive baggage brought along by senior and field grade officers. While the French, one veteran complained, made officers carry their own packs, 'in our army . . . every company has a whole tail of carts just to transport officers' baggage.'[29] Yet, these were only contributing factors. To be sure, officers' baggage was an impediment and the Austrians were unused to foraging but even so, marching on good roads, the army covered about ten miles a day, about equal to the normal French movement rate. But, unlike the French, the Austrians were not capable of getting the last ounce out of their troops by forced marches. These, an integral part of Napoleonic strategy, were alien to the thinking of Austrian commanders and probably beyond the capability of their troops.

Mack's advance to Ulm

Though not fully organized, the Austrian army took the offensive on 5 September. That day advance elements of the army, 29 battalions and 40 squadrons, set out from camp at Wels. On 8 September they crossed the Inn at Schärding and Braunau and entered Bavaria, encountering no resistance. On 5 September, Prince Schwarzenberg had appeared in Munich and called upon the Elector Maximilian to place his army at Austria's disposition, but the Bavarian temporized, withdrawing his army, about 22,000 men, north into the Main valley. Having already concluded a secret alliance with Napoleon, Maximilian left Munich on 8 September.

Mack had established a careful schedule for the advance. Every nine days another echelon was to follow the first: 17 battalions and eight squadrons' between 6 and 15 September, 13 battalions and eight squadrons between 16 and 25 September, until the entire army, 88 battalions and 148 squadrons was assembled by the end of October on the line of the Lech west of Munich to await the arrival of the Russians.[30] But, on hearing that the French already had crossed the Rhine at Strassburg, he decided to speed up the advance. After entering Munich on 12 September, he hustled his troops some 50 miles west to the Iller, to watch for the French debouching through the Black Forest.[31] The hasty movement dislocated his schedule. Much of the army was strung out along the 138 miles between the Inn and the Iller, while supply arrangements, sketchy from the outset, broke down. Archduke Ferdinand, the nominal army commander who had arrived in Munich on 19 September, was perturbed and demanded a withdrawal eastward.[32] Mack, however, simply ignored him. He had the emperor's backing and was convinced that Napoleon would follow the traditional invasion route through the Black Forest. Then too, after detaching troops to watch the Channel coast and to garrison France, the enemy would barely dispose of 70,000 men. As for a French advance from the northwest, Mack held that this would violate the Prussian enclave of Ansbach, something he was sure the French would not dare. He planned to strike at the heads of the French columns as they debouched from the Black Forest.

To strengthen his position he already had called on General Jellacic from the northern Tyrol to deploy from the shores of Lake Constance north towards Biberach, thus guarding the left flank. To guard the north and watch the Bavarians, on 23 September Mack posted a corps under General Kienmayer near Ingolstadt. He also asked that the movement of reinforcements from Italy to Germany be expedited

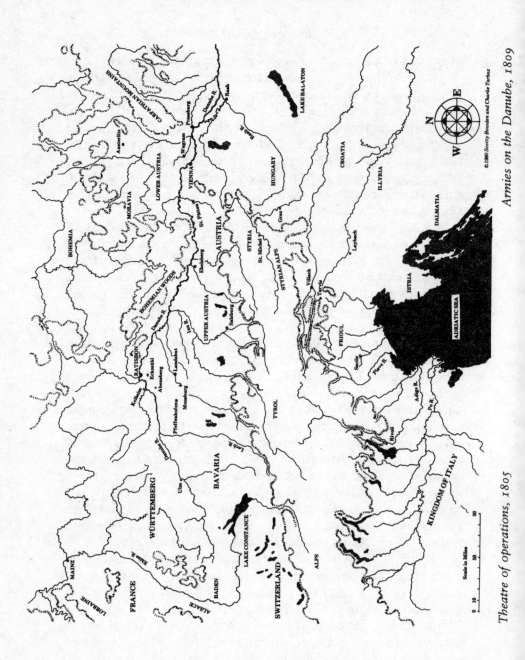

Armies on the Danube, 1809

Theatre of operations, 1805

and ordered fortifications thrown up at Memmingen, Ulm and Ingolstadt. Mack expected that by the end of the month he would have 50,000 to 55,000 men between Memmingen and Ulm, a stretch of about 30 miles, 11,000 under Jellacic to the south and some 12,000 with Kienmayer at Ingolstadt.[33] Additional troops were moving up on the lines of communication, and above all, he confidently looked towards the imminent arrival of the Russians.

But Mack was deluding himself. Kutusov had marched ten days late and his rear column had been detached to the Turkish frontier. He reached Teschen on the Moravian frontier on 22 September where the Austrians provided wagons to enable part of his troops to move faster. Even so, he could not be expected on the Inn before late in October and his army proved to be ill-equipped and had to draw substantial quantities from the meagre Austrian stocks.[34] Mack also ignored the fact that his own army was suffering under the strain of the rapid advance. The weather had turned bad. Attrition through illness and desertion was beginning to decimate many units; supplies fell short, and the fortifications at the key points had barely progressed and most of the works were poorly laid out and indifferently armed.

Even more ominous were the rifts in high command where generals no longer were on speaking terms. As Paget reported 'from the very outset of the campaign there existed a degree of jealousy and misunderstanding among the general officers' which by the end of September had 'arrived at such a position that no communication took place among the commanders in chief *but in writing.*'[35] Mayer, the chief of staff, had supported Ferdinand's recommendation for consolidating the army closer to the Lech and as a result had been bitterly assailed by Mack. And with Ferdinand and Mack at odds, the matter had to be laid before the emperor who arrived at Landsberg, 30 miles southwest of Munich on 22 September. Francis, it appears, already had made up his mind. Soon after the offensive started he had asked Archduke Charles for his opinion and had received the answer that Mack was exceeding his authority and violating all strategic principles.[36] Undeterred, however, Francis now proceeded to back his general. Mayer promptly was relieved and transferred to command a Grenadier brigade, while Ferdinand was informed that Mack's dispositions had imperial approval.[37] Having made a very bad decision, the emperor returned to Vienna on 26 September. By this date Napoleon had arrived in Frankfurt and issued final orders for the destruction of the Austrian army in Germany.

The disaster at Ulm

Napoleon at first was slow to believe that he faced such a massive coalition. By late August, however, the danger had become evident and Napoleon was not the man to permit the allies to assemble their forces undisturbed. On 24 August he sent an ultimatum to Vienna demanding immediate troop reductions in the Tyrol and Venetia. Two days later he issued movement orders for his army to march into Germany.

The newly designated *Grande Armée* was perhaps the finest force Napoleon ever commanded. Training, personnel and morale were excellent and its new corps organization combined maximum control with maximum flexibility. Predominantly infantry organizations, each corps combined two to four infantry divisions, a brigade or division of light cavalry, several batteries, and a small number of support troops. The exact composition of each corps varied purposely, both to confuse the enemy and to reflect its assignment and the talents of its commander. In 1805 it ranged from Soult's IV Corps with 41,000 to Augerau's VII Corps with 14,000 men. Ney's VI Corps, 24,000 strong, was about average. Out of approximately 350,000 troops available that summer, Napoleon committed 194,000 to the operations in Germany – seven corps, to which an allied corps formations, primarily Bavarians, must be added. In addition there were three major formations under his personal control – the Army Cavalry Reserve, the Army Artillery Reserve, and the Imperial Guard, then numbering over 6000 picked men. Some 30,000 men remained on guard along the Channel coast; Massena with 50,000 was to deal with Archduke Charles while Gouvion St Cyr guarded his rear with 18,500 in central Italy.[38]

In rough outline, Napoleon's strategic plan called for Lannes' V Corps and the cavalry reserve under Murat to go across the upper Rhine and into the Black Forest to draw Mack's attention while five corps, I Bernadotte, II Marmont, III Davout, IV Soult, VI Ney, would execute a huge wheeling manoeuvre into Swabia so as to hit the Austrians on their right flank and rear. The Bavarians under Wrede moved alongside Bernadotte's I Corps while Augereau's VII Corps, which had to march all the way from Brest to the upper Rhine, was to follow as a strategic reserve. The movement of 194,000 men and some 300 guns from the coasts to the Danube was an unparalleled administrative feat; no other contemporary army could have accomplished it with such speed and efficiency.

On 25–27 September Soult's IV Corps accompanied by the Guard and screened by Mùrat's cavalry went over the Rhine at Strassburg and entered the Black Forest; VI, IV, and III Corps moved a day later and crossed the Neckar on 1 October. Together with Marmont's II and Bernadotte's I Corps they swung southeast, their strategic objective the Danube to the east of Ulm along a wide stretch from Elchingen to Ingolstadt. If they crossed to the south (right) bank, Mack's lines of communications and retreat were threatened, while his link-up with Kutusov already had become problematical. For Mack to stay where he was spelled disaster. As Napoleon wrote to Bernadotte from Strassburg on 27 September, 'If I have good fortune and Mack dreams away another three or four days on the Iller and in the Black Forest, I shall have encircled him and only fragments of his army will escape.'[39]

And this was what happened. After weeks of manoeuvring, Austrian advance guards and the French exchanged their first shots on 2 October. At this point Mack still was not certain about the main direction of the French thrust. A few days later, on 5 October, he heard from Kienmayer that the French were advancing through Prussian territory towards Donauwörth.[40] The next day, Mack began to concentrate his army around Ulm and Günzburg, and on 7 October ordered General Auffenberg with eight battalions and 13 squadrons, about 6000 men, to Wertingen to provide the advance guard for an attack on Napoleon as he was crossing the Danube. That day, 7 October, Soult (IV), Murat, and the Guard already were across the River at Donauworth, followed the next day by Lannes (V) at Münster and Davout (III) and Marmont (II) at Neuburg. Standing passively at Wertingen, Auffenberg was attacked and destroyed by Murat's horse and infantry elements of Lannes' corps. From prisoners taken here Napoleon learned that the bulk of Mack's army still was at Ulm and that he had cut off the Austrians' line of retreat eastwards.

Once across the Danube, Napoleon formed his forces into three groups. Murat and Lannes were to strike directly at Ulm, supported by Ney (VI) whose corps still was on the north bank but preparing to launch across at Günzburg. Bernadotte (I), Marmont (II), and the Bavarians were to hold Ingolstadt and advance to Munich. Napoleon with Soult (IV) and Davout (III) went to Augsburg where a major base was being established. From there he was ready to support either of the other two groups and by moving west on Memmingen could block Mack's escape south to the Tyrol.

Although the *Grande Armée* had remained an infantry host, with the day of the cavalry and artillery masses still in the future, its

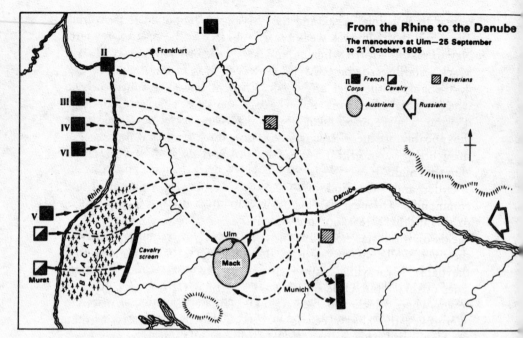

The manoeuvre at Ulm, 25 September to 21 October 1805

skirmisher covered battalion columns, better led and with greater elan than the Austrians, had once again proved superior to the line. Moreover, having established what he considered a secure operational base around Ulm, Mack had surrendered the strategic initiative to Napoleon who had used it to achieve a 3:1 numerical superiority in Bavaria and a 5:1 superiority in the encounters around Ulm. The fighting had lasted for only one week, but after losing the opening engagements the Austrian army was disheartened. Dissension in the high command filtered down to lower levels, morale was shaken, and in and around Ulm formations camped in disorder. Especially hard hit were the cavalry and artillery units; some squadrons had fewer than 50 combat capable troopers.[41]

By now even Ferdinand realized that he was merely a figurehead. A letter from Emperor Francis informed him to follow the advice of *Feldmarschall Leutnant* Mack in all military matters.[42] Reconfirmed in authority, Mack became even more erratic in his conduct, yet with little drive or perseverance. On 9 October he tried to cross to the north bank of the Danube below Ulm in order to sever French communications, but encountered Ney's troops near Günzburg. After a confused night action he retreated to Ulm and now decided to retreat to Bohemia. Assuming that Mack was about to retire to the Tyrol and that Ulm was weakly held, on 10 October, Napoleon told Ney to take the town while he moved towards Memmingen to block Mack's southward route. Mack, however, was busy crossing to the north bank of the river and on 11 October gained a minor success when 25,000 Austrians under Schwarzenberg defeated Dupont's division, a mere 6000 men, left in an isolated position at Haslach. Inexplicably, neither Schwarzenberg nor Mack exploited this success for a break-out north and instead the Austrians tamely returned to Ulm that night.

Order and subordination were fast disappearing in the army's command.[43] The next day a stormy council of war persuaded Mack to try another break-out towards Bohemia. On 13 October, Werneck's division marched out towards Elchingen on the north side of the river, while Riesch's division moved towards Günzburg to cover the flank. Meanwhile Napoleon was preparing to attack on both sides of the Danube. He fell on Riesch and drove him back into the town, where Mack and the remainder of the army stood inactive. Werneck, rather slowly, continued to move northeast. Perceiving that the trap was snapping shut, Archduke Ferdinand and Schwarzenberg decided to break out towards the north. Mack tried to dissuade them but about midnight on 14 October Ferdinand and 12 squadrons of cavalry rode out of the doomed fortress. Ney stormed the Michelsberg just outside the walls the next day. Surrounded, Ulm lay defenseless under direct fire. Clearly the end was in sight. Perhaps Mack still could have broken out with part of his army, but his will was shattered. He tried to delay surrender by negotiations, bargaining for time in the hope that the Russians might arrive. On 17 October, however, he agreed to capitulate by 25 October unless relieved earlier. He did not stick to this. On 19 October he had an interview with Napoleon who informed him that Werneck had been caught by Murat and had surrendered and that the outlying detachment at Memmingen had been taken by Soult (IV). And when Napoleon's chief of staff, Marshal Berthier, gave his word of honour that the Russians were in no position to arrive in time, Mack caved in and agreed to surrender the remainder of his army, 51 battalions, 18 squadrons, and 60 guns, 23,500 men, the next day. Officers were released on parole; the rank and file became prisoners of war. Schönhals recorded that 'in this fashion, after a campaign of only twelve days, an army fell into the hands of the enemy, not because it was defeated in battle, but because of miscalculations, overconfidence, obstinacy, and lack of unity in command.'[44]

And this was not all. Kienmayer's corps escaped to join Kutusov, and, after riding hard for eight days, Ferdinand, with only 1800 remaining, managed to reach Bohemia. Jellacic withdrew into Vorarlberg, but, slow and methodical, was overtaken by Augereau (VII) and forced to capitulate on 14 November. Altogether, of the troops which had invaded Bavaria, almost 60,000 were lost in the initial campaign. On his arrival in Vienna, Mack was arrested and, when the war was over, court-martialled in 1806. He wrote voluminously in his own defence, asserting that his own best efforts had been frustrated by lack of cooperation from Archduke Ferdinand and his fellow generals, as well as by the poor training of the troops.[45]

The Battle of Caldiero

News of the debacle at Ulm arrived in Vienna like a bolt from the blue. On 19 October Cobenzl informed Colloredo that 'we have every hope that the two armies [Mack and Kutusov] will affect a junction ... there no longer is any danger that they may be cut off.'[46] In Italy, however, Charles had expected disaster in Germany. After rendering his opinion on Mack on 9 September, he had left the capital in a gloomy mood. Arriving at army headquarters in Padua on 20 September he found what had become the all too familiar story of the Austrian forces at the outset of a campaign. He reported that the army lacked money, bread, horses, supplies, and men. Pontoons and engineering stores were in short supply, soldiers were walking about inadequately clothed, without boots, and even without serviceable muskets.[47] He duly advanced to the Adige,[48] but already on 26 September he wrote to Emperor Francis that while he had dispatched seven regiments to Innsbruck, he now was too weak to undertake any major offensive operations.[49] Contributing to this reversal of plans was Charles's overestimate of the opposing forces. He believed that these numbered 102,000 foot and 6000 horse; in reality Massena only had some 45,000 in the field with another 5000 garrisoning Mantua, Peschiera, Verona, and Legnago.[50] Even after detaching reinforcements to Bavaria, and discounting the 6000 men in Venice, Charles still possessed a slight numerical edge. Convinced, however, that disaster was likely in Germany, he already had decided that his main duty was to preserve what might well constitute the Monarchy's last field army.

For his part, Marshal Massena had orders to stand on the defensive unless he received definite orders, though, as common in the Napoleonic system, he was expected to exploit any special opportunities.

On 5 October Charles received orders from Vienna confirming his decision to await the outcome of events in Germany before committing his army.[51] By this time both sides already had agreed to an armistice pending the arrival of news from Germany. The agreement stipulated six days' notice before hostilities would commence. On 11 October Massena heard that the *Grande Armée* had arrived on its projected line of departure along the Rhine-Main and decided to support it by an advance. He gave notice that day and prepared to cross the Adige. During the night of 17–18 October his light infantry managed to secure a bridgehead across from Verona at Veronetta and consolidated it the next day. Then fighting died down. Convinced that little good news could be expected, Charles already had initiated a retrograde movement, shifting men and supplies to a prepared position some miles east of the Adige at Caldiero.

On 24 October, having just been informed about the surrender at Ulm, he wrote to the emperor that he intended to fight a battle in this position, hoping to inflict enough casualties on Massena to deter him from pursuing the retreating army.[52] For his part, Massena had received instructions to attack Charles and prevent him from breaking off contact. For three days, between 29 to 31 October, the French, 39,000 foot and 4000 horse, attacked the Austrians, 42,000 infantry and 6000 cavalry. Although the Austrians had a slight numerical edge and fought in prepared fieldworks reinforced by some permanent fortifications, élan and the manoeuvrability of the French in broken terrain almost brought them success. On the second day Massena in person led Molitor's division against the centre of the Austrian position and reached the main trench. Charles was forced to commit his last reserves – a Grenadier brigade under Prince Hohenlohe-Bartenstein. The next day the French concentrated against the Austrian left wing where Major General Nordmann led a stout defence. Fighting continued until nightfall when Massena, having lost two generals, 134 officers, and about 7000 men, withdrew. Austrian losses were on the same order, two generals, 120 officers, and 5700 men.[53]

The battle of Caldiero, Austria's solitary major success in this war, has been much overrated by patriotic historians. The French actually considered it their victory.[54] Massena was repulsed, but hardly destroyed and when the Austrians began their withdrawal on 1 November, he still was able to strike at their rear guard . On 2 November he severely mauled Major General Hillinger's detachment, inflicting 400 casualties and taking 1800 prisoners. It was not until 5 November that the Austrians broke clear. Abandoning supplies, they reached the Isonzo on 11 November and crossing it, disappeared into the Julian Alps. Massena, having detached a force to blockade Venice and concerned about a possible Austrian irruption from the Tyrol into his rear, and also temporarily out of touch with the *Grande Armée* did not choose to pursue, but halted along the Isonzo.

The French advance on Vienna

Kutusov had reached Braunau in the last week of November and had managed to assemble some 27,000 exhausted Russians, only half of the number promised, near that town. They were joined by Kienmayer's corps as well as some units collected along the lines of communications, bringing the Austrian total up to some 16,000. In addition, Major General Maximilian Count Merveldt was forming a new corps, about 20,000. Merveldt tried to persuade the Russians to advance in order to restore the situation around Ulm. Of course, it was much too late for that. On 23 October, Kutusov was informed by Mack, passing through on his way to Vienna, about the debacle and, realizing the danger to his army, the Russian commander began his retreat two days later. Marching from Braunau to Wels and then along the right side of the Danube via Linz, Amstetten, Sankt Pölten, repeatedly pressed by French cavalry, he crossed the river at Mautern on 9 November and burned the bridge there. An attempt by Marshal Mortier's scratch VIII Corps, a hastily thrown together formation, 7500 strong, against combined Austro-Russian of over 25,000 was a predictable failure. In heavy fighting near Dürnstein on 11 November, Gazan's division almost was destroyed, the remainder broke off contact. Casualties on the Austro-Russian side also were heavy; most importantly Major General Baron Schmitt, Kutusov's able Austrian chief of staff, was killed in action.[55] The Russians had successfully extricated their army, though Napoleon already was preparing to spring another trap by advancing in a wide arc through Vienna into their rear.

By this time the Austrian position had worsened even further. Originally they had hoped to induce Kutusov to make a stand on the right side of the Danube, perhaps in a fortified position at Mautern, 40 miles upstream from Vienna. By this time very few Austrian troops remained with Kutusov. Kienmayer's corps had left him at St Pölten and marched to Vienna, arriving there on late 10 November. Also at Vienna was a 13,000 strong reserve corps of *Feldmarschall Leutnant* Carl Prince Auersperg, former captain of the imperial lifeguard, a ceremonial body. In addition, Merveldt, with about

6000, six line battalions, eight battalions *Grenzer*, and 14 squadrons, had left Kutusov and marched south to Styria in order to join up with Archduke Charles. Napoleon, however, had already made his own dispositions. While his main body followed Kutusov, he had detached Augerau (VII) to follow Jellacic into the Vorarlberg; Ney (VI) and the Bavarians were to seize the Tyrol and the passes into Italy, while Marmont (II) was to move to the Styrian-Hungarian border to block Archduke Charles's escape route. On 5 November, with the single road south of the Danube crowded and also to pursue Merveldt, he detached Davout (III) south towards Styria and Leoben. An early winter already covered the Alps with heavy snow. On 8 November, Davout caught up with Merveldt's poorly handled corps at Mariazell. The largest part of the Austrians was forced to surrender; only a pathetic remnant of 2000 reached Hungary.

Napoleon's advance on Vienna continued, delayed by occasional Austrian and Russian rearguard actions. In these actions the Austrians under Major Generals Count Nostitz and Schustekh acquitted themselves bravely enough. Schustekh, for instance, managed to defend the crossing of the Traun on 1–2 November in a bitter encounter. These engagements, however, could not do much beyond holding up the French for a few hours or days. Their greatest difficulty was that there was only a single road from the Enns to Vienna as well as supply difficulties. These were alleviated by the Austrian failure to destroy essential supplies in their magazines. Vast quantities of supplies and ammunition, including 45 cannon at Braunau, were captured intact, additional stores were seized at Linz. By this time the Austrian central command was falling apart. Kutusov had taken over command of the main army, while according to Sir Arthur Paget, 'general Consternation and Dismay' were taking hold in Vienna.[56] On 4 November the emperor summoned a council of war, attended by Generals Liechtenstein, Gyulai, Fleischer, Crenneville, Klein, and Gomez, chaired by the president of the *Hofkriegsrat, Feldzeugmeister* Maximilian Count Baillet de Latour. It achieved little. The capital was to be evacuated and all remaining troops transferred to the left bank of the Danube where, together with Russian forces, they were to deny a French crossing. Only a few troops were available, and Kutusov had no intention of standing in an exposed position. Altogether, the plan was not sound. Schönhals commented that it 'certainly did not exhaust the limits of human or military wisdom.'[57]

The seizure of the Tabor bridges and the occupation of Vienna

Of course, defence of the imperial capital and residence was virtually impossible. Its fortifications where outdated, some parts of the Inner City walls near the *Hofburg* had been razed to make room for an expansion of the palace, and the curtain walls around the suburbs had been allowed to fall into disrepair.[58] Few troops were available. There were Kienmayer's battalions, shrunken by attrition and detachments, and now part of Auersperg's corps, a total perhaps of 16,000 and 40 guns. Also available, though of no combat value, were two regiments of civic guards, 3000 in all. The citizenry, 240,000 in 1805, might have been able to help in a last ditch stand, but the government was not interested in arousing popular sentiment and the population was disaffected. Soldiers had been used in June to quell a bread riot, leaving ten dead and over 100 wounded. If the lower classes were sullen, the well to do were indifferent to the outcome of the war. They feared the plundering Russians and preferred to hand the city over intact to the French. Many, following the example of the court, left town by boat or wagon. On 3 November, already, Paget had written to his mother that 'You can have no idea of the consternation which prevails here, I don't know which is most feared, the arrival of the Russians or their retreat, or that of the French. Everybody who possesses or can hire a horse is moving off.' Five days later, he reported that 'there is a considerable degree of discontent here, which has not diminished by the departure of the Emperor having taken place without any notice of it having been given to the Public.'[59]

Moreover, official evacuation of the city was undertaken with very little regard to military considerations. Much attention was given to saving the archives including the papers of the Bohemian Chancery that were of no conceivable interest to the French, but nothing was done to remove the thousands of muskets and hundreds of cannons from the arsenal, or the clothing depot at Stockerau, or the fodder from government magazines. For that matter, it was much the same everywhere during this campaign. Later that month Murat found 300,000 rations at Pressburg, and smaller quantities fell into French hands in almost all the towns, fortresses, and magazines throughout Bohemia, Austria and northern Hungary.[60] There even were instances where officials in areas not touched by the fighting complied with French orders and sent in requisitioned supplies. For that matter, Austrian soldiers still did not understand that war had changed since the days of Maria Theresa. When Kienmayer was marching to Vienna in November, he sought an interview with Murat and asked him not to press too hard towards Vienna because his (Kienmayer's) soldiers were badly in need of rest.[61] Clearly, the Habsburg Monarchy was not prepared to mount comprehensive resistance.

Even so, the episode of the Tabor Bridge north of Vienna was an extraordinary display of confusion, dereliction of duty, and possibly treason. The bridge in question actually was three wooden structures and some connecting causeways carrying the main road north to Moravia across a number of waterways, canals, and branches of the Danube. Together these structures were referred to as the Tabor Bridge and as the lowest permanent crossing of the Danube, they played an important part in Napoleon's scheme for getting Murat's cavalry and Lannes' V Corps into the rear of Kutusov's army.[62] With the strategic importance of the bridge clear, the *Hofkriegsrat* had ordered Auersperg to destroy it as soon as the corps had removed to the left bank of the Danube. Auersperg's corps evacuated Vienna on 11 November, but he failed to carry out his orders. Count Wrbna, who had been appointed imperial commissioner for Vienna to represent the Crown and citizens, persuaded Auersperg not to proceed with demolition. He claimed that the bridge was required for rapid communications between the court, Vienna, and the French. Since 8 November, Emperor Francis in fact was negotiating with Napoleon, using *Feldmarschall Leutnant* Ignaz Count Gyulai as his chief contact.

Auersperg had taken precautions to rapidly destroy the bridge if this became necessary. The southern end was secured by a wooden gate, guarded by pickets from the Szekler Hussars. At the far side a battery was trained down the causeway with additional guns deployed to the rear. Firewood, straw, and gunpowder charges had been placed among the bridge timbers. All these preparations were completed on 12 November.

That day elements of Lannes' corps and Murat's cavalry entered Vienna. During the night Count Wrbna once again urged Auersperg not to destroy the structure. Next morning the city fathers did not hesitate to provide a guide for a French Hussar detachment in an attempted *coup de main* and also there was much coming and going by horse and carriage across the bridge, with rumours spreading that an armistice was in the offing. All this was confusing to the simple *Grenzer* on duty and they were further confused when several senior French officers, followed by a mass of generals, including Murat and Lannes, presented themselves at the gate and announced that an armistice had been concluded and the bridge be yielded intact. While the sentries hesitated, the French pressed forward and moved to the centre span of the one-mile long bridge. At this point Colonel Geringer of the Szekler Hussars appeared and was told the same story. It was an outright lie, but he was confused, especially when he noted Austrian officials, including Wrbna, among the throng, and rode off to consult his corps commander.

While he was gone, French grenadiers pushed forward to the north bank. Again, the puzzled Austrians did not open fire and when Auersperg appeared he found his own guns pointing inland. Murat now informed him that while in consideration of the alleged armistice his corps would be allowed to withdraw, the bridge and the captured guns would have to be retained.

'The failure of Auersperg to deny the bridge,' Duffy wrote, 'denotes a failure of the will and intellect, if not downright imbecility.'[63] It also was symptomatic of the state of mind then prevailing in the army and the civil administration. Auersperg was relieved of his command, court-martialled and convicted of gross dereliction of duty, though like Mack he was reinstated in grade some years later. No punishment was meted out to the Vienna civic authorities or to Count Wrbna. The mysterious traffic across the bridge in the hours before the French appeared also has remained unexplained.

Kutusov, however, appreciated his peril and already under pressure from Bernadotte who had crossed to the north bank to support Mortier, he left Krems on 13 November and moved off northward in the direction of Brünn in Moravia. With the French across the Danube at Vienna, he posted Prince Bagration with a rearguard in a narrow defile at Schöngrabern, 8000 including a weak Austrian brigade under Major General Nostitz. Murat, Lannes, and Soult pressing north to intercept Kutusov ran into the blocking force on 15 November. They were able to persuade Nostitz to accept the story of the fictitious armistice, but the Russians were not taken in.[64] On the contrary, they now bluffed Murat with a specious story that Kutusov had accepted an agreement that French pursuit be suspended while he retired to Russian Poland. When fighting resumed on 16 November, Bagration's forces made a most gallant stand, several battalions fighting to the last man, that provided time for Kutusov to reach Moravia where he was joined on the 19th by Buxhowden's first column. Bagration also managed to extricate himself and together with the arrival of the Russian Imperial Guard and the Austrian reserve corps, now commanded by Liechtenstein, elements of Kien-mayer's corps, and the rest of Buxhowden's army, the combined Russo-Austrians numbered well over 80,000 by the end of the month.

10 Pontooneer privates, 1798. Corsican hat, dark blue German cut coats and breeches. Black sailor boots. (Plate from the Vienna Army Museum.)

11 Archduke Charles and Staff in the Battle of Ostrach, 21 March 1799. Note the Hussar officer on the left still wearing the peakless shako with plume, cords and flounders tied around the top. Cavalry advancing on right is wearing bicorns. (Print from the Vienna Army Museum.)

12 Austrian troopers billeted in Bavaria, c. 1797–1808. Hussars on left and centre, Cuirassier on right. The Hussars still wear the peakless shako, but the Cuirassier has taken off his new style helmet. (Etching by C. Steinler from the Vienna Army Museum.)

13 Miner and sappers, about 1800. Officers and men. The Corsican hat has become standard, but the senior officer in the centre still wears the old fashioned bicorn. Coats grey of German infantry cut. Trousers and belting white. (After a plate by Ottenfeld.)

14 Austrian infantry (Hoch- und Deutschmeister Regiment No. 4) in combat. Fusiliers and officer wearing the classic helmet with brass front plate. Crest black over yellow for other ranks; black over gold for officers. The 'F II' cypher on the front plate was changed to 'F I' in 1806 when Emperor Francis renounced the throne of the Holy Roman Empire. (Knötel plate.)

15 Archduke Charles and Staff in the Battle of Caldiero, 29–31 October 1805. Austrian Grenadiers in left foreground, Austrian line infantry in shakos and grey coats on right. (Watercolour by L. Rüss, 1844, from the Vienna Army Museum.)

16 'An accidental encounter.' Dragoons in a provisional encampment. Civilian wagon pressed into service on left. (Coloured print by J.B. Secle from the Vienna Army Museum.)

17 Austrian troops about 1809. German and Hungarian Grenadiers on right, artillery in bicorns and brown coats on left. Mounted senior officers in centre.

18 Austrian *Landwehr*, 1809. An idealized contemporary picture. In reality, most men wore a simple grey smock and a black cocked hat. (The Vienna Army Museum.)

19 Bombardment of Würzburg, October 1813, by Austrian (left) and Bavarian (right) troops.

20 Fieldmarshal Carl Prince Schwarzenberg
(Print from the Vienna Army Museum.)

21 Austrian infantry in
combat, 1813. On left
German Grenadier,
German Fusilier in centre,
and Hungarian Fusilier
on right. The original
caption on this Knötel print
indicated the figure on
the right as a Grenadier
– this appears wrong.
Grenadiers usually
carried sabres as well as
bayonets.

22 Fieldmarshal Schwarzenberg reports victory to the allied monarchs during
the Battle of Leipzig, 19 October 1813. Emperor Francis standing in centre
under flags. In background Austrian troops advancing in column. (By P. Kraft
from the Austrian National Library.)

23 Austrian troops in camp somewhere in France, October 1815. On Napoleon's
return from Elba a large Austrian army advanced into France but saw no
combat. Generally Austrian relations with the French were good. (Painting from
the Vienna Army Museum.)

Additional forces were drawing near. Archduke Ferdinand was collecting a corps south of Prague in Bohemia, another Russian division was approaching, and above all, Archduke Charles's undefeated Italian army was within 12 days' march.

The prospect was enough to give Napoleon pause. *The Grande Armée* had marched steadily since it had left the coast. Now its equipment and weapons were in poor shape; losses by combat, illness, and straggling had reduced forces immediately available to 50,000. Therefore Napoleon halted at Brünn to await developments.

The evacuation of the Tyrol and Charles's march to Hungary

Commanding in the Vorarlberg and the Tyrol, Archduke John had been obliged to release two strong formations, Auffenberg and Jellacic, to the army in Bavaria. Auffenberg was lost in the debacle; Jellacic made his way back to Vorarlberg in early November. By this time, however, John already had decided to retreat from his positions covering the northern frontier of the Tyrol and was under considerable pressure from Ney and the Bavarians who had entered Innsbruck on 5 November. The Tyrolean levies, reorganized in 1802–4, about eight regiments strong, proved of limited combat value and John, abandoning his supplies, was moving towards the Drave valley in Carinthia in an effort to meet up with the Italian army. Contact with Jellacic and a small brigade-sized detachment under Prince Rohan in southern Vorarlberg was lost. The prince, infiltrating south along mountain paths, escaped, but Jellacic, as already mentioned, was trapped by Augerau on 14 November. Only his cavalry evaded the French. Rohan then tried to operate on the Italian plain hoping to break through to Venice. After operating for some time in Massena's rear, he was engaged by St Cyr's superior forces on 24 November at Castelfranco. Rohan was wounded; his troops, about 2500 strong, surrendered to St Cyr's corps.

By this time John, with some 20,000 left, had managed to reach Styria where on 26–29 November he linked up with the Italian army in the vicinity of Marburg. Altogether, the combined armies numbered around 85,000, 155 battalions and 96 squadrons, a formidable force. Archduke Charles was out of touch with the situation of the army in the north.[65] Although at this point he was but ten or 11 days march from Vienna, he did not turn northward against Marmont and into the rear of Napoleon. Instead, he moved rather slowly. At the end of November the army went into camp along the Mur where it rested until 2 December. Charles has been criticized for this. 'This delay, this indecision in a critical period,' a Prussian critic wrote, 'can in part be explained by the condition of the troops, but it cannot be justified.'[66] The condition of his army undoubtedly was an important consideration, though perhaps decisive was the archduke's reluctance to hazard Austria's last effective field army and his desire to preserve it to provide leverage during the expected peace negotiations.

Leaving camp on 2 December, Charles marched to Körmend in northern Hungary. Altogether his army had covered some 370 miles in 34 days, not a bad march performance, but hardly impressive.[67] By the time he arrived in Körmend on 6 December the decision already had come about on the field in Austerlitz.

The decision at Austerlitz and the Treaty of Pressburg

From the viewpoint of Austrian military history the Battle of Austerlitz, one of Napoleon's most perfect achievements, has little importance. Emperor Francis had become a fugitive at Olmütz where Tsar Alexander also had established his headquarters. His army was reduced to a pathetic remnant, 16,000 at the most, with regiments down to weak battalions and squadrons. Relations with the Russians were poor. The Russians sneered at the Austrians and behaved in Moravia as if in enemy territory. Tsar Alexander had assumed supreme command, with Kutusov acting as his chief executive officer. Alexander's military experience qualified him to drill a battalion, but his ambition was to beat Napoleon in a great battle. He did not listen to cautious counsels, but to his entourage of vainglorious young officers. There was little Austrian input in his decisions, except for General Weyrother who since the death of Schmitt was chief of staff to Kutusov.

Alexander, apparently with the approval of Francis, decided to force Napoleon into battle. Contributing to this decision was a lack of proper housing, fuel, and above all food for the army in the area around Olmütz.[68] Kutusov proposed a withdrawal eastward, but was overruled. 'We are now perhaps upon the eve of a decisive battle,' Paget reported to Lord Mulgrave, and continued 'I do not feel sanguine.'[69] In fact, the allies had nothing to lose by waiting. Considerable reinforcements were moving up; Prussia had promised armed mediation and Napoleon's forces were experiencing supply difficulties. Nevertheless, on 27 November the decision was taken to force Napoleon into battle and the allied army moved out of the encampment at Olshan west to the area of Austerlitz. And this exactly was the ground Napoleon had selected for battle.

The allies had very little intelligence about Napoleon's position or strength and made little effort to gather it.[70] They did, however, have a plan elaborated by Weyrother. At Austerlitz, the French position had a six mile front with some 60,000 deployed and an additional 10,000 under Davout being fed in during the battle on 2 December. Weyrother's plan, typically complicated and making no allowances for terrain or enemy reaction, called for an envelopment of the apparently vulnerable French right wing by four columns advancing across the marshy Goldbach stream. The Russian right and a weak centre were to hold until the flanking manoeuvre had succeeded. In the event, the advance across the Goldbach met unexpected strong resistance and bogged down in disorder. By late afternoon, feeding in more troops, Alexander had denuded the centre permitting Napoleon to swing his left forward to come down on the rear of the confused mass on the Goldbach. Few allied formations held, most were swept away. The Russians suffered about 25,000 casualties; the small Austrian contingent lost 5992. By the end of the day the allied army had ceased to exist as a fighting force. 'For the present,' a depressed

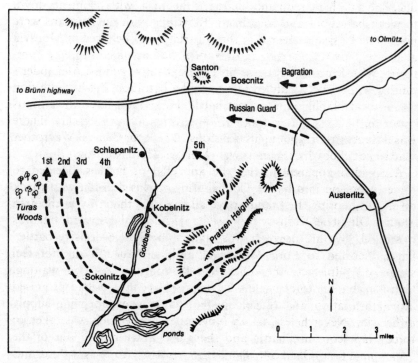

Weyrother's plan for Austerlitz

Paget noted, 'nothing more is to be hoped than they may have made a safe and effectual retreat.'[71]

The outcome of the battle changed everything. Prussia, prepared to intervene, hastily changed its tune and accepted Napoleon's offer of Hanover in return for its benevolent neutrality; the Russians made no attempt to resume hostilities or to come to terms, but withdrew their battered army into Poland. Austria now was isolated and on 6 December agreed to an armistice. There was little hope or spirit for continuing the war. The only troops left were those collected under Ferdinand, 10,000 at the best and Merveldt's ten raw battalions in Hungary. The Hungarian *insurrectio* had been reluctantly mustered, but Count Joseph Pallfy, second in command of this body, informed the French that the kingdom was neutral and would not fight. There still remained the army under Archduke Charles which on 25 December Paget described as 'in every respect in the highest Order.' He continued that with Napoleon's troops exhausted, if the king of Prussia moved into Bohemia and Charles moved to Vienna, the situation might yet be retrieved.[72]

But the ambassador was whistling in the dark. On 22 December Charles had advised Francis that the Monarchy 'is shaken, its components have been wrenched from their foundations.' Peace, he added, was 'indispensable.' As yet, the people still respected the monarch, but soon they would 'demand an accounting for the economic ruin, the bloody sacrifices, and the horrible consequences of this war.'[73] Thoroughly frightened, the Austrians signed the Treaty of Pressburg the day after Christmas. It ceded Venetia, Dalmatia and Istria to the Kingdom of Italy, recognized Napoleon as king, and also conceded royal status to Napoleon's German allies, the rulers of Bavaria and Württemberg, who received Tyrol and Vorarlberg. In addition, Austria had to pay a large indemnity. These changes in Germany prepared the way for the formation of the Confederation of the Rhine and the formal dissolution of the Holy Roman Empire the following year.

Colloredo and Cobenzl resigned, the latter replaced by Count Philip Stadion, a choice endorsed by Archduke Charles. Having emerged from war with credit, especially when compared to the sorry performance by Mack, Auffenberg, Auersperg, Merveldt and others, the archduke now became the leading political-military figure. Austrian to the core, he almost was relieved by the disappearance of the Monarchy's ties to the German Empire. He was no francophile as sometimes was hinted, but he did regard Russia as Austria's permanent rival while he believed that the French threat would disappear with the death of Napoleon. For the moment his programme was for Austria to husband her resources, restore her army, and enter into future conflicts only on her own terms and with overwhelming strength.[74]

VI

Archduke Charles and the Second Reform Period, 1806–9

EARLY in 1806 Archduke Charles resumed his efforts to overhaul the Austrian military establishment. The results, however, were fragmentary. Before military reforms could become effective, a thorough reform of Austrian society and state was required and neither the archduke nor his opponents were willing to go that far. The conservatism of the rulers and their dislike for radical innovations, combined with the very nature of the Habsburg Empire, its diverse political institutions and people, all discouraged such fundamental changes. From the outset the aim was much narrower – improvement of the military administration and the fighting components of the army. But even in this limited objective Emperor Francis, who, like all Habsburg rulers since the days of Wallenstein, feared the concentration of military powers in one hand, did not fully support his brother; instead he instigated intrigues against him and his projects. And Charles himself was unprepared to fully accept the military implications of the French Revolution, especially popular mobilization and a strategy aiming at the rapid and complete annihilation of the enemy. As a recent historian observed: 'A service whose most influential reformer was a conservative contending against soundly entrenched reactionaries, could never become fully reconciled to the techniques and to the energy and activity demanded of modern war.'[1] In the end, though much was accomplished, much was left undone. When war came in 1809 the Austrian army still was not prepared to face the striking power and mobility of the *Grande Armée*.

Renewed struggle for command and control

The debacle of 1805 posed a challenge to the entire Austrian military and political system and first and foremost to the structure of the supreme command. The response, however, was inadequate. Even after Ulm and Austerlitz the emperor and the archduke, together with courtiers, politicians, and senior officers, would not abandon their ambitions and at once resumed the struggle for personal power and influence that had disrupted reforms in 1804–5. Moreover, both sides adopted methods that boded ill for future co-operation and the common good.

Charles was not blameless. He was convinced that the outcome of the war left no other alternative but his restoration to supreme command and already during the last stages of his withdrawal into northern Hungary he had begun to clamour for clarification of his future position. His first request was that General Mayer be appointed to replace the elderly Zach as his chief of staff. Beyond that the archduke demanded the removal of ministers and senior officials who had worked against him and the return of the *Hofkriegs-rat* to a subordinate position in the military hierarchy.[2] He pressed his demands by repeated threats of resignation and predictions of dire disaster. 'Austria, 'he wrote to the emperor, 'faces a terrible crisis. Your Majesty stands alone at the end of a short but horrible war; your country is devastated, your treasury empty, your credit lost, the honour of your arms diminished, your reputation tarnished and the economic well being of your subjects ruined for many years. The devotion of your people is shaky, you have no allies.'[3] Only the immediate centralization of military affairs in the archduke's hands could bring salvation. As for the *Hofkriegsrat*, Charles declared that because of its very nature it had to be 'subordinated to the War Minister or the Supreme Commander ... a deliberative body can never infuse the army with a sense of purpose and direction like a single figure.'[4]

Although perturbed by the tone of the archduke's communications, Emperor Francis readily acceded to the archduke's request for General Mayer and the dismissal of Colloredo, Cobenzl and several other senior officials. Also dismissed was General Lamberti, the emperor's adjutant general. Except for Count Stadion, with whom Charles maintained cordial relations, their replacements, however, were a change for the worse. Moving into more prominent positions in the imperial entourage were his private secretary, Jakob Szvetics, a courtier with a tarnished reputation and a willingness to spy on his superiors, and Baron Anton Baldacci, a court toady and a zealous intriguer. Lamberti was replaced by Colonel Johann Baron Kutsch-era, soon promoted to major general, a singularly unsavoury charac-ter, given to crude sexual excesses in the innumerable brothels of

Vienna. These worthies formed the nucleus of a court faction opposing Charles and did much to deepen the continued gulf between the two brothers.

Of course, Charles already had given the ever suspicious emperor reasons for caution: Late in 1805 there had been covert contacts between officers representing the archduke and Napoleon, culminating in the meeting of the two men at Stammersdorf on 27 December where Napoleon had offered Charles the Austrian imperial Crown. The archduke, to be sure, had rejected the proposal, but the very fact that it had been made scared Francis and from now on he trusted him far less than his own advisors. Then too, Charles had made a very poor choice in selecting Mayer as his chief of staff. Mayer was an unstable personality, showing a great proclivity for intrigues. He was friendly with Szvetics and cultivated him to have access to the emperor's ear, while at the same time he was hostile to Grünne. In fact, the two men hated each other violently and as a result there was no co-operation between the archduke's two closest subordinates.[5]

His suspicions aroused, Francis refused at first to give in to Charles on the issue of the *Hofkriegsrat*. On 13 January 1806 he informed the archduke that he was willing to appoint him *Generalissimus* in complete control of all armies and operations during the war, while in peace he was to become the emperor's major advisor in all military affairs. But the emperor insisted that the *Hofkriegsrat* continue as an independent body, to relieve, as he put it, the archduke of the 'irksome burden of administrative detail.' On the face of it the argument was not unreasonable, but it was an attempt to avoid giving the archduke a clear mandate. Above all, the emperor wished to avoid giving Charles a major voice in political matters and this the archduke would not accept. He replied to Francis that 'as a just monarch' he could not expect him to once more assume 'the protection of the monarchy which, just when the army was about to be combat ready, had been deliberately disorganized either through ignorance or evil intent.'[6] Only a more perfect restoration of the command structure existing between 1801 and 1804 was acceptable.

In the end there was a compromise favouring Charles who on 10 February 1806 was appointed *Generalissimus* to command all forces in war while in peace he was to 'supervise and direct' the entire military establishment including the *Hofkriegsrat*. While this body continued as a separate agency, its major functions were controlled by the archduke. Count Latour continued as its president until the end of the year when he was replaced by *Feldzeugmeister* Count Wenzel Colloredo. There now were four major military departments, the *General-Militärdirektion*, the *General-Grenz-Direktion*, the *General-Artillerie-Direktion*, and the *General-Genie-Direktion*. Count Grünne, the archduke's head of chancery, also headed the first directorate functioning as a war ministry, while the remaining three military directorates also operated under the archduke's control. The president of the *Hofkriegsrat*, a position filled by Count Wenzel Colloredo from 1806 to 1809, supervised the remaining departments and sections dealing with finances, supply, recruitment, and medical services.[7]

Success of this arrangement, however, was more apparent than real. Deep rifts continued beneath the surface. There was much resentment of the archduke's pre-eminent position and the emperor's suspicions of his brother were intensified by continuing allegations that there was a French agent at the very centre of the military administration. These allegations were spread by men close to Baldacci and Szvetics, but they also were believed by the young Empress Maria Ludovica, the emperor's third wife.[8] The identity of this agent, whose existence is accepted by historians, has never been established. Grünne was often mentioned, though this never has been proved and on balance appears unlikely. But the allegations served to discredit Charles and set the stage for another attempt to remove him from his singular position.

The occasion was provided by Prussia's ill-timed decision to resist Napoleon's growing domination of Germany. Though it would have been wiser to postpone an open break until the Russians could again operate in central Europe, King Frederick William mobilized and during August and September 1806 Prussian columns slowly moved south. Except for Saxony, Prussia had no ally, but the king apparently hoped to surprise Napoleon and cause his new German allies, the Confederation of the Rhine, to defect. In the event, Frederick William did neither. Even so, during the late summer and early autumn there was a great amount of agitation for Austria to join in the new war against Napoleon. As always, Charles opposed such a course, declaring that the army was not ready, that he did not believe that the Prussians could succeed or that they would receive adequate Russian support, and that there was no money. Moreover, the archduke was concerned about a Russian military presence in Serbia and on the Dalmatian coast. Still, to prepare for all eventualities, Charles deployed an 80,000 strong army of observation in Bohemia.[9]

The force was being assembled when news of Jena and Auerstädt arrived. Stadion now suggested that Austria had only three choices: to join Prussia, to join France, or to prepare for an all-out defence.

He advocated the third course of action and Charles agreed.[10] On the other hand influential court circles, including Kutschera and Baldacci, still favoured entering the war on Prussia's side. They were supported by Fassbender who had retained some connections and on 17 November wrote from Prague that he had recently talked 'with many well informed officers, Klenau, Bubna, Vincent, Stutterheim . . . who all tell me that the army is in excellent shape, but that the Archduke Charles remains the greatest obstacle to any beneficial action.'[11] This too was the opinion of the Prussian ambassador in Vienna who wanted to spend 10,000 florins to purchase influence in the archduke's entourage. News of the battle of Eylau in February and the subsequent lull in operations brought renewed pressure from the war faction. Even Stadion wavered, but Charles remained firm, while dissolution of the expensive army of observation removed any immediate force to carry out such schemes.[12]

The Battle of Friedland in June 1807, followed by the Treaty of Tilsit where the volatile Tsar Alexander agreed to a partition of Prussia and even joined Napoleon's measures against British commerce, put Austria in a most precarious position. A small corps under Bellegarde, about 28,000, had been concentrated in Galicia to prevent any territorial exchange at Austria's expense, but in the event this was not necessary. Agitation against Charles continued. In March 1808, the emperor had taken the extraordinary step of asking both Mayer and General Klein to aid Kutschera in spying on the archduke and to submit 'sub secretissimo silentio' reports on how best to restore the Hofkriegsrat to an independent and powerful position.[13] Needless to say, the endless intrigues and continuous efforts to undermine the archduke's position hampered any consistent programme to rebuild the army.

Charles on strategy and grand tactics

Except for the instructions laid down in the outdated *Generalsreglement* of 1769 the Habsburg army lacked a common strategic doctrine. This Charles believed had contributed to the poor showing of senior commanders during the last campaigns. Most had passively awaited orders, showing little or no initiative, conduct which Charles hoped to remedy by providing systematic strategic indoctrination. To this end he published in 1806 the manual, *The Fundamentals of the Higher Art of War for the Generals of the Austrian Army*.[14] Although attributed to Charles, the book was a collaborative effort. The first draft had been produced jointly with Lindenau who contributed the first section dealing with the nature of war and armies in 1803. Then the two authors sent it for comment to General Mayer who substantially revised major parts.[15] But even if Charles was not the sole author, the work was published under his name and certainly reflected his basic concepts on strategy, generalship, grand tactics and the nature of war during the period when he actually held command. The official history found that it represented the 'highly developed military literature of the second half of the eighteenth century,' modified somewhat by the archduke's recent campaign experiences.[16]

The manual was divided into three major and not always logical sections: the first dealing with the nature of war, the composition of armies, operational plans and the use of fortresses, followed by a section considering the placement of magazines, movement, field fortifications, winter quarters, and the defence and attack of river lines. The third section dealt with miscellaneous matters such as the protection of convoys, demonstrations, raids, war against the Turks, lessons of the French Wars, and a brief conclusion which in good eighteenth-century fashion tried to establish immutable rules of war.

Old and new concepts could be found side by side. While on the one hand the manual declared that because 'war was the greatest evil that can befall a state or nation' it should be concluded rapidly, and, breaking with the cordon system, asserted that to accomplish this the 'real art of war is how to concentrate superior numbers at a decisive point,' it insisted on the other hand that a general should never select a line of operations that would endanger his communications.[17] Mindful of the experiences in Flanders the archduke warned that operations should never begin with sieges, though he also demanded that magazines be laid down along the main line of operations.[18] In grand tactics he recommended advance in parallel or convergent columns, but insisted that these remain aligned and had to operate closely because unexpected circumstances could delay the best planned manoeuvres.[19] Continuing, the manual recognized mobility and open order fighting as among the major lessons of the French Wars, but cautioned 'one always must observe the basic rule that only a small portion of the troops may be employed as skirmishers while the main body must be kept as a reserve in closed order to decide the issue.'[20] Such observations already had been made in the archduke's 1796 *Observationspunkte*.

Overall the manual did not break with the formal traditions of eighteenth-century close order fighting and it was far removed from the total nature, the impetuosity and improvisations of Napoleonic warfare. Characteristic of eighteenth-century philosophy it asserted the existence of permanent laws in war 'which shall always remain the same because they are based on irrefutable mathematical verities.' The manual described these as the 'need to calculate the means required to achieve a desired objective,' and understanding that the combat of 'equal forces can never achieve a decisive result' and that to attain a decision 'one must have superiority in numbers, or quality of generalship.' And finally, the *Fundamentals of the Art of War* stated that 'because of constant attrition, the security of the line of communication remains a basic requirement.'[21]

The manual was silent regarding the responsibilities and the initiative expected of senior commanders and its emphasis on careful planning, supply, and precise alignments of large formations in battle tended to check individual enterprise. Under the old Austrian fighting system each general officer had his assigned place in the line of battle where his duties were rigidly circumscribed by precise orders. The manual did not change this. Moreover, during the period 1806–9 there were no large-scale manoeuvres and commanders therefore had little or no experience in the independent handling of large formations and the employment of combined arms. When in 1809, after corps formations were introduced hastily at the outset of the war, most corps commanders showed little initiative and instead waited for orders that often did not arrive or arrived too late.

Contemporaries were not unaware of these shortcomings. Some Austrian officers commented that the French battle command and staff structure was much less centralized and that while Austrian senior generals were content to execute orders, French commanders were expected to make their own decisions. At least one writer asserted that the insistence on fixed rules of war was dangerous and that social and technological developments had fundamentally altered the character of conflict, a statement Lindenau described as 'sheer nonsense.'[22] However, later writers generally have considered the manual as conservative and not progressive. Delbrück concluded that Archduke Charles was not a strategic innovator but a disciple of the eighteenth-century system of attrition strategy.[23] Most recently an Austrian military historian wrote that in the last analysis this conservatism was due to the archduke's dominant concern to keep the army in being so as to not risk the collapse of the Habsburg state.[24]

For the enlightenment and instruction of regimental officers Charles directed the publication of a series of teaching manuals. In all there were eight of these pamphlets, the first published in 1806. Under the general title *Contributions for the practical instruction of officers of the Austrian Army*, they elaborated tactical doctrine.[25] The first pamphlet discussed advance guards, the second and third, both dated 1807, dealt with reconnaissance and skirmishing. The fourth pamphlet, 1808, concerned the defence and the attack on villages and woods, while the fifth, appearing the same year, considered the attack on and the defence of field fortifications. Later pamphlets, appearing after Charles no longer held command, elaborated fire and movement, demonstrations, convoys, procurement and winter quarters. By order of the *Hofkriegsrat* these teachings were to be treated confidentially though they were widely distributed. They were issued on the scale of one copy for every battalion of line, *Grenz*, or *Jäger* infantry, while in the cavalry the distribution was one copy for every two squadron division. Altogether 474 copies were issued and the series was offered for individual purchase at a reduced price.[26]

The *Contributions* closely followed the overall formalism displayed in the *Fundamentals of the Art of War*. The section on skirmishing, for instance, merely repeated earlier statements that neither the American nor the French Wars had changed the fundamental rules of combat. Skirmishing merely had added a new, but clearly subordinate, element and decisions could only be achieved by formations ranged in closed order.[27]

Reform of the combat arms: infantry

The archduke considered infantry 'able to fight in every type of terrain' the single most important arm.[28] Therefore the new regulations for infantry published in 1807, of which he and Lindenau were the chief authors, assume particular importance in considering the fighting techniques of the reformed Austrian army. Some writers have argued that the regulations were innovative, even revolutionary, while Charles himself believed that they greatly streamlined procedures. A few days after Austerlitz he had told his brother Joseph that 'in tactics as in all sciences the simplest is always the best,' a statement he repeated in the regulations. The Austrian official general staff history, however, did not consider his regulations simple.[29] On the contrary, it concluded that 'they were even more complicated than the regulations of 1769 and incorporated all the refinements and artifices of Frederician drill.'[30]

The regulations did eliminate some of the obsessive detail of the earlier codes, reduced the elaborations of ceremonial drill, stressed the use of columns and masses, devoted considerable space to fire, and provided instructions for skirmishing.[31] However, most of the innovations already had been introduced in the provisional regulations of 1805, while the methods of deployment and the sections dealing with conduct in garrison and the field were left unchanged from the Theresian period.

In organization the infantry regiments returned to the 1769 pattern. On the peace establishment regiments were composed of three battalions and two Grenadier companies; two field battalions of six companies each, and one garrison battalion of four companies and two Grenadier companies. The war establishment was the same as the peace establishment except that the third battalion was augmented to six companies, while the Grenadiers were detached into separate elite battalions and brigades. Altogether there now were 46 German and 15 Hungarian infantry regiments of the line. In the German regiments the companies were to have 180 men while the traditionally stronger Hungarian units had 200 men in each company. Few companies, however, were up to full strength. There also existed 17 *Grenz* infantry regiments, four Karlstadt, two Warasdin, three Slavonian, two Banal, two Banat, and four Transylvanian, which also formed three battalions of six companies each. In addition, around a cadre of officers and non-commissioned officers from the Tyrolean *Jäger* corps, eight new *Feldjäger* battalions were raised in Bohemia, Moravia and Galicia in 1808 with an additional battalion organized the following year.

All units continued to wear the 1798 uniform, a short single-breasted white jacket, brown in the case of the *Grenzer*, with a high collar, small cuffs and short turnbacks in regimental colours. German regiments wore white breeches with knee-length black gaiters, while Hungarian and *Grenz* regiments sported tight light blue-pants and half boots. Pigtails and powdered hair already had been abolished in 1805 and the hair now was cut short. The head was covered by the helmet, though a light shako, tapering toward the bottom, was making its appearance. Grenadiers, of course, continued to wear their black bearskins and the *Jäger* retained the pike-grey uniform.

Fur-covered leather back-packs, *Tornister*, were becoming general issue as were the M 1798 muskets and bayonets. The *Jäger* battalions were equipped with carbines for the first two ranks, while the third rank and all non-commissioned officers had short rifles. All infantry carried 60 rounds of ammunition, preassembled into cartridges, in a thick leather pouch, except for rifle-armed men who carried the makings for 100 rounds.[32]

The regulations of 1807 retained the three-rank formation, though it had been recognized for many years that the third rank was not useful for delivering fire. It was, however, thought necessary for the charge in line and, as already laid down in 1805, it also was to be used for extending the line or for skirmishing. Kneeling by the first rank when firing was abolished for good and the practice of providing for some modest amount of target shooting, ten rounds a year for all soldiers and 23 rounds annually for the two corporals and 12 privates designated as sharpshooters in each company, was continued. However, rapid fire continued to be considered more important than aimed fire. Fire was to be delivered by individual ranks along a battalion, division, company or platoon front, with fire by divisions and companies preferred 'because this permits maintaining a continual discharge at a high rate.'[33] Of course, this basically was a variant of the Frederician rolling fire, formalistic and difficult to control in combat.

The regulations considered the line as the 'ideal formation' not only for fire but, curiously de-emphasizing firepower in favour of shock tactics, advocated its use even when coming to grips with the enemy with the bayonet. Archduke Charles held that the line could be used to charge cavalry. A three deep line, he believed, had little to fear from cavalry if its flanks were securely anchored and he instructed that volley fire was to cease when the enemy had closed within 50 paces. Then, with the enemy disordered by the last shattering volley, the line was to charge with the bayonet. Ceasing fire just when the attacker had entered into the most effective musket range in order to charge in linear formation was a rather questionable tactic and in 1809 led to rash attacks that seldom brought the desired result.[34]

All movement, whether charging, advancing, or retiring was done by the battalion as a whole. For movement the regulations recommended the battalion column formed from the line on the right flank company, a rather old-fashioned technique slower than the French method of forming simultaneously from both flanks to the centre. Columns also were recommended for movement on the battlefield, while attack columns were to be employed against fortified places and woods. Movement were to be carried out at the 'ordinary' or the 'manoeuvre' pace, 90 to 95 steps per minute for the first and 105 steps for the second. A third tempo, the double or charging pace existed, at 120 steps, but rarely was used because it tended to disrupt alignments. It should be recognized, of course, that under the pressure of combat, and especially during a charge, alignments disappeared as the men pressed forward.

Perhaps the best known, and often overrated, innovation of the 1807 regulations was a variant of the square, the 'mass.' Considering

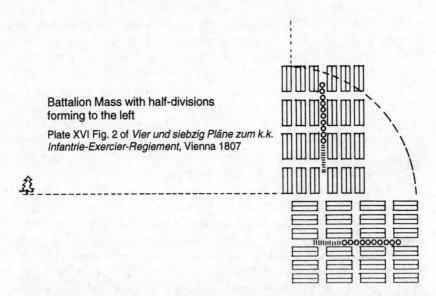

Battalion Mass with half-divisions
forming to the left

Plate XVI Fig. 2 of *Vier und siebzig Pläne zum k.k.
Infantrie-Exercier-Regiement*, Vienna 1807

the conventional three-rank square as too fragile against cavalry and incapable of manoeuvre, Charles introduced masses, that is closely packed columns with the depth never to exceed double the width. The so-called 'division mass' comprised three two-company deep columns, about 9 yards deep, and with a half-company frontage about 30 to 35 yards wide. These columns were to operate abreast but separated by 54–60 paces. Another recommended formation was to draw up the battalion in two divisions of three companies each. In defence divisions were to volley independently against the enemy and, if they were not under direct attack, they were to charge the attacking enemy column from the flank. For the charge, each division mass was to operate independently though in concert with the others. Requiring a considerable measure of independence from company grade officers, this innovation was not well liked and employed only rarely.

On the other hand, the battalion mass, one company wide and six companies deep, was used frequently in 1809 and later. It could manoeuvre either in open or closed order, and in closed order, with the files touching the pack of the men in front, it could withstand cavalry charges. Manoeuvring, though with difficulty, on flat ground at Aspern, closed battalion masses advanced in the presence of hostile cavalry and shattered the charges of six Cuirassier regiments with volleys delivered at short range. Such battalion masses also were considered useful for placing the maximum number of troops in a limited area. They were, however, extremely vulnerable to artillery fire and

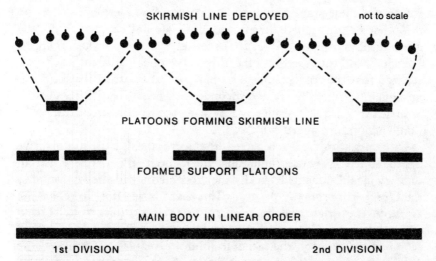

Skirmisher deployment according to the 1807 Manual. Plate 52 in Vier und siebzig Pläne zum k.k. Infanterie-Exercier-Reglement *Vienna, 1807.*

Charles prescribed that masses were to utilize cover whenever possible. Essentially a revival of tactics employed against the mounted Turkish hordes on the Hungarian plains, they tended to lack flexibility.[35]

The regulations of 1807 also provided instructions for fighting in open order and skirmishing but the two sections dealing with these matters gave skirmishers little scope.[36] Such *tirailleurs* were to be found from the third rank composed of the 'brightest, most cunning, and reliable' soldiers in the battalion.[37] Skirmishing was conceived basically as defensive, screening the closed formations against hostile skirmishers. Though the individual skirmisher was given some latitude in the use of terrain and in loading and firing, the skirmish screen was tightly controlled with orders transmitted by the battalion drums. Up to a third of a company, six platoons, could be moved as skirmishers. Normally the skirmish chain, with six paces' intervals, was deployed within 300 yards of the main body. Two platoons formed the first line, supported by two more platoons 100 paces to the rear and with two more platoons in reserve another 100 paces back.[38]

Rigidly controlled and regimented, the Austrian skirmishers rarely were equal to the French. Some observers blamed this on national aptitude. The able Radetzky, probably the best young general to come out of these wars, observed ruefully that 'operations *en tirailleure* can only be conducted in a very limited manner because we do not understand this kind of fighting.'[39] A German officer, on the other hand, argued that it was not national character but 'too much drill' that made the Austrians less effective skirmishers than the French.[40] And the Austrian official history concluded that 'it was not realized that the soldier, unless he has natural aptitude for skirmishing, must be carefully trained for independence.' Instead, the Austrians tried to get quick results by following the totally wrong approach of relying on formalized drill.[41]

Of course, this also reflected the methodical and conservative approach to war predominating throughout the entire Austrian military establishment. Basically they repeated ideas already found in the *Observationspunkte* of 1796. There was little effort to return the *Grenzer*, the original light infantry, to their skirmish role. A new manual for the *Grenz* infantry, published in 1808, merely was a modified version of the general infantry regulations.[42] Even the *Feldjäger* operated without receiving any instructions specially designed for their service. A short manual, *Instruction of Skirmishers*, appeared in 1810 but consisted merely of instructions for the individual man with no tactical content.[43]

Reform of combat arms: cavalry and artillery

For economic reasons cavalry remained 35 regiments: eight of Cuirassiers, six of Dragoons, six *Chevaulegers*, 12 Hussars, and three *Uhlans*. Cuirassiers and Dragoons were designated as heavy cavalry, the remainder as light. The heavy regiments comprised of six squadrons with 135 in each squadron; the light were larger, eight squadrons of 150 troopers in each regiment. The Szekler Hussars, a *Grenzer* formation, were the exception with only six squadrons. In addition, each regiment contained a number of supernumerary dismounted troopers who on mobilization provided the cadre for a reserve squadron, 60 strong in the heavy and 90 strong in the light regiments.[44] Austrian cavalry was inferior in number to the French and suffered from a shortage of suitable remounts.

Armament continued unchanged. All troopers carried a cut and thrust weapon; Cuirassiers, Dragoons and *Chevaulegers* were equipped with the heavy, straight cavalry sword, the Pallasch, the Hussars had their curved sabre. *Uhlans*, of course, carried lances but also were armed with a slightly curved sabre. In addition, there was a liberal allocation of firearms. All cavalry had two pistols and each squadron had eight short rifles and eight carbines, except the Dragoon and *Chevaulegers* regiments, where all troopers were carbine armed with 16 rifles per squadron. In earlier days, especially against the Turks, Austrian cavalry had made considerable use of mounted fire, but for some time now this practice was discouraged and shock action with the *armes blanches* was considered the primary task for cavalry.[45]

Cavalry regulations had been frequently updated, the last time in 1804, and new regulations issued in 1806 for the most part confirmed earlier arrangements. The 1806 regulations stressed that the officers were the most important element in combat, even poorly trained and mounted cavalry under good leaders was superior to a better trained and mounted unit led by poor officers. The two-squadron division continued as the main tactical element while the two deep line was recognized as the standard formation. Cavalry was to act offensively whenever possible and the frontal charge, normally delivered at 12 pace intervals between divisions, was recommended. The troops were forbidden to receive any attack at the halt. All charges were to be made with flank guards and the regulations noted that a reserve should be retained under all circumstances. In making a charge, careful attention was given not to blow the horses. Speed was to be gradually increased from a walk to a trot, then to a canter and finally to a restrained gallop with only the last 80 or so paces before impact at full career.[46]

Columns and even masses were to be used for movement and deployment, but the regulations did not utilize compact columns for the charge, a practice increasingly common in the French mounted arm. On occasion, the thin two deep lines were at a distinct disadvantage in a clash with French cavalry. An even greater disadvantage was the lack of any precise instructions for multi-regiment charges. Together with the absence of large scale exercises which might have revealed this shortcoming, this led to the use of single regiments, even divisions and squadrons, for futile attacks.[47] The tendency to splinter cavalry strength, though opposed by Archduke Charles, was further reinforced by the new, and not always well understood, battle movements which called for large formations manoeuvring in column during deployment. Fearful of cavalry charges against their flanks, commanders often insisted on cavalry support and received it in the form of small detachments. Instead of developing capabilities of acting as an independent strike force on the battlefield, a role cavalry had repeatedly performed in the wars of Maria Theresa, the Austrian mounted arm was becoming a support element.[48] Combat capabilities of the arm were further lessened by the fact that although the regulations contained a section on the use of horse artillery, the *Kavallerie Batterien* were only partially mounted and in any case not trained to support cavalry charges. In 1809 these batteries would be used primarily as mobile field artillery.[49]

During the Prussian Wars the Habsburg artillery repeatedly had swung the military balance in favour of Austria. It continued as a powerful instrument, though its materiel had not changed and it always suffered from a shortage of trained gunners and auxiliary personnel, the absence of permanent tactical formations and control over its own transport. Charles managed to make some needed reforms in artillery organization in 1808, though these fell short of making Austrian artillery as effective as that of the French.

The archduke realized that the regimental guns flouted the principle

WAR ESTABLISHMENT OF THE IMPERIAL-ROYAL FIELD FORCES AS OF
1 MARCH 1809

Type		Man	Horses	Totals Men	Horses
Inf.	46 German line inf. rgts 2 Gren., 18 Fusil. coys., 1 depot div. of 2 coys. Total 5170 man.	237,820			
	15 Hung. line inf. regts 2 Gren., 18 Fusil. coys, 1 depot div. of 2 coys. Total 5065 men.	75,977			
	4 garrison batts, 1114 each.	4456		318,253	
Spec. corps.	9 *Jäger* batts, 9 depot coys. 1084 men.	9756			
	9 pioneer divs, 398 men each	3582			
	1 *Mineur* batt. of 5 coys.	637			
	1 sapper batt. 6 coys.	760			
	1 batt. pontooners, 6 coys.	770		15,505	
Artill.	1 *Bombardeur* corps, 5 coys.	1075			
	4 artillery rgts 16 coys; 2811 men each	11,276			
	1 batt. *Artillerie-Handlanger*, 8 coys.	1179			
Grenz troops	17 *Grenz* inf. regts, 2 field batts, 1 res. batt. each	57,889			
	1 *Tschaikisten* batt., 6 coys., 1 res. div.	1719			
	1 rgt *Szekler* Hussars, 8 sqds, 1 res. sqdn.	1478	1408	75,002	1408

Cavalry	8 rgt Cuirassiers, 6 sqdns, 1 res.				
	sqdn. 1031 men, 975 horses each	8248	7800		
	6 rgts Dragoons, 6 sqdns, 1 res.				
	sqdn., 1031 men, 975 horses each.	6186	5850		
	11 Hussar regiments, 8 sqdns, 1 res.				
	sqdn., 1481 men, 1414 horses each	16,291	15,554		
	6 rgt *Chevaulegers*, 8 sqdns, 1 res.				
	sqdn.; 1479 men, 1414 horses each	8874	8472		
	3 rgts *Uhlans*, 8 sqdn., 1 res. sqdn.;				
	1481 men, 1414 horses each	4443	4242	44,042	41,918
Staff troops	Staff inf. 1 div., 10 indep. coys.	2856			
	Staff Dragoons, 1 sqdn., 10 indep. wings	898	873	3754	873
	Grand total			470,656	44,199

This table includes artillery, miners, and sappers on the peace establishment and does not include *Landwehr*, volunteer units, and free corps. The Szekler Hussars include two additional field squadrons.

of concentration and he gradually withdrew these pieces. Normally the 3-pounders were combined into eight gun brigade batteries; the relatively few 6-pounders were sent to the artillery reserve. To replace the drafted infantrymen who had been used to assist gun crews and to provide the brute force needed for traversing and moving the pieces, an *Artillerie Handlanger Corps*, eight companies reinforced to eight battalions on mobilization, was created. These auxiliaries served not only with the brigade batteries but also with the artillery reserve. Transport still was provided by the *Fuhrwesen Corps*, but it now was militarized and in 1809 its officers received equal status with other commissioned personnel. From late 1808 on transport cadres were kept with the batteries. In addition, the artillery reserve was subdivided further. The 6-pounders, usually grouped with two 7-pound howitzers, were classified as support batteries (*Unterstützungs Batterien*) and together with the cavalry batteries, four light 6-pounders and two short 7-pound howitzers, formed the corps artillery reserves in 1809. Heavy pieces, together with some 6-pounder batteries, were designated as position batteries, four 6 or 12-pounders assisted by two 7-pound howitzers. These constituted the *Haupt-Dispositions-Reserve* of the army, sometimes augmented by 18-pounders. If there was time, these were normally held in a fortified place where spare artillery materiel and other ordnance supplies were stocked. In contrast with the cavalry batteries, brigade, support, and position batteries were foot artillery with only the officers and a few non-commissioned officers mounted.[50]

Battery designation	Type of gun		Vehicle type				Crew	
	Cannon	Howitzer	Ammo. 2 wheel	Cart 4 wheel	Bagg. cart	Forage wagons	Gunners	Auxil.
3-pdr bgde batt.	8	–	8	–	2–3		32	32
6-pdr bgde batt.	8	–	8		2–3	–	32	48
6-pdr support batt.	4	2	6	6	3	–	20	46
12-pdr posit. batt.	4	2		3	3	–	20	46
6-pdr cav. batt.	4	2	3		24 pack horses	6	32	–

Adapted from Maj. Semek, 'Die Artillerie im Jahre 1809,' *MkkKA* 3rd ser. III (1904), 74.

The new artillery organization, 742 field guns in 108 batteries, aimed to provide concentrated fire but in practice this was not always realized. Smoothbore artillery's effectiveness was much influenced by proper siting and ability to target and few senior Austrian field commanders appreciated its potential and limitations even though early in 1809 a senior gunner was appointed as chief of artillery to assist corps commanders. Moreover, there developed a real gap between the 'scientific' artillery specialists and field generals which tended to interfere with efficiency. Finally, the individual battery commanders, described by Charles as 'often old and frail, and having been slowly advanced up the ladder,' still tended to regard the individual piece as a discreet fire element, while generals often lacked feeling for the proper use of artillery. As a result the archduke's instructions that artillery should always act as part of a combined arms team as often were neglected.[51]

The following table shows the ammunition immediately available to each battery in its limberboxes and ammunition carts:

Type and calibre of gun	Round shot	Canister heavy	Canister light	Grape	Shell
3-pounder	90	12	2	–	–
6-pounder	94	26	–	–	–
12-pounder	123	40	–	12	–
6-pounder cav. gun.	94	26	–	–	–
7-pdr how.	–	–	12	–	72

Adapted from Maj. Semek, 'Die Artillerie im Jahre 1809', *MkkKA*, 3rd Ser. III (1904), 84.

Additional ammunition, between 130 and 180 rounds per gun, were carried by the corps reserve park which also held extra rounds for the infantry. Austrian powder was renowned for its strength, the ammunition carefully manufactured and reliable.

Austrian artillery fired solid shot, common shell, and canister. Round shot was fired more than any other type of ammunition and was effective against formed troops in direct as well as ricochet fire. At Essling in 1809 a large Austrian battery caused considerable casualties on French troops deployed in closed formation in the open. At closer range the most common anti-personnel load was canister which in the Austrian service came in three different sizes indicated on the table below. Common shell, finally, was fired by howitzers which could throw the projectile over a wide range of elevations and which, if they exploded, had a danger radius of about 25 yards.

Type of gun and calibre	Solid shot-shell		Canister		
	Range without ricochet in paces	Range with ricochet in paces	Type/weight	Range	
3-pounder	500–1200	1400–1500	1½ oz	300	400
6-pounder	500–1400	1600–2100	1½	300	400
			3 oz	400	600
12-pounder	500–1600	1800–2400	1½	300	400
			6 oz	600	700
			grape shot	900	1000
Howitzer	680–1100	900–1800	3 oz	400	500

Adapted from Kriegsarchiv Wien, *Krieg 1809*, Vienna, 1907, I, 106.

The artillery preserved its old *Reglement* dating to 1757 which set a most progressive humane tone, with promotions to officer rank almost always from within the corps. Regulations for field artillery published in 1809 merely elaborated the service of the guns and its only tactical recommendation was that batteries or half batteries should always cover each other in action.[52]

Officers and men

In 1805 many generals had given a disappointing performance, showing little ability or enterprise, common purpose or even technical proficiency. Charles would have liked to conduct a major purge, but this clearly was impossible without the emperor's wholehearted support. Lacking this, he hoped to raise competence through education. In addition to the various new instructions, in 1808 the archduke was instrumental in founding a professional military journal, the *Österreichisch-militärische Zeitschrift*, edited and issued by Major General Gomez, the head of the War Archive in Vienna.[53] The journal was primarily devoted to essays in military history, a subject Charles believed provided important lessons and inspiration.

Of course, little immediate result was to be expected. For one thing, the Austrian officer corps never was studious, but an even more important reason was that there was no change in the composition of the generalcy, totalling 422 in 1807, including six fieldmarshals, 25 *Feldzeugmeister*, or generals of cavalry, 121 *Feldmarschall Leutnants* and 162 major generals. While Charles managed to retire 25 generals, the remainder still averaged 63 years of age. These men were products of the Theresian army which has been described as notably lacking in mental agility and a sense of professionalism.[54] They neither had the intellectual capacity to evaluate the importance of new techniques nor the imagination to break the bonds of their own experience. Moreover, with the passage of time these worthies became less disposed to expose themselves to hardship and danger, though, of course, there were some notable exceptions. Still, while in the French Republican and Napoleonic armies conspicuous bravery in action was one sure way to promotion and the personal example of generals often inspire troops in action, casualties among the Austrian generals were far below those suffered by their adversaries. During the wars from 1792 to 1815 the Austrian army lost a total of 49 generals killed in action while the French, admittedly fighting for a longer period and in more theatres, lost 219 generals.[55] Casualty rates of senior officers may serve as indicators of the intensity of fighting and the prowess of individual armies and they also provide for a turnover in higher command.

If the Austrian army showed surprising resiliency and recuperative powers during these long wars, much of the credit must go to the junior officers and especially the rank and file. Since the days of Maria Theresa there had been efforts to humanize discipline and to raise morale by better treatment. The artillery *Reglement* of 1759 was exemplary in this respect, stating that 'we must seek in the artillery to encourage the men in their duties more through love of honour and good treatment, than through brutality, untimely blows and beatings.'[56] In 1807 Charles introduced a new *Dienst-Reglement* for the infantry animated in much the same spirit.[57] The code sharply condemned brutality as destructive to the concepts of honour. The soldier must be disciplined but never be treated as a convict. 'Love of his Monarch and an honest life ... obedience, loyalty, resolution, these are the soldierly virtues. In one word, a soldier must be a nobleman.'[58] *Esprit de corps* was the foundation for true discipline. 'The confidence of a regiment in its capabilities, pride in its tradition and the determination to safeguard its reputation constitute the *esprit de corps*. When such ideas have permeated to the common soldier ... all duties and tasks will be carried out willingly.'[59] The well-written statutes remained, with some modifications, in force to the very end of the Habsburg army.

Introduction of the new service regulations was accompanied by implementation of the shortened service obligations already sanctioned by the emperor in 1805. Although discharges were to be staggered in order to prevent a sudden exodus of trained men and re-enlistments encouraged with bonuses and better pay, the archduke feared that this would lead to a substantial decline in troop strength. Moreover, the Habsburg army had experienced considerable difficulty in obtaining trained replacements in war time. Therefore, a commission was established to inquire into setting up a reserve. After much deliberation the commission, chaired by Archduke John, came up with such a system which was introduced by decree on 12 May 1808.[60]

The decree established two reserve battalions for each of the 46 German line infantry regiments. Officers were to be provided by the regiment while the rank and file was to consist of men subject to conscription who had been deferred. Reservists were to receive annual training; four weeks the first year, three weeks thereafter. While undergoing training they were to be subject to military discipline and jurisdiction, otherwise, though regarded as soldiers on furlough, they were to be treated as civilians. If it became necessary to call up the reserves, the youngest were to go first and if this did not provide sufficient numbers, men for active service were to be chosen by lot. Because conscription did not apply to Hungary, no reserve battalions were created for the Hungarian regiments. Instead, after a long and bitter debate the Diet of 1808 promised an increased number of recruits, 20,000, but as usual made it clear that this was a voluntary non-binding concession. In the event, few of these men were mustered the next year.[61]

The *Dienstreglement* of 1807 as well as the reserve legislation cannot be considered steps towards the creation of a popular force, they were designed to improve the professional army. Although the 'participation of the people in this great affair of state' as Clausewitz called it, was the real cause of the transformation of war, Charles and most other senior officers could not accept this and the very nature of the Habsburg Empire made such a course extremely difficult if not impossible.[62] Therefore, when after 1805 there again were suggestions that Austria should adopt some form of popular army, perhaps a militia such as had been tried in limited form in 1797, Charles remained opposed. Militias, national guards, and all such bodies he wrote to Duke Albert, not only were politically dangerous and unreliable, they also 'make it appear as if we have large masses of combatants and so induce a false sense of security.'[63] His sentiments were shared by other generals including Schwarzenberg and Radetzky, while Emperor Francis also had grave misgivings about such a radical step.[64]

In the late spring of 1808, however, there was a temporary change of mind. There appear to have been two considerations. One was that the economy was hard pressed to sustain the costs of a large regular army; the second was the shock produced when Napoleon dethroned the king of Spain. Even Charles conceded that the establishment of a militia had become necessary in order to supplement 'the inadequacy of the military resources still remaining to us after fifteen years of fighting and fifteen years of misfortune.'[65] Archduke John had worked out plans and an imperial patent establishing the *Landwehr* was issued on 9 June 1808. Service was made compulsory for every male between the ages of 18 and 45 in the Hereditary and Bohemian lands unless he already was serving with the colours or in the reserve or belonged to exempt categories. Original estimates held that Austria would raise 180,000 and Hungary 50,000 men, but the nature of the empire prevented full exploitation of the manpower potential. Because the Poles in Galicia were suspected of harbouring sympathies for Napoleon it was unsafe to introduce the scheme in that province though a larger number of men were enrolled as reservists. In Hungary the Diet refused to introduce the *Landwehr* though it gave the king permission in advance to mobilize the *insurrectio* 60,000 strong for the next five years in case of war. Charles thought it wise not to press the matter further.

The *Landwehr* was to be divided into 'normal' and volunteer units, organized in three directorates each headed by a member of the imperial family. Bohemia was under Ferdinand d'Este, Upper and

Lower Austria were to be supervised by Maximilian d'Este, and Inner Austria was entrusted to Archduke John. Presumed establishment was set at 170 battalions, each composed of four to six Fusilier and two rifle armed *Schützen* or *Jäger* companies. Between five and ten battalions formed a brigade, though in practice no such larger formations were used for operations and the *Landwehr*, as far as it did see active service, fought in battalions attached to line formations. Equipment and training of these formations remained indifferent. Although several of the volunteer units designed and procured special uniforms, the majority was issued a simple grey smock and a 'Corsican' hat turned up on one side. For arms the state provided all types of muskets, M 1776, 1780 or 1784, while the rifles represented a mixture of private arms, cavalry *Stutzen* or Dragoon rifles, and even some Crespi experimental breechloaders and air rifles. Under the command of officers recalled from the retired list, the *Landwehr* was to train on Sundays and attend a three week camp annually. Many of the officers were old and useless for service, training was sketchy, few units ever went to camp, and in 1809, except for the volunteer units, the bulk of the force showed low fighting spirit.[66]

The Military Border code of 1807

Reorganization of the Military Border had been underway since 1802 but before a new code could be drawn up Austria had become involved in war. The unlucky campaign hastened the introduction of a new Border code. There were apprehensions about the effects of French propaganda on the *Grenzer*, especially in the several thousand returned prisoners of war. 'It grieves me to report,' wrote an Austrian police agent late in 1806 from Agram (Zagreb), 'that the Military Border no longer remains steadfast in its allegiance to the House of Austria. Especially among the men returned from captivity there are many who have succumbed to French influence and are spreading false doctrines.'[67] To counteract these developments the code was hurriedly debated by the *Hofkriegsrat*, approved by Archduke Charles, and signed into law by the emperor on 7 August 1807. Although the preamble to the code, titled 'Basic Law for the Karlstadt, Warasdin, Banal, Slavonian, and Banat Borders,' declared that it 'provided a constitution for Our loyal and brave *Grenzer* more in keeping with the times and with their national character,' it was little more than an elaboration of the Theresian settlement. Two principal, yet conflicting, motives were behind the document and underlined the cross purposes of this institution. On the one hand there was the desire to lighten the lot of the *Grenzer*, and on the other there was the need to call on them for the maximum number of trained soldiers. As always the second objective won out.

The code consisted of seven major titles and 155 lengthy paragraphs enumerating the rights and obligations of the *Grenzer*, limiting some of the worst abuses and creating a special group of administrative officers subject to the control of the regimental commanders. Supplemented by regulations issued by Archduke Ludwig, acting as director general of the Border, the code went into effect on 1 May 1808. Included in the regulations were provisions for a new service uniform for the *Grenzer* consisting of a brown button-up jacket with short skirt and tight light blue Hungarian trousers. Crossbelts, pouches, and other leather equipment were black as was the newly introduced leather shako. The amphibious *Tschaikisten* battalion retained its dark blue uniform.

Introduction of the new code did not solve the basic problems of the Military Border, especially the increasing poverty of the region. Essentially the last of the numerous eighteenth-century reform schemes it did not envisage and was not designed to deal with problems of the new century, especially the question of nationalism. Across the frontier in Serbia and Bosnia there was a national revolt against Turkish misrule which since 1804 had engaged the hearts and also the active support of the *Grenzer* while at the same time the continued economic hardships, aggravated by the continual heavy drain on manpower, were beginning to alienate the *Grenzer* from their old loyalties.

Moreover, the military bureaucracy was not about to let go. While Charles attempted to get the army ready for another contest with Napoleon, the *Hofkriegsrat* continued to worry about paperwork. In October 1807, Count Colloredo complained that strength returns and other periodic reports from the Military Border had been coming in late and threatened stern action against offenders. Also, there were objections to the code within the Border administration. *Feldmarschall Leutnant* Hiller, appointed commanding general of the Karlstadt regiments, complained that the new code did not resolve the basic economic-social problems of his units which held the poorest land in the region. Much annoyed, Charles blamed Hiller as the 'originator, or at least the spreader, of false rumours' causing unrest among the *Grenzer*.[68] But Charles was wrong. While Hiller was insubordinate and disliked the archduke, the grievances of the *Grenzer* were real enough.

The decision for war

In the spring and summer of 1808 there appeared to be a shift in the fortunes of Napoleon. Although a French army easily defeated the Spanish regulars, popular resentment against the alien invaders made Spain a difficult country to control. While King Charles IV had been forced to renounce his throne and Napoleon had made his brother Joseph King of Spain, the people would not accept him and the revolt against French rule continued to spread. On 1 July 1808, Dupont's corps was forced to surrender at Baylen, the first French surrender in the field for well over a decade. Britain seized the opportunity and intervened with an expeditionary force under Sir Arthur Wellesley who in the first week of August defeated another French corps under Junot. To be sure, Napoleon rapidly transferred major combat elements from Germany to Spain and in November began an offensive which destroyed the Spanish armies and drove one British expeditionary force to evacuate with heavy losses. The Spanish revolt, however, continued and from now on was supported from the base at Lisbon where Wellesley was preparing for operations in conjunction with a reconstituted Portuguese army.

Napoleon's discomfiture in Spain raised hopes of the war faction in Vienna. These now included the Count Stadion, the beautiful third wife of the emperor, Maria Ludovica, as well as Archdukes John and Ferdinand, Baron Hormayr, an Austrian nationalist born in the Tyrol which he wanted to liberate from Bavaria, and such figures as Baldacci, Kutschera, and Generals Stutterheim, Merveldt, Bellegarde and Vincent. Also important was the financial situation. Count O'Donnell, the finance minister, declared that the state could only continue to maintain the present level of military expenditures for another six months. By the end of August 1808 even Charles agreed that war had become unavoidable.[69] On 20 August he submitted a memorandum to the emperor outlining the war readiness of the army and calling for additional preparations.[70]

The decision for war was accompanied by a 'national' revival in Austria pushed by a swarm of publicists, some native and others imported. Their appeals flooded both the German-Austrian lands as well as the German states, appealing not only to national but also to democratic feeling. Francis and his beautiful young wife toured the western provinces among scenes of patriotic fervor. At heart, of course, Francis was fearful of the consequences of stirring up national passions and he was none too firm in his support for war. At the same time, the ruling groups in the Habsburg Empire ignored almost entirely the predominantly non-German character of the state, but except for a few pamphlets translated into Czech, the non-German majority was left out of the propaganda effort as it already had been left out of the *Landwehr* scheme. In the German speaking areas of the Monarchy, however, there existed a unique, if short-lived, popular enthusiasm for war.

If the emperor still had reservations, shared among others by Archduke Joseph, Palatine of Hungary, and Count Grünne, while Charles began to have doubts. On the other hand the chancellor, Count Stadion, the empress, and the entire imperial entourage continued to favour war. The case for war was strengthened by news from Paris about French losses and discontent in the capital. Stadion felt that the emperor and the archduke still needed persuasion and to that end recalled Count Metternich, then ambassador to Paris. Metternich arrived in Vienna early in December and submitted three appreciations in which he claimed that Napoleon had lost the support of the French people, that despite having made an alliance with France in October at Erfurt, Russia would remain neutral and that this would be more valuable than 'mismanaged and uncertain support.' Finally he argued that because of commitments in Spain, Napoleon could count on only 206,000 men for war against Austria, of whom 78,000 would hail from the Confederation of the Rhine and 21,000 from the newly created Duchy of Warsaw. The loyalty of these Germans and Poles to Napoleon, the ambassador asserted, would be weak and Austria, with or without allies, at the least would have numerical equality. Austria, he concluded, could look forward to war with confidence.[71]

Both the estimates about the Tsar's intentions and about the weaknesses of Napoleon's military establishment were badly mistaken, but they decided the issue in Vienna. A hasty conference held the night of 23 December 1808 around Chancellor Stadion's sickbed decided to strike in the spring.

VII

Archduke Charles and the War of 1809: the Ratisbon Phase

IN contrast to the campaign of 1805, the war of 1809, much embroidered by patriotic legend, occupies an honoured place in Austrian military history. And yet there were striking parallels with the events in 1805. Undertaken on the basis of false assumptions and with the army still not ready for combat, hostilities opened when senior commanders already had lost heart. Within a few weeks the initiative passed to Napoleon while the Austrian leadership as so often before merely hoped to avoid defeat rather than to achieve a decisive victory. If, nonetheless, the army managed to inflict the first major setback on Napoleon in person, the credit belongs to the regimental officers and the troops.

The coming of war

Developments preceding the war in 1809, one Austrian writer concluded, 'were of unprecedented confusion. There was no co-ordination between diplomatic efforts and military planning and matters were further complicated by personal rivalries.'[1] The transfer of major French elements to Spain and their apparent difficulties there had encouraged the war party in Vienna to challenge Napoleon. By January 1809, however, Napoleon had driven one British army out of northern Spain and scattered most of the Spanish insurgents. Worried about reports from Vienna and rumours of conspiracies in Paris, Napoleon left Spain and arrived in Paris on 24 January.

By this time Austrian efforts to forge a new coalition against Napoleon had faded. Stadion had hoped to bring Russia into the new alliance, but Tsar Alexander, bound to Napoleon by the Treaty of Erfurt of October 1808, would not make any promises. Nonetheless, when in February 1809 there were reports of Russian troop concentrations on the Transylvanian frontier, both Stadion and Archduke Charles remained convinced that the Tsar did not contemplate any major hostile action.[2]

Negotiations for Prussian support had been underway since October 1808 and a provisional agreement under which Prussia would assist Austria with 80,000 men, half regular and half *Landwehr*, with Austria furnishing 40,000 muskets, had been reached. But this was not a definite undertaking and in March 1809 the cautious Frederick William III repudiated it. By then, however, Austria had committed herself too far to reconsider and troop concentrations as well as the initial plan of operations had been made on the premise of Prussian co-operation.[3]

Austria also lacked concrete assurances from Britain. London had been approached in October 1808, but Foreign Secretary Canning, who had a low opinion of Austria after the 1805 debacle, was reluctant. Following the evacuation of Sir John Moore's intervention force from Spain and after learning from John Mordaunt Johnson, his confidential agent in Vienna, that Austria was in earnest, he changed his mind. Britain promised £750,000 in specie and 4 millions in bills of exchange. Although the bulk of the funds arrived only in July, the prospect served to bolster Austrian credit notes.[4] The British government also promised a major diversionary effort in northern Germany, but repeatedly delayed, this operation finally was cancelled and instead there was an abortive expedition into Holland in July 1809, too late to affect the campaign on the Danube.[5]

Austrian military preparations had begun in January and on 8 February 1809 a Crown Council reaffirmed the decision for war and decided to place the army on its full war footing. By this time Charles had lost much of his earlier confidence. He told General Mayer, his chief of staff, that 'I did not vote for war; let those who did assume responsibility.'[6] Years later he wrote that he had changed his mind because 'given the general conditions and the state of the military establishment our chances for success were minimal.'[7] Nonetheless, on 12 February, Emperor Francis appointed him supreme commander of all field armies as well as of all branches of the military establishment. The archduke was empowered to appoint or dismiss commanders in the field, to make promotions up to the rank of *Feldmarschall Leutnant*, to award the Order of Maria Theresa, and to allocate gratuities. All military and civil officials were ordered to give him any and all assistance.[8] Charles now had authority such as no servant of the dynasty had held since the days of Wallenstein.

However, without confidence in his army, Charles was ill-suited for the position. Delbrück, the great Prussian military historian, remarked that the Austrian leadership in 1809 did not miscalculate physical resources, but 'overestimated the capabilities of the man whom they placed in command.'[9] Harsh words perhaps, but justified during the first phase of the war. Additional complications were created by the continued bickering and infighting at the highest levels of the government and within the army hierarchy. Altogether it was not an auspicious beginning for a war that had to be fought aggressively and with single-minded resolution.

Austrian strategic considerations and plans

Austrian military planners in 1809 faced a most difficult situation. The aim was to break the Napoleonic hegemony in Europe and this required that a major defeat be inflicted on the French army and the war be carried into France. However, though weakened by withdrawals for Spain, there remained substantial French and allied forces in Germany, Italy, Poland and Dalmatia. Clearly, Austria's best chance was an early offensive in the decisive theatre of operations, Germany, while the secondary theatres would have to be neglected. The next question was the selection of the major line of operations. The shortest route followed the valley of the Danube from Vienna to Strassburg, but, because Prussian cooperation still was expected, and also because it would cut the opposing forces in two, a more northerly approach, the Main valley was chosen.[10] On 25 December 1808, Archduke Charles instructed Mayer to draw up operational plans. He informed his chief of staff that he intended to strike with the major part of the field army out of north-western Bohemia while a smaller body was to operate along the Danube. The so-called 'sedentary troops,' that is the *Landwehr, insurrectio*, and militias, were to guard strategic positions along the frontiers.[11]

Mayer submitted his plans on 16 January. Two weeks later, on 2 February, the archduke activated corps formations in the field army and told Mayer to develop specific operational plans aimed at the destruction of French and allied forces in Germany. However, disregarding his own axioms regarding the concentration of all forces in the primary theatre, Charles also gave orders for offensive operations in Italy, the Tyrol, Dalmatia and Poland. It appears that Charles at this point was overly optimistic and still counted on Prussian support.[12]

In compliance, Mayer submitted a more elaborate set of plans, discarding, however, the unrealistic paper strength of over 470,000

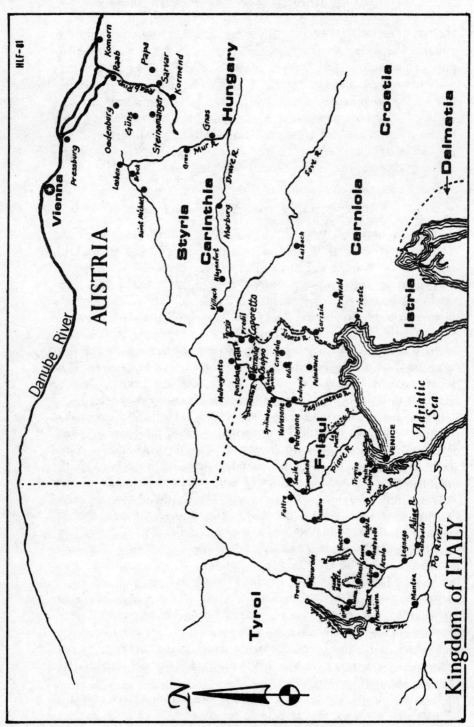

The Italian theatre of war, 1809, and the area of Archduke John's retreat

Field forces	
Line infantry	181,109
9 *Jäger* batts	10,200
34 *Grenzer* batts	38,525
Reinforcements for third batts	21,960
Light and heavy cavalry	31,697
	283,401
Sedentary troops	
Depot batts	73,200
First reserve of 46 German rgts	27,600
Second reserves of 46 German rgts	32,200
Third batt. of *Grenz* rgts	20,400
Landwehr	152,159
Reserve cavalry sqdns	5,356
	310,815

Adapted from KA, FA 1809, Hauptarmee, F 1/ad 19, tables.

men assumed for the field forces and instead assuming a much lower figure, 283,401 as the actually available number. As possible strategic targets he named Bamberg, Munich, Dresden, Warsaw, Innsbruck and Verona and proposed assembling seven corps in north-western Bohemia, two corps along the Inn, two in Inner Austria, and one in Galicia.[13] The plan, made in accordance with instructions, was deficient in regards to concentration of a main mass, but reflected the actual assembly areas of the troops which already had been ordered in January.[14]

By mid-February, however, relations between Mayer and Archduke Charles, long tense because of the ongoing quarrel with Grünne, reached breaking point. Worried about reported French military activities in Germany and concerned that his army was not combat ready, Archduke Charles changed his mind and wanted to switch the main effort from Bohemia to the Inn, placing the army in a position to protect Vienna. By contrast, Mayer insisted that only an early offensive, undertaken before the end of March, could bring favourable results. Annoyed, and undoubtedly egged on by Grünne, the archduke now took steps to secure the removal of his uncomfortable subordinate. The fact that Mayer was drinking heavily and allegedly babbled about the conflict in public provided the immediate cause for his abrupt dismissal. On 19 February the emperor informed Charles that General Mayer was to be relieved at once because he had 'openly criticized measures taken by the Monarchy, shown himself faint hearted, and had spread public alarm.'[15] Mayer was relegated to Brod, an obscure garrison on the Turkish frontier. His successor was Major General Johann von Prohaska, a man of modest capabilities, considered to be under the influence of the archduke's Second Adjutant General, Wimpffen.[16] Now there was no more opposition to switching the main army from Bohemia to the Danube.

Opposing forces on the eve of war

Charles did have good reason to worry about the state of the army. Although mobilization had been underway for some time, there existed grave deficiencies. As usual, remounts and draft horses were in short supply and the trains inadequate, and, as events would show, poorly controlled. The long marches to the assembly areas had caused wastage of men and horses, while some equipment, especially pontoons, had failed to arrive. Replacements were needed and time was required to assimilate these in their units.[17] Still, no army is ever quite ready to fight and Austrian armies had experienced similar deficiencies in earlier campaigns.

A much more critical problem was the hasty last minute introduction of new higher tactical formations. On 2 February 1809 an army order activated corps in the field army.[18] Although in 1798 Charles had opposed adoption of the similar legion system because there had not been time to school commanders to handle the new formations, he did not hesitate this time. Actually, the corps system had been under consideration for some time and had been authorized by the emperor in August 1808.[19] Details had been worked out by autumn of that year, but no attempt had been made to acquaint high-ranking officers and staff with the new order.

There were two types of corps: nine line and two reserve. The line corps were composed of 25 to 30 battalions, 16 squadrons, and between 64 to 84 guns. Each corps comprised of three divisions, including one advance guard division. Advance guard divisions were formed from light troops, two regiments of cavalry, four to six battalions of *Jäger*, *Grenzer* or volunteers, and two light batteries, organized in two brigades. By contrast, the line divisions had no cavalry or artillery and consisted of two or three infantry brigades, each two regiments of three battalions. The average strength of a line corps stood at 29,000 to 31,900 men and 2200 horses. Reserve corps were formed from the heavy cavalry and the detached Grenadier battalions. The larger I Reserve Corps consisted of a 12 battalion

Grenadier brigade and three heavy cavalry brigades of two regiments each; II Reserve Corps had a five battalion Grenadier brigade and two heavy cavalry brigades.

Corps artillery was divided into brigade, cavalry, and support or position batteries. Each brigade had its own foot battery, 3 or 6-pounders, while cavalry brigades normally had a 6-pounder cavalry battery. The divisional artillery was formed by 6-pounder support batteries, one per division, normally held at corps level. Together with the two or three 12-pounder position batteries of the corps artillery reserve they were employed under the direction of the corps *Artilleriechef*.[20] This was feasible because a corps fought as a compact body and rarely deployed on a frontage exceeding 3000 yards. Thus the entire formation could easily be directed by an energetic commander with a competent staff.

The Austrian command and control structure, however, was defective. Highranking officers, including corps commanders, were selected by seniority and birth rather than by merit and experience. In early 1809, Archduke John handled the Army of Inner-Austria, while command of the nine corps was entrusted to two archdukes, Ludwig (V) and Ferdinand (VII), three princes, Hohenzollern (III), Orsini-Rosenberg (IV), and Liechtenstein (I Reserve), and the remainder, except VI Corps which was led by Hiller, to members of the old high aristocracy. None of these men had any experience or schooling in operating under the corps system and this increased demands on their staff. Archduke Charles later held that too much reliance had been placed on the staff officers.[21]

The staff was not capable of handling the corps system. The officers of the Quartermaster General Staff still were primarily trained in mapping, mathematical computations, horsemanship, drawing and penmanship. Many were personally brave and on paper quite capable of elaborating plans for moving troops. In the field, however, it was a different matter. The new system created much confusion and the Austrian general staff lacked a common doctrine and manuals of procedure. And this became especially critical when because of the small size of the permanent staff untrained officers had to be assigned for duty when the army was activated.

Functions and compositions of corps staffs were outlined on 6 March 1809 by General Prohaska. The chief of staff was to advise the corps commander in all matters, but clearly was to remain his subordinate. He was assisted by a number of general staff officers looking after reconnaissance, march routes, quartering, and the operations journal. In addition, the chief of staff controlled the technical corps troops, engineers, miners, and pontooneers. The other major official at corps headquarters was the adjutant general responsible for internal administration and the direction of staff troops, military police, and medical services. The adjutant-general also supervised discipline and strength returns. In addition, corps headquarters housed the chief of artillery, the chief surgeon, the chief commissary, and a great number of other officers and functionaries. Altogether, the official history concluded that while the absence of staffs at the division level required large corps staffs, administration in the field consumed too much valuable time.

The headquarters of the main army performed political as well as military functions. An army order of 6 April 1809 constituted four major as well as a number of minor departments. Among the major departments the first, the Secret Chancery, handled all correspondence with the emperor, the ministries, and with allies and enemies. In addition, it looked after promotions and disbursed secret funds. The second department, the Operations Chancery, issued orders and kept the secret operations journal, while the third department, the Detail Chancery looked after reports and returns. The curiously named *Armee-Generalkommando*, the fourth major department, dealt with transport, supply, pay, medical, and disciplinary matters. Other important officers and officials included the directors of artillery, engineers, and the commissary general, as well as the army minister, Count Zichy, who was supposed to assist the *Generalissimus* in procuring supplies. Altogether, with its subsidiary staffs, bureaus, escorts and attached personnel, headquarters became extremely large and its movement and activities slow and often inefficient.

A British historian concluded that among the major causes of Austrian defeats was the 'hopeless over-centralization of affairs in the Field Headquarters, which rendered it impossible to get out orders in time to meet a sudden emergency.'[22] The concept of decentralization had not been accepted in the service and army headquarters still sent out detailed orders to each unit. Instead of delegating authority, the Austrians merely added more officers and clerical help. On several occasions, this system caused critical delays.

In March 1809, headquarters and six corps, I (Bellegarde), II (Kolowrat), III (Hohenzollern), IV (Rosenberg), V (Archduke Ludwig), and I Reserve Corps (Liechtenstein) were located in northwestern Bohemia. The other two corps of the main army, VI (Hiller) and II Reserve Corps (Kienmayer), were concentrating along the Inn. Archduke John's Army of Inner Austria, VIII Corps (A. Gyulai) and

IX Corps (I. Gyulai), was assembling in Carinthia and Carniola. A small corps, mainly reserve *Grenzer* units under General Stojevic, was forming in Croatia. Finally, near Cracow there was Archduke Ferdinand's VII Corps. Altogether, the eight corps of the main army numbered 200,000 men, the Inner Austrian Army, including reserves, had about 60,000, while VII Corps mustered about 30,000 men. Stojevic had some 10,000 and additional formations, free corps and some Landwehr units were becoming available.[23]

At this moment the French and allied forces in Germany were not yet concentrated. They had been weakened by the withdrawal of some 230,000 veterans for the war in Spain and their cantonments were widely dispersed. Late in December, Napoleon had ordered the creation of a new Army of the Rhine and issued instructions for the concentration of the approximately 100,000 French troops in Germany around Nuremberg and Ratisbon, while also calling on Baden, Württemberg, and Bavaria to prepare their contingents. After returning to Paris, Napoleon had taken additional measures, calling up conscripts of the classes of 1809 and 1810, dispatching his chief of staff, Marshal Berthier, to Germany to take temporary command, and recalling Marshals Lannes, Lefebvre and Bessières from Spain. Even so, French preparations were somewhat slow. The emperor expected war, but did not expect hostilities to start until May when the weather had turned more favourable. By the end of March the dispositions of French and allied forces in Germany were as follows: III Corps (Davout) with three integral and two attached divisions was moving from Erfurt to Bamberg and shifting towards Ratisbon. The Bavarian VII Corps (Lefebvre), three divisions, was forming at Munich, Freising, and Landshut. II Corps (Oudinot) with two divisions and IV Corps (Massena), four divisions, were moving from Frankfurt and Strassburg into Bavaria. The excellent Württemberg VIII Corps (Vandamme) and Rouyer's division were mustering east of the Rhine. The two divisions of heavy and the three brigades of light cavalry available were assigned to the various corps. In all, the French and allied forces in Germany numbered some 170,000 men at this point, with additional forces, including the Imperial Guard moving up partly in forced marches or in wagons, but could not arrive before the end of May.[24]

In Italy, Viceroy Eugene was mustering French and Italian forces, but at the moment only had some 30,000 available for operations. However, he also could count on the Army of Dalmatia, actually no more than a small corps of two veteran divisions under Marmont, about 12,000 men but with a strong artillery component. Finally, and still in the process of organizing, was the Army of the Grand Duchy of Warsaw under Prince Poniatowski, 20,000 at best.

In overall manpower and artillery the Austrian armies outnumbered their opponents, though as French reinforcements arrived the balance would become much more equal. Also, after three years of reconstruction, the Austrian army had improved while the French had deteriorated somewhat. While the Austrian infantry had improved, the French foot no longer was as good as it had been at Austerlitz. Too many new recruits had to be assimilated and many of the best regimental officers were away in Spain or dead. Lack of training forced the French to adopt massive assault columns, though some of the best divisions, notably those of III Corps could advance in column, deploy into line, and fight in open order. French cavalry was excellent and still superior in its massed formations to the Austrian horse. Initially, the French were much inferior in artillery, but their batteries were bravely and imaginatively handled. Overall, while the Austrian army was better than that of 1805 and the French had declined, they still enjoyed marked superiority of morale and with more experienced generals and staff, the advantages of flexibility and better command.

The Austrians hoped for defections from the contingents of the Confederation of the Rhine. But all of Napoleon's German allies remained loyal and did well. Bavarian troops, constituting the largest contingent, 30,000 men, provided steady infantry, excellent light horse and artillery. Württemberg's fine corps distinguished itself, while the Saxons contributed indifferent infantry and artillery, but perhaps the best heavy cavalry in all of Europe. Smaller contingents also did well, including the Hesse-Darmstadt brigade in IV Corps.[25] On the other hand, the Austrians faced trouble in Hungary. When in January 1809 Emperor Francis asked the Palatine Archduke Joseph for the additional recruits conceded by the Diet of 1808, the palatine pleaded to defer the call-up. 'The spirit of this country,' he wrote, 'is so bad that this action might precipitate real trouble, so that while our troops are engaged abroad we may face a more dangerous enemy at home'.[26] Fears about internal complications inhibited the Austrian conduct of the war then and later.

The Austrian change of operational plans

If the Austrians had struck late in March they would have caught the French still concentrating and, throwing the enemy off balance, might have been able to inflict a major defeat after which they could have used their numerical preponderance to retain the initiative. But Charles hesitated and lost this fleeting opportunity.

From early February on there were indications of increased French activity. On 6 February, for instance, it was reported that the French were concentrating near Erfurt, establishing a base at Ingolstadt, and were fortifying Passau and Ratisbon. As such intelligence mounted, Charles became worried that if he attacked along the Main, as Mayer urged him to do, the French would advance along the Danube towards Vienna.[27] It is possible, however, that if he had advanced before the end of March, his army, constituting a single mass of manoeuvre while the French still were dispersed, might have gained initial victories which could have swayed Prussia to abandon her neutrality. But after mid-February such speculations became redundant. Mayer was dismissed and on 13 March, leaving behind I and II Corps in Bohemia, Charles began to transfer his army to the south bank of the Danube.[28]

The change has remained controversial. Some observers, including Radetzky, later concluded that it had imposed a fatal delay, a delay long enough for Napoleon to arrive in Germany and rally his forces.[29] In defence, General Prohaska rationalized that an offensive west out of Bohemia would have been difficult. Communications were poor and the enemy might have attacked the heads of columns as they emerged from the Bohemian mountains. Moreover, Prohaska argued, if the enemy assembled at Ratisbon the army either had to leave Vienna uncovered or attack across a defended river. Finally, a main advance from Bohemia would have severed communications with the army in Italy.[30]

None of these contentions appear valid. The three weeks' delay gave the French time; Vienna was not protected and there was little strategic co-operation with the troops in Italy. The two corps left behind to manoeuvre from Bohemia operated to no good purpose, while shifting the main body exhausted troops, ruined equipment, and strained supply arrangements.[31]

The advance to Ratisbon

The main army arrived on its new line of departure, Braunau-Schärding, on 8 April with General Jellacic, eight battalions, eight squadrons and two batteries, detached to Salzburg. Charles issued new orders that day. Hostilities were to open on all fronts on 10 April. In Germany the two parts of the main army were to attack towards Ingolstadt. Archduke John was to take the offensive across

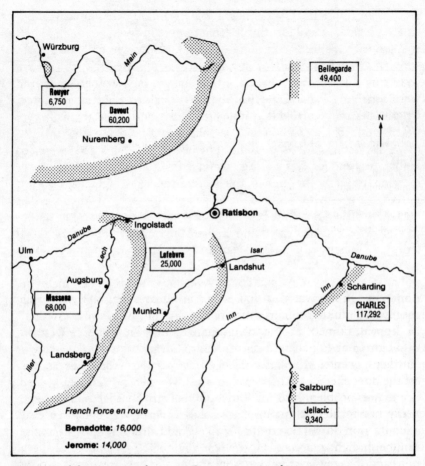

Position of the opposing forces in Germany, 9 April 1809

the Piave in Italy, detaching General Chasteler with 12,000 men to support a revolt in the Tyrol. In the east, VII Corps was to move on Warsaw, defeat the Poles, and then return to the Elbe to secure the main army's rear against Saxony. 'It is my intention,' Charles wrote, 'that all movement be rapid and decisive.'[32] The next day the archduke issued a war manifesto to the troops. 'Companions in arms, the eyes of the world, the eyes of all who still retain a sense of national honour are focused on you. . . . Europe looks for freedom under your banners . . . your German brethren wait for redemption at your hands.'[33]

The manifesto, composed by Friedrich Schlegel, a German exile in the Habsburg service, made no appeal to the Slavic majority in the

TRANSPORT ALLOCATION CHART 1809

Formation	Field chest	Rations	Field forge	Admin. wagon	Pack-horse
for each					
Line inf. regt	1 (4 horse)	10 (4 horse)	1 (2 horse)	1 (2 horse)	26
Grenzer inf. regt	1 (4 horse)	6 (4 horse)	1 (2 horse)	–	?
Jäger battl.	1 (2 horse)	6 (2 horse)	–	–	12
Pioneer battl.	1 (2 horse)	4 (2 horse)	1 (2 horse)	–	4
Cavalry regt	1 (4 horse)	3 (4 horse)	1 (2 horse)	1 (2 horse)	–
Legion battl.	1 (2 horse)	–	–	–	9
Vienna volunt. battl.	1 (4 horse)	2 (4 horse)	–	1 (2 horse)	–

Despite a directive dated 9 March 1809, senior officers brought numerous private vehicles and packhorses, and units added unauthorized conveyances. Source KA, *Krieg 1809* I, 96-7.

Monarchy. If the war of 1809 is perceived as a national war, this ignores the multinational nature of the Habsburg Empire. At that, the appeal, aimed at Napoleon's German allies had no effect. Although Charles had told corps commanders that Bavarians might join them, events, Hiller grumbled in his diary, 'revealed that it was just the opposite.'[34]

A major problem was the slow rate of advance. To sunder the enemy before he could concentrate, and Charles was confident that he could not do so before 18 April, it was necessary to reach the Danube in eight marches. However, encumbered by a large artillery train and by massive columns jamming the two available major roads, hampered by bad weather and the absence of reliable maps, the advance immediately fell behind schedule. After only two days of marching Charles discovered that his army needed a day of rest for recuperation, maintenance and to allow the trains to catch up.[35]

Austrian sources frequently blamed the bad roads and weather for the slow pace of advance, but conditions were no better for the French. The reasons were more complex. Fearing to provoke popular resentment and concerned about discipline, Charles never accepted the system of direct requisitioning practised by the French. Requisitioning was restricted to replenishing magazines and during the advance each corps was followed at one day's distance by its supply column, including the heavy field ovens to bake the bread rations. Then too, the corps commanders were not used to march troops in corps formations and continued to use the old order of march. Their formal columns were too wide for the available roads, while the inclusion of the brigade batteries in the column led to frequent traffic stoppages. Matters were not improved when on 12 April III Corps had to move across the line of march of IV and V Corps. That night troops bivouacked badly mixed up and their condition was not improved by an order for a general issue of a half-litre of wine to all. 'Unfortunately,' the official history records, 'there was no wine to be issued.'[36]

Meanwhile to the north, I and II corps, led by Bellegarde, also made little progress. Described as a 'gallant man and an extremely brave soldier, but lacking the enterprise required of a field commander,' Bellegarde clearly was over his head in an independent role.[37] His indecision was compounded by the failure of his light cavalry to provide intelligence. In fact, throughout the campaign the Austrian light horse failed in this vital function so that Austrian commanders lacked knowledge of the enemy's actual position.[38]

The Battles of Abensberg and Eggmühl

In the second week of April, owing partly to a failure in communications, Berthier still had his forces dispersed. Davout's right wing north of Ratisbon was separated by some 70 miles from Massena's left wing at Augsburg, the interval only lightly covered by Lefebvre. On direct orders from Napoleon, Berthier instructed Davout on 16 April to hurry to Ratisbon, but this still left the French divided and offfered an opportunity for Charles to turn against the separate wings. That day the Austrian main body had reached Landshut, pushed aside a weak Bavarian division, and crossed the Isar. To exploit his advantage, Charles decided that V and VI Corps, supported by I Reserve Corps, would guard his flank while the bulk of his army would march to the Danube west of Ratisbon for a link-up with Bellegarde. 'My operations,' he explained, 'will most probably move to the Danube where it appears the enemy is concentrating.'[39] However, he did little during the next three days. Some authors claim that he had another epileptic seizure, others hint that he lacked strategic inspiration and resolve.[40]

But time was running out. On the morning of 17 April Napoleon had arrived in Donauwörth and recognized the dangerous situation. Although unsure about the location of the main enemy body which he assumed to be around Landshut, he set about to organize his *bataillon carrée* formation in which the various corps marched independently but in supporting distance, and were able to come together rapidly when the main body of the opponent had been located. Urging Massena and Oudinot to hurry, he instructed Davout to leave Ratisbon where the marshal had arrived on the 17th and move on Ingolstadt to join up with Lefebvre. Lannes, just arrived from Spain, was ordered to form a provisional corps.

On 18 April, Charles, realizing that Davout was at Ratisbon in strength decided to move against him, keeping his left wing under Hiller facing west. The next day Davout, leaving only one regiment behind, led his corps out of the town. The Austrians, moving late and in four columns without much mutual support, failed to block his progress though III and IV Corps had a number of running fights with Davout's rearguard. By nightfall Napoleon had united his right wing and centre near Ingolstadt. Charles now was in the peril from which the French just had escaped. Perceiving that the Austrians were over-extended on 20 April Napoleon launched Lannes in an attack passing south of Abensberg that drove a wedge between Charles and Hiller. Charles withdrew east to take up a position some 14 miles wide between Eggmühl and the Danube, sending word to Bellegarde to move to the river to threaten French communications and directed Kolowrat to seize Ratisbon.

On the morning of 21 April, Napoleon, not certain about the position of the major part of the Austrian army, sent the greater part of his forces southward in pursuit of Hiller, that is V, VI and II Reserve Corps. Pushed back to Landshut, Hiller put up a stout defence, but with Massena now coming up he evacuated the town with Bessieres and Wrede in pursuit. Meanwhile, in accordance with orders, Davout had moved against the Austrian position but found himself heavily outnumbered, 30,000 against 75,000 at best. Even so, fighting in broken terrain well suited to French tactics, his veterans gave a good account of themselves. Informed that Davout had the Austrian main force, Napoleon ordered Lannes and Massena to march north before dawn the next day, 22 April. Charles had been reinforced by Kolowrat whose corps had required 24 hours to cover the seven miles from Ratisbon and planned to use II and I Reserve Corps to drive in Davout's left flank. As usual, the Austrian attack started late and was poorly supported by the other corps, though shortly after noon Davout's situation became difficult. But then Lannes' columns crashed into the Austrian left flank and Charles had to withdraw.

Under pressure, the retreat degenerated into a partial rout. Though some units stubbornly defended villages and defiles, Rosenberg's corps lost most of its guns and ammunition carts. To halt the French

NAPOLEON'S GREAT ADVERSARY

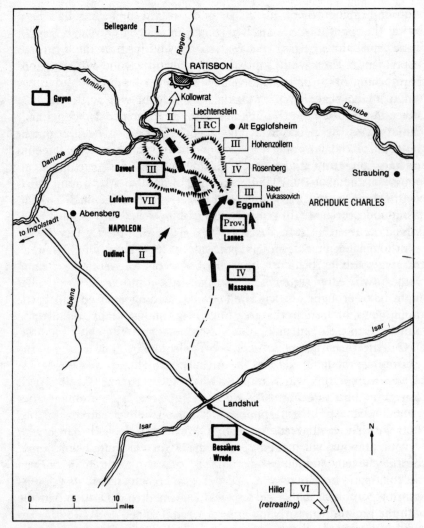

Battle of Eggmühl, 22 April 1809

cavalry pursuit, Charles towards evening committed part of his mounted reserve, 29½ squadrons near Alt Egglofsheim. Fighting as separate regiments without the support of their guns which had already been pulled back, the Austrians were worsted by some 66 squadrons and 18 guns. Even so, the unequal combat had gained time and about 10.00 that night the exhausted French broke off pursuit.[41]

Meanwhile, utilizing the intact bridge at Ratisbon as well as a pontoon bridge further north, Charles extricated the bulk of his army during the night and next morning. But casualties had been heavy, on 22 April alone he had lost 10,700 men and his mood had turned despondent.[42] Even while combat still went on around Ratisbon, on the morning of 23 April, he sent a message to his brother advising him to make peace. 'With half the army in dissolution, I have no choice but to cross the Danube at Ratisbon and make for Bohemia.' The army had to be saved at any price. No reliance, he continued, could be placed on either the *Landwehr* or the *insurrectio*, on the contrary, the army might 'well be needed to deal with events in the interior of the Monarchy.' An end to hostilities, he told the emperor, was imperative and the sooner the better because 'once the enemy has entered the lands of Your Majesty they will be ruined and like Prussia occupied for many years.'[43]

Although the French renewed pressure the next morning, Charles got away, leaving behind a brigade of infantry for the final defence of the town. After the French stormed Ratisbon a vigorous pursuit might have brought disaster to Charles, but Napoleon was worried about news of insurrectionary movements in Germany and determined to take the enemy capital to end the war quickly. Sending Davout after Charles, he now turned against Hiller.

Given the state of Charles's army and the shaken resolve of its *Generalissimus* this was a mistake. During the retreat Charles tried to negotiate an accommodation with Napoleon. 'Your Majesty,' he wrote on 28 April, 'has announced to me your arrival by cannon shots without leaving me time to compliment you. I hardly had heard of your presence when the losses I sustained caused me to realize it painfully.' He continued to suggest that 'perhaps Fortune has chosen me to assure my country a durable peace,' and closed the letter assuring Napoleon that 'I feel flattered, Sire, to have measured swords with the greatest captain of the age . . . I beg your Majesty to believe that my ambition always leads me towards you and that I shall be equally honoured, Sire, to meet you either with the sword or the olive branch.'[44]

Napoleon ignored this abject communication which did much damage to Charles in the eyes of his contemporaries. At court there were renewed efforts to remove him from command. Stadion, Baldacci, Kutschera, and above all the empress urged his dismissal, but there was no one to replace him.[45] Meanwhile, with only Davout's infantry following him, the Austrians for once almost matched the French marching speed. Averaging 12 miles a day, between 28 April and 16 May the army covered 200 miles without a rest.[46] Making its way down through Bohemia into Austria, it arrived on 16–17 May at the historic Marchfeld, east of Vienna on the left bank of the Danube. Together with Bellegarde, who had joined during the retreat, Charles now had over 90,000 men. Despite the rapid march, however, the capital already had fallen to Napoleon.

Although the Ratisbon campaign could not compare with some of his earlier victories, Napoleon, with a hastily assembled and improvised army first had seized the initiative from Archduke Charles and then, in a classic manoeuvre, with one corps holding the enemy, attacked his flank to defeat him. If Eggmühl was neither an Ulm nor an Austerlitz, it still was a well run series of battles illustrating superior generalship and flexibility. On the Austrian side as the official history noted sadly, the 'army still was not equal to the requirements of mobile warfare.' The staff had been unable to co-ordinate movements, while commanders had displayed little initiative, rarely supported each other, and always kept back too many reserves. At Eggmühl, for instance, Charles committed only about one half of his available troops, the remainder standing to arms but contributing little. On a tactical level, the French remained more mobile and maintained their superiority in broken terrain.[47]

As was his unfortunate habit, Charles blamed his subordinates. While he was justified to assert that they had been unable to handle independent commands, he conveniently forgot that he had done nothing to train them for such roles.[48] For that matter, Charles was not on good terms with his corps commanders, did not give them much discretion and rarely revealed his plans to them. His orders issued through Grünne, an officer cordially disliked by most other high-ranking officers, often were obscure or ambiguous. During the retreat to Bohemia he abolished the corps system, though he retained the designation, and resolved to return to the old and familiar fighting form in which the entire army would fight as one body, tightly controlled, with carefully chosen positions and with as little risk as possible. Prohaska, criticized for the shortcomings of the staff, was dismissed on 8 May and replaced by General Wimpffen who protested that he lacked the qualifications for the job.[49]

Hiller's retreat and the capitulation of Vienna

Following the French breakthrough south of Abensberg on 20 April General Hiller with three corps found himself temporarily out of touch with the main body of the army. Driven out of Landshut, he retreated south-eastward where on 24 April at Neumarkt, some 24 miles from Landshut, he turned on his pursuers. With 23,000 foot and 4000 horse he attacked the Franco-Bavarians under Bessières and in a brief engagement inflicted 2500 casualties, including 900 prisoners, on the enemy. It was however, impossible to exploit this success. Hiller now was aware of Charles's retreat and realized that Massena and Lannes were across the Isar. Continuing his retreat, and with his rearguard hard pressed, he crossed into Austrian territory at Braunau two days later. That day, 26 April, Legrand's division of Massena's IV Corps stormed Schärding on the Inn. With the line of the Inn compromised and the road to Vienna open, Hiller now fell back to the next tributary of the Danube, the river Traun.[50]

By this time he was receiving conflicting instructions. From Charles there came rather vague instructions that Hiller was to bring his corps across the Danube at the first possible opportunity, while from Vienna, with the emperor now interfering in the conduct of operations, he was advised to gain time so that preparations could be made to defend the capital. On 28 April Archduke Maximilian arrived and advised him that he was to retire to Linz where a fortified camp had been prepared. Linz, Maximilian assured him, was to become the base where the army was to reunite.[51] Hiller, who did not like the Archduke Charles since he felt that he had slighted him in the past, chose to obey the imperial instructions. Archduke Charles was incensed and later wrote that Hiller was 'an able man, but devoured by ambitions which he pursued by devious means' who 'as soon as he no longer was under my direct supervision . . . deliberately failed to rejoin the main army.'[52]

Arriving in Linz on 2 May, Hiller received a typically ambiguous message from Charles telling him that the archduke intended to cross the Danube further downstream, though no exact location or date was provided. Also, Hiller discovered that nothing had been done to fortify the town and that, a few volunteer units excepted, the Landwehr was not disposed to fight. Upper Austria had mustered 15 battalions, 12,200 men, but when the French actually entered the land on 26 April, the bulk of the force, about 75 percent, deserted.[53] However, with his rearguard brigades in contact with the enemy and hoping to buy time, Hiller decided to stand at Ebelsberg, a small town on the east bank of the Traun, a few miles southeast of Linz.

The position was strong, though already outflanked by Lannes who had crossed the river at Wels. Even so, on 3 March Massena decided to make a frontal attack across the 500-yard long bridge over the Traun which the Austrians, hoping to save some transport, had failed to blow. There was heavy and bloody street fighting in which the 4th, 5th, and 6th battalions of Vienna Volunteers distinguished themselves, proving an exception to the general dismal showing by the *Landwehr*. The castle and ridge dominating the town remained in Austrian hands and Hiller had ample reserves. However, above all concerned to preserve his army, he refused to engage these forces and by noon an additional French division was across the river. About 2.30 in the afternoon the battle was lost and Hiller, who had spent the decisive hours calmly lunching on the castle terrace, was in retreat. Casualties were heavy on both sides with many of the wounded dying in the fire which swept through the wooden buildings.[54]

While Hiller's personal conduct during the action was, to say the least, inappropriate, his decision not to commit additional troops was correct. He probably could have driven the French out of Ebelsberg, but he lacked strength to follow up and he realized that his rear was menaced by Lannes. With the only major field force still standing between Napoleon and Vienna, retreat was obligatory and, under pressure, Hiller moved east and on 10 May arrived at St Pölten some 15 miles from the capital. Assured by Archduke Maximilian, commandant of the city, that Vienna would be defended, Hiller detached his five battalions of Grenadiers to assist in the defence and then managed to get his army across the Danube to Krems on 11 May.[55] Assurances notwithstanding, Maximilian lost his nerve and in the evening began to evacuate Vienna, abandoning very substantial stocks of war material.

In 1809 Vienna was the largest city in central Europe with over 200,000 inhabitants. Located on the right bank of the Danube, and with a small branch of that river dividing the city from a large island on which there was the Prater park and the suburb of Leopoldstadt, the city in turn was divided into the walled Inner City, housing about 50,000 inhabitants in narrow streets, and a semi-circle of suburbs. The fortifications of the Inner City were old fashioned and only 48 guns were mounted, but there was a wide, if overgrown glacis, and additional guns were held in the arsenals. The suburbs, of course, had no fortifications except for the excise walls. Beginning on 5 May, however, efforts were made to improve the works and 8000 men, including 600 soldiers, were employed to clear the glacis and build hasty fieldworks.[56]

There was a substantial garrison, 14 battalions *Landwehr* and 6000 civic militia, stiffened by eight ½ line battalions and the five Grenadier battalions sent in by Hiller. In addition, Archduke Maximilian's appeal for volunteers had received an enthusiastic response, though at the approach of the French many of these recently recruited patriotic defenders slunk away. The Viennese were not known for heroic steadfastness. While the fortifications clearly were inadequate, an aroused citizenry might have made Napoleon pay dearly for the conquest of the city as the example of Saragossa in Spain had revealed. But neither the Archduke Maximilian nor the population were prepared for a fight to the bitter end. As in 1805, the imperial court, archives, library and other institutions were packed up and left Vienna, as did many of the leading citizens. When on 11–12 May, French advance element seized Prater Island and threw a few shells into the streets there was near panic and Maximilian, informed that the archduke would not arrive until 18 May, decided to evacuate the city.[57] If the capital had been defended Napoleon might have been caught with one part of his army still fighting in the streets, while the other had to turn against the relief army.

But this was not to be. Late in the evening of 12 May Maximilian marched out, accompanied by a disorderly throng of soldiers, carts, carriages, and horses. At the north end of the Tabor bridge he met a disconcerted Hiller to whom he declared 'I hereby hand this entire mess (*Boutique*) and the command over to you.' Hiller at once ordered the bridge destroyed and spent the rest of the night trying to create some order.[58]

In his haste to evacuate the city, Maximilian made no attempt to destroy the hundreds of guns in the arsenals or the stores in the magazines, and even abandoned a war chest of 4 million florins. Also left behind to surrender the city was Major General O'Reilly with 17 senior and 163 junior officers and 2000 men, not to mention the volunteers and the city militia.[59] Vienna formally capitulated on 12 May and during the next two days the French entered Vienna in force. The population quickly came to terms with the new masters. 'Intimate relations,' one contemporary reported, 'soon sprung up between the society ladies and French officers... while soldiers and girls from the lower classes mingled on the bastions ... where scenes took place that made Vienna look like Sodom and Gomorrah.'[60]

The legend that in 1809 Austria, or at least the German-speaking areas were animated by strong patriotic feelings and wholeheartedly supported the war, still is commonly accepted by historians. But it is not based on fact. Austrian leadership distrusted the population, there was much patriotic posturing, but when put to the test only few *Landwehr* units fought well, and, except for the Tyrol, there was no popular resistance. Little had changed since 1805. The real heroes, as so often before, were the lower ranking officers and the common soldiers.

Operations in Italy

In 1809 both sides regarded Italy as the secondary theatre and both the Austrian as well as the French commanders in chief lacked experience. Archduke John, of course, had held a number of commands, but his one independent role had led to disaster at Hohenlinden. On the French side Prince Eugene de Beauharnais, viceroy of Italy, never even had commanded a regiment, let alone an army, in the field. Napoleon hoped that Eugene's status as an honest and respected administrator would compensate for other shortcomings and, between May 1808 and January 1809, he sent him elaborate notes and instructions on military affairs. As the danger of war became more evident, Napoleon urged his step-son to stand on the strategic defensive, with the main line of defence based on the fortresses of the Quadrilateral and the Adige river. Eugene, however, had become more confident and intended to regard the Adige merely as a 'worst case' position. Instead, he now contemplated an earlier offensive scheme combining a thrust from the north Italian plain towards Laibach in Carniola supported by a northward strike from Dalmatia.[61]

In early April 1809, however, Napoleon's main concern was to avoid provoking Austria by premature concentrations. 'I intend,' he informed Eugene, 'to remain stationary all of April and I do not think that the Austrians will want to attack.' Therefore, Eugene's Army of Italy remained dispersed. Nonetheless, Eugene made efforts to increase combat readiness of his troops, six French and two Italian infantry divisions, two Dragoon and one light cavalry division, as well as the two-brigade Royal Italian Guard, and the army artillery park. On paper these amounted to 68,000 men and 250 guns, but the divisions were understrength and included a high percentage of raw recruits. Marmont's Army of Dalmatia, actually one corps, consisted of two veteran divisions and corps artillery of some 78 guns. Although some divisions and observation detachments, about 30,000 men in all, were well forward of the Adige, the Austrian attack in April took Eugene by surprise.[62]

Archduke John's Army of Inner Austria, VIII and IX Corps, with one division detached from VIII Corps to support the planned uprising in the Tyrol, was to be supplemented by 42 *Landwehr*, Croatian *insurrectio*, and volunteer troops. The total came to 76,390

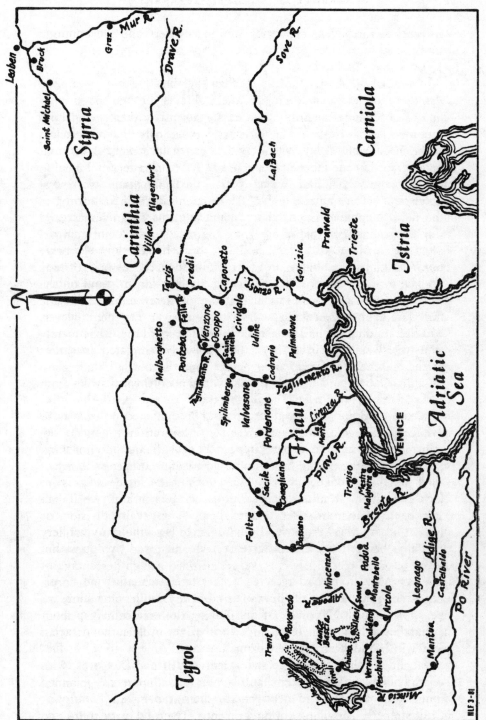

Archduke John's theatre of operation, 1809

men and 148 guns, not counting the Tyroleans, but if the poorly trained and unreliable second line troops were subtracted, only 46,000 were available for the initial offensive.[63]

On 9 April the Austrian army reached the Villach-Tarvis area and from there advanced in several parallel columns through the mountains to Pordenone where it defeated Eugene's rearguard in a brief encounter. On 16 April, the viceroy, having collected additional troops, about 40,000 but with only 64 guns, attacked the Austrians at Sacile, east of the Piave near the head of the Adriatic. After severe fighting, Eugene fell back losing 3000 killed and wounded, 3500 prisoners, one eagle and 15 guns.[64] Although he still had fresh troops, John did not conduct an energetic pursuit and this gave Eugene time to make an orderly withdrawal to the Adige where he halted. Following at about six miles per day, John arrived before the new French positions at Caldiero on 27 April and the next day he repulsed a foolish sortie by Eugene. But before he could make any move of his own, he was recalled to join the defeated main army and by 15 May, after a number of rearguard actions, his main forces were back in Carinthia holding the line Villach-Laibach. The French-Italian pursuit meanwhile was divided into two main columns, one under Eugene and the other under MacDonald.

John had attempted and failed to slow the pursuers at the Piave on 8 May, but in the narrow valley passes towards Carinthia the reinforced blockhouses at Malborgeth and Predil impeded the French advance. The heroic defence of these two positions by a handful of gunners and some 250 Croat *Grenzer* in each fort, few of whom survived, was one of the most impressive events of the campaign, called the 'Austrian Thermopylae.' Of course, these little forts, really blockhouses with an additional redoubt, could not hold up an army. Malborgeth was outflanked before being stormed by a French division on 17 May; Predil held out under heavy bombardment for three days before its defenders were overwhelmed by a two regiment assault on 18 May.[65]

On 19 May, John had received orders to march north and join with Kolowrat, then on the north bank of the Danube near Linz, in operations against Napoleon's rear. Judging this enterprise hopeless, he marched to Graz where he hoped to be met by Jellacic's detachment which had been recalled from Bavaria. While waiting for his arrival, he missed a chance to fall against either of the two divided French columns, each weaker than his own force. In the end, Jellacic, a remarkably unlucky and inept general, did not manage to join John in full strength. Moving from Bavaria into Styria, he blundered into

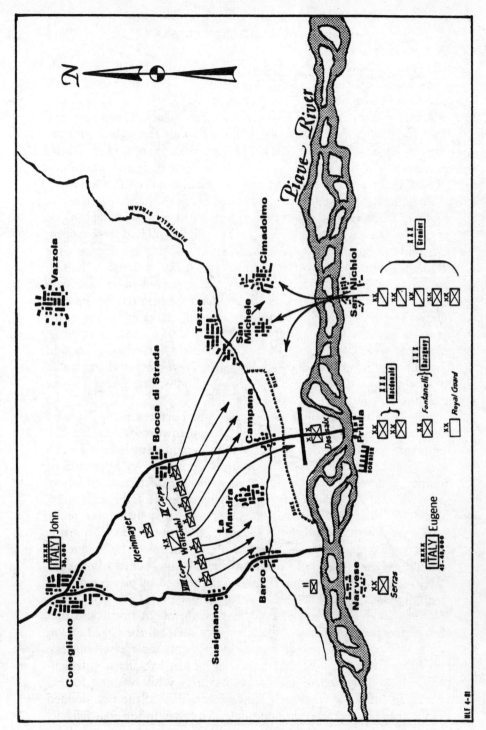

Rearguard action on the Piave, 8 May 1809. Situation at 8 am. John turns to throw Eugene back across the Piave. (This map and the two following, courtesy Robert M. Epstein, Prince Eugene at War, *1809.)*

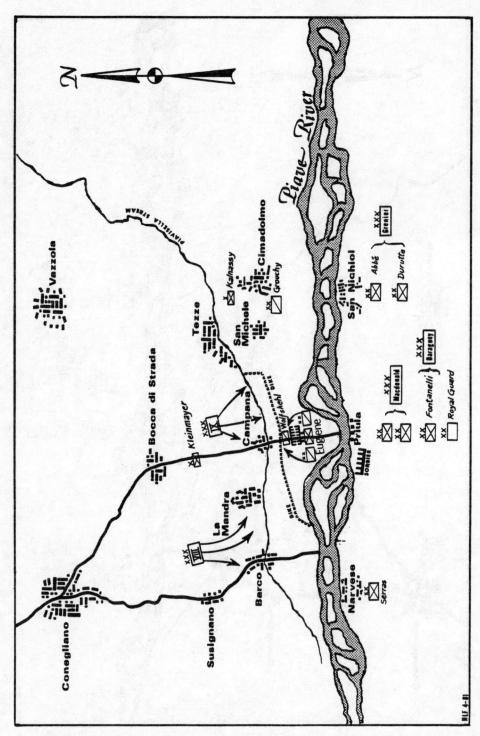

Rearguard action on the Piave, 10.30 am. Eugene has enveloped Austrian cavalry, but Austrian infantry has deployed.

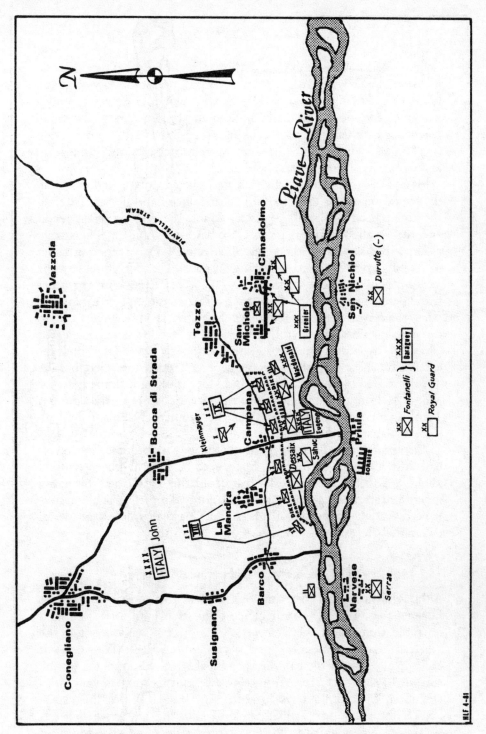

Rearguard action on the Piave, Situation as of 4.30 pm. Eugene has elements of his army across the swollen river; Austrians are holding along the dike, but will retreat during night.

Eugene's left column and on 25 May at Sankt Michael near Leoben his detachment was badly mauled by Seras' division. Only scattered fugitives made it to Graz. Chasteler was luckier. Leaving behind a small brigade, Buol's, to maintain a regular presence in the Tyrol, he reached Carinthia, but missed linking up with the main army moving to Hungary where John hoped to be reinforced by the Hungarian and Croatian *insurrectio* and other levies.[66]

In any case, Chasteler's division had played only a minor role in the liberation of the Tyrol and it had sustained heavy losses. Entering the country on 10 April, Chasteler found the population in revolt and the small Bavarian garrison, six battalions and one squadron, either wiped out or on the verge of surrender. Two French brigades in transit from Trent to Augsburg also came under attack by the armed population; one managed to escape back to Trent, the other surrendered in Innsbruck. Things changed at the end of the month when the Bavarians were able to send Lefebvre with elements of two divisions against the Tyrol. On 13 May the Bavarians defeated Chasteler at Wörgl south of Kufstein and six days later they re-entered Innsbruck. By this time the general had been recalled, but the Tyroleans, led by Andreas Hofer and other leaders, won the battle at Mount Isel on 29 May and drove the Bavarians out of the country. Tyrol again was liberated and for the moment Napoleon had no troops to spare for its reconquest.

But apart from diverting parts of the Bavarian corps, the revolt had little influence on the war. Eugene, to be sure, had been worried about a possible threat to his rear from the Tyrol, but the hardy mountaineers were neither organized nor willing to provide a strategic diversion in the Italian plain and Chasteler's defeat at Wörgl eliminated any strategic threat.

The sideshows in Dalmatia and Poland

Although Marmont's corps in Dalmatia was part of the forces under Eugene, there was little strategic co-ordination until after John had retreated from the Adige. Marmont's major task was to contain the greatest possible number of Austrians and in the event Major General Stojevic and his reserve battalions and levies proved no match for the seasoned French veterans. At first Stojevic made a small advance into Dalmatia, but within days his offensive stalled before the expert French musketry and artillery fire. Conducting an active defence, Marmont merely garrisoned a few strong points and abandoned all others, and by requisitioning pack mules managed to make his corps mobile. In early May he counterattacked and drove into the Lika region of western Croatia. And when the Bosnians, instigated by Marmont, raided across the almost totally undefended frontier regions further east, burning a number of *Grenzer* villages and destroying several homeguard detachments, Stojevic's corps virtually dissolved as men deserted to protect their homes. With French forces threatening Croatia from Carniola where *Feldmarschall Leutnant* Moibelle had surrendered Laibach without a fight, the Croatian Military Border appeared lost and from Pest, where the *Hofkriegsrat* had moved to avoid Napoleon's capture of Vienna, precautionary orders were issued for an evacuation of military personnel, records, and stores. In the meantime, the Austrians were unable to block Marmont's fast advance along the coastal road north to Senj and then across the Karlstadt region to Carniola where he joined Eugene.[67]

The operations of VII Corps, about 35,000 strong, in Poland were equally without result. On 15 April Archduke Ferdinand crossed the frontier and on 19 April defeated some 14,000 Poles under Ponia-towski at Raszyn, six miles southeast of Warsaw. The Poles now evacuated the capital and withdrew east towards Lublin where a small Russian auxiliary corps was approaching. In addition, a number of fortresses remained in Polish hands. Turning north, Ferdinand now attacked Thorn but was repulsed. Meantime Ponia-towski boldly sent detachments into Austrian Galicia and raised a revolt there. Ferdinand's position was becoming precarious.[68]

While the Austrian armies had been defeated or pushed back on all fronts and Vienna had been occupied, they had not been destroyed and there were signs that they might still be able to fight. Increasingly Napoleon was worried that his forces before Vienna were outnum-bered by Charles's army across the Danube and that his dispositions were scattered by the need to watch Kolowrat, and to prevent John from joining his brother. To be sure, John was in no hurry to combine with the main army and Kolowrat would be repulsed at Linz. But with four corps as well as the Army of Italy still away from his main army, and with local uprisings in his rear and in Germany becoming constant embarassments, Napoleon decided that the only way to resolve the growing impasse was to eliminate the Austrian main army. This set the stage for the second and decisive phase of the war of 1809.

VIII

The War of 1809:
Aspern-Essling and Wagram

In May and July 1809 the Austrian army led by Archduke Charles faced Napoleon in two major battles. In the first, at Aspern-Essling, Napoleon was defeated, though in the second he won a costly victory that ended the war. Still, the Austrian army displayed unexpected tenacity and skill and regained much of the reputation it had lost at Ulm. These two battles, together with the campaign of 1796 and his army reforms, constitute Charles's main claim to military greatness. 'To defeat Napoleon at Aspern-Essling,' Chandler commented, 'was tribute enough to Charles's abilities, but even at Wagram he denied the Emperor the complete victory he wanted.'[1] Even so, the battles also illustrated the limitations of the Habsburg army and the archduke's manifest reluctance to entrust the fate of the dynasty to the field of battle.

On the eve of Aspern-Essling

Between 16 and 17 May Charles assembled his army on the March-feld where after combining with Hiller's troops and the Vienna garrison he disposed of slightly over 105,000 men. At this point Napoleon only had 82,000 available and the archduke came under much pressure to take immediate offensive action. Emperor Francis urged him to 'get the armies scrapping,' while Empress Maria Ludovica complained that Charles 'has become indifferent to a soldier's honour and only longs for peace.'[2] But Charles had no wish to venture a major attack across the Danube. Although he let it be known that this still was his 'favourite project,' he welcomed and probably inspired Wimpffen's memorandum of 17 May advocating a Fabian strategy. By remaining on the left bank of the river, the new chief of staff argued, the army retained freedom of manoeuvre.

Replacements, stores, and materiel were close at hand and just by staying in position, the army tied down a large part of Napoleon's total forces. In the end, Napoleon would have to attack across the Danube and if repulsed, his entire army might well be annihilated during the retreat. On the other hand, if the Austrians crossed the river and suffered defeat this might spell the end of the Monarchy. Why therefore, Wimpffen asked, risk total disaster? 'Fabius had saved Rome as Daun had saved Austria not through rashness but through delay . . . these are the examples we should follow.'³

This was the strategy adopted. After some further discussion, Charles decided that no attempt would be made to contain the French attack along the water's edge, but to allow the enemy to transfer a considerable body of troops and attack him when he was getting ready to debouch into the plain beyond.⁴ Undoubtedly he remembered Prince Eugene's great victory at Zenta in 1697 where the Turks had been caught in a similar situation.

In the days before the battle Charles reordered his forces. He already had decided that under Austrian conditions the command and control system was impractical and that a return to the traditional tightly run battle was necessary. While corps designations remained, there now was a single army advance guard commanded by Klenau. The two reserve corps were amalgamated forming the Grenadier Corps and the Cavalry Corps which, commanded by Liechtenstein, the archduke kept under his immediate control. The Cavalry Corps was weakened when the corps commanders, having lost their mounted troops, requested cavalry to protect their infantry in the open plain. Charles therefore reallocated some cavalry to each corps. Together with the basically defensively oriented regulations of 1806, the result was that during the coming battle the mounted arm did not act as a major striking force but was employed primarily to protect infantry formations.⁵ The 292 available guns, organized in 18 brigade, 11 cavalry, and 13 position batteries, remained with their respective formations.⁶

Napoleon realized that he had to force a decision. He was troubled by unrest in his rear, concerned about the approach of John's army, and worried by the possibility of Prussian intervention and a change in Russia's position. Moreover, he held the Austrians in low esteem and surmised that the main army was retreating into Moravia. He did not think that it was in any condition to deliver a major battle on the northern bank of the Danube. Therefore, following a hasty reconnaissance, he decided that the most feasible crossing was some four miles downstream from Vienna where the islands of the Lobau divided the Danube into three separate channels, 700, 250, and 125 yards wide respectively. To divert Austrian attention and forces during the actual operation, a diversion was to be made, or at least threatened, at Nussdorf on the further side of Vienna. Disregarding the danger posed by the rising waters and the rapid current, Napoleon also underestimated the potential threat of waterborne destructive devices and in the interest of speed and economy ordered the construction of a single series of three bridges across the arms of the Danube. The last, and shortest, was to be placed from the main Lobau island to the Muhlau salient on the other bank.[7]

Lobau island was occupied on 19 May. By evening of the next day an improvised pontoon bridge was thrown across the last arm of the river and IV Corps accompanied by cavalry began to cross to the Mühlau salient and then fanned out into the Marchfeld. Klenau's outposts were driven off and Aspern and Essling, the two villages flanking the crossing were occupied. Deceived by the lack of major Austrian reaction, and by reports from his cavalry patrols that there was no indication of major enemy forces in the vicinity, Napoleon concluded that the archduke was in fact retreating to Moravia. By this time the rising waters and a series of hulks, floating mills and fireships already had twice broken the single vital link across the Danube and progress was somewhat slower than planned. Still, by mid-morning on 21 May, Whitsunday, 23,000 men, three infantry and two cavalry divisions with 44 guns, were deployed in the bridgehead area. Molitor's and Legrand's divisions commanded by Massena were ordered into Aspern, Boudet's division, temporarily assigned to Lannes, occupied Essling while the cavalry under Bessieres held the centre. About noon, Napoleon toyed with the idea of calling off the entire operation, but shortly thereafter Molitor's outposts came under attack by Austrian advance elements and fell back to Aspern. The battle had begun.

Not expecting attack, Napoleon had not issued orders to fortify the two villages, but even so Aspern and Essling constituted strong positions. Both were within a few hundred yards from the river, too close to be turned. Approximately a mile and a half apart, they were joined by a shallow flood dike, remnants of which also encircled some of the buildings. Both villages were built of stone and timber. At Aspern the church and the adjoining walled cemetery, providing cover against musket though not against artillery fire, enfiladed the streets; in Essling the three-story granary, its stone walls up to a metre thick and its windows provided with iron shutters, was a natural stronghold. To the front of the villages the ground was generally flat with a very slight slope north towards a five to six miles distant line of hills with a partial escarpment at the foot along which flowed the Russbach river. To the northwest was the Bisam Hill on which the Austrians had an observation post. A number of small villages dotted the escarpment and the plain.

Aspern-Essling: the first day

Although the Austrians were well aware of the French activities, they remained uncertain about Napoleon's real intentions. On the afternoon of 20 May, Charles's main body, formed in six columns, was drawn up along the northern edge of the plain between the Danube and Wagram. From right to left, Hiller's VI Corps formed the first column, Bellegarde's I Corps the second, and Hohenzollern's II Corps the third. Rosenberg's IV Corps was divided into two columns. Rosenberg in person was to lead the fourth column, primarily Dedovich's division, while Hohenlohe was to command his own as well as Rohan's division making up the fifth column. The Cavalry Corps was positioned between the third and the fourth column in the centre with the Grenadier Corps in reserve some two miles to the rear. V Corps remained behind to watch the French in the Nussdorf sector. About ten in the morning on 21 May, Charles gave orders to advance for a concentric attack against the French. Hiller, Bellegarde, and Hohenzollern were to attack Aspern, Rosenberg Essling, while Hohenlohe was to swing his column past Essling to Gross-Enzersdorf and on to the Danube.[8]

The scheme looked good on paper, but depended on concerted action by major formations with approach marches of different lengths. There was further delay when on encountering the French outposts the Austrians deployed from marching into fighting order. In the end the slow and unco-ordinated development of the Austrian attack gave the French time to hastily improve their positions and negated the full effect of Austrian numerical superiority, 83,000 foot, 14,000 horse, and almost 300 guns, that should have been crushing. While Hiller mounted his attack against Aspern around two, Bellegarde was just completing his deployment and Hohenzollern's column did not arrive until one hour later. On the left wing, the Austrians were not ready to come into action until four, by which time Liechtenstein's cavalry which had pushed ahead slightly already was disordered.[9]

Even so, Hiller achieved at least partial tactical surprise through a combination of a low ridge and a sudden dust storm and after short preparatory fire by three batteries he sent four battalions to storm Aspern. After penetrating into the village, the assault column was halted by French reinforcements in the church-cemetery position. Hiller failed to send in additional troops and instead deployed so as to cover an eventual retirement of the assault force. By this time the second and third columns were coming into action on the north edge of the village. Liechtenstein's cavalry, however, was in trouble. Advancing in two lines, it received cannon fire and at the same time discovered the French horse drawn up opposite. Liechtenstein then tried to charge, but ill-trained for action in large formations, his second line had crashed into his first. Meanwhile Bessieres with 7000 sabres had counter-charged, though the arrival of advance elements of the fourth Austrian column had caused him to retreat after a short melée. For the moment, Liechtenstein's cavalry was no longer capable of offensive action and the Austrian centre was thinly covered.[10] An hour later, Rosenberg began to attack Essling while Hohenlohe managed to take Gross-Enzersdorf. The French, however, expertly handled by Lannes, defended Essling throughout the afternoon without losing any ground.

On the right wing, Hiller, Bellegarde, and Hohenzollern finally had sorted out matters and shortly after four were preparing for a concerted attack on Aspern. But with a frontage of only a few hundred yards, congestion hampered proper deployment. Aware of the weakness of the centre, Charles now tried to shift some of Hohenzollern's II Corps to the left. While this still was in process, Napoleon hurled his Cuirassiers forward. With Liechtenstein's horses standing behind the infantry and unable to do anything, the Austrian masses had to repel the charge of Napoleon's heavy cavalry and they did so in great style. Holding firm and firing only when the enemy closed to within 15 paces, they inflicted heavy casualties and on occasion, as prescribed by regulations, even counter-attacked with the bayonet. Even so, the French attack had left the Austrian centre dangerously stretched.

Meanwhile Hiller and Bellegarde had continued their assault on Aspern where the struggle went on from house to house, roof to cellar, and from gravestone to gravestone in the cemetery. By nightfall the Austrians held most of the village though they had not expelled the French entirely. Fighting now died down all along the front with only sporadic firing during the night.[11]

During the afternoon's intense combat the single pontoon bridge over the Danube had been breached repeatedly. It had been repaired and on the first day about 8000 French reinforcements of all arms

AUSTRIAN TROOPS ENGAGED AT ASPERN-ESSLING, 21–22 MAY 1809

Formation[1]	Infantry[2] battalions	Cavalry[3] squadrons	Guns	Remarks
1st Column VI Corps	26	20	60	Includes Advance Guard
2nd Column I Corps	22	10	50	
3rd Column II Corps	27	8	50	8 sqdns det. to Cavalry Corps
4th Column IV Corps	14	8	30	
5th Column IV Corps	12½	8	22	Part of cavalry det. to Cavalry Corps
Cavalry Corps	0	84	42	Includes 44 Cuirassier sqdns
Grenadier Corps	16		12	
Totals	117½	128	266	

[1] Tactical deployment was in columns and not by corps.

[2] Regiments now at variable strength. Included are seven volunteer (*Freiwillige* or Legion) battalions.

[3] Includes two regiments of *insurrectio* cavalry and two squadrons of free corps cavalry.

All units at variable strength due to losses. Estimates show variations of up to 8000 foot and 2000 horse, counting gunners and other artillery personnel.

had reached the battle. During the night Napoleon sent urgent orders to Davout to bring up his corps and with the bridge holding for much of the night, Lannes' own II Corps, more cavalry, as well as the Imperial Guard entered the bridgehead. Charles received no reinforcements. By dawn on 22 May Napoleon had some 50,000 infantry, 12,000 cavalry, and 144 guns against Austrian effectives remaining at about 80,000 infantry, 14,000 cavalry, and 280 guns. The odds had improved, but still were heavily weighted in favour of the Austrians.[12]

Charles was very pleased with the results of the first day. To be sure, in effect he had fought near the water's edge and not further inland as planned, but he was unaware that he had only engaged part of Napoleon's army and that the bulk had remained on the south bank of the Danube. Moreover, he did not know that the bridge had been repaired and that the enemy had received reinforcements. For the next day he planned to repeat his methodical attack, throwing a series of heavy assaults against the wings of the French bridgehead

Armies on the Danube 1809
©1980 Scotty Bowden and Charlie Tarbox

194

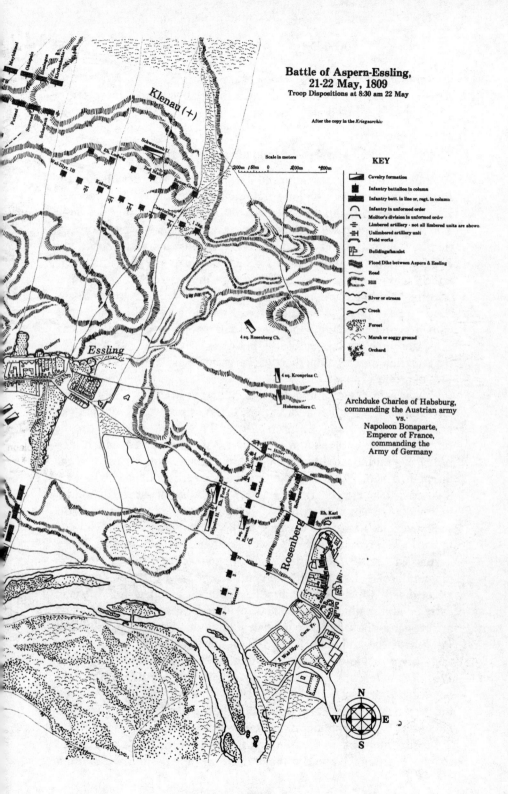

Battle of Aspern-Essling,
21-22 May, 1809
Troop Dispositions at 8:30 am 22 May

After the copy in the *Kriegsarchiv*

Klenau (+)

Scale in meters
200m /60m   0   200m   400m

KEY

Cavalry formation
Infantry battalion in column
Infantry batt. in line or, regt. in column
Infantry in unformed order
Molitor's division in unformed order
Limbered artillery - not all limbered units are shown
Unlimbered artillery unit
Field works
Buildings/hamlet
Flood Dike between Aspern & Essling
Road
Hill
River or stream
Creek
Forest
Marsh or soggy ground
Orchard

Essling

4 sq. Rosenberg Ch.

4 sq. Kronprinz C.

Hohenzollern C.

Archduke Charles of Habsburg,
commanding the Austrian army
vs.
Napoleon Bonaparte,
Emperor of France,
commanding the
Army of Germany

Eh. Karl

Rosenberg

195

and holding in the centre. Napoleon, of course, had no intention of remaining passive. Instead he decided to strike at the Austrian centre which he presumed to be weak.

Aspern-Essling: the second day

At dawn the Austrians attacked both Aspern and Essling. In the former Massena succeeded in regaining the entire village in a counter-attack, while in Essling, Lannes' garrison also beat off the Austrians. The loss of Aspern was due to a remarkable display of insubordination by Major General Wacquant who had lost his nerve during the night and already asked Hiller for permission to fall back. Although Hiller had angrily refused, Wacquant evacuated his positions.[13] Aspern would be contested throughout the battle, absorbing most of the energies of two Austrian corps. At Essling too, the French had gained ground and now Napoleon had room to deploy II Corps, three divisions strong, backed by Bessières' cavalry, for an attack on the Austrian centre at the juncture between Hohenzollern's corps and Liechtenstein's cavalry.

At seven in the morning the French attack went in, the divisions advancing in dense battalion columns. They suffered heavy punishment but pushed the Austrians back. To relieve pressure on the centre, Charles ordered the attack on Aspern resumed and hastily brought additional batteries as well as the Grenadier Corps to the threatened spot. Although the most advanced elements of Lannes' divisions, their closed ranks decimated by Austrian fire, had stalled, the white-coated foot also was wavering and retreating into the shelter of Liechtenstein's cavalry. Bessières now threw in his cavalry, formed up in two massive blocks of 4000 and 5000 horsemen. When it charged against the Austrian cavalry two regiments of *insurrectio* Hussars broke in panic and the nearby Infantry Regiment Zach No. 15 began to waver. At this moment Charles galloped forward and steadied the regiment. According to legend, memorialized in many pictures and in a famous equestrian statue outside the imperial palace in Vienna, the archduke seized the regimental colours as he led the unit forward. However, he later told an inquirer: 'You know how heavy the colours are. Do you really believe that a little chap like me could have gone off with them?' Whatever the exact circumstances, his personal intervention stabilized the line and provided time for the Grenadier Corps to mount a counter-attack.[14]

Shortly after nine in the morning the crisis of the battle had passed for the Austrians. Napoleon maintained his new position for another hour, but with his troops wavering in the face of intensive Austrian fire he decided to withdraw. To continue offensive action he needed reserves and the bridge had parted again which meant that Davout's corps now approaching could not cross. About ten he ordered Lannes back to the Aspern-Essling line. In fact, he now realized that a general retreat was inevitable, though it could only be carried out under the cover of darkness. Until then the perimeter around the bridgehead had to be held.

In the centre the Austrians pressed forward slowly, delayed by repeated charges from Bessières' cavalry. About two in the afternoon, Charles pulled back his units and massed some 150 cannon against the French centre. It was during this intensive bombardment that Lannes was hit by a cannon ball that smashed his leg. Napoleon too came under fire and at the insistence of his guardsmen retired out of range to the Lobau. Fighting was most intense on the wings of the French position. About two in the afternoon Rosenberg's IV Corps, supported by Merville's Grenadier Brigade led forward by Charles, forced Boudet out of Essling, but the general and a few hundred Grenadiers were able to hold out in the granary. Essling had to be held and Napoleon dispatched General Mouton with some Imperial Guard battalions to retake the village. Mouton penetrated into Essling but was in danger of being cut off by Austrian reinforcements. General Rapp with two additional battalions of Middle Guard Fusilier Grenadlers was sent to extract Mouton. Interpreting his orders liberally, Rapp induced Mouton to attack once again. Rosenberg lost his nerve and fell back towards Gross-Enzersdorf.[15]

The last Austrian attack of the day against Essling, led by Charles in person, had failed. Attempts to pierce the French centre also did not get very far when Napoleon sent in elements of the Old Guard. On the right wing Hiller's seventh attack finally made progress and by four he had taken all of Aspern and environs, except for the ditch and dike leading to Essling and some enclosed grazing land between the houses and the river. When *Feldmarschall Leutnant* Vogelsang hesitated to carry out orders to take the position at all cost, Charles, who meanwhile had arrived on the spot, ordered that the position had to be taken at once. 'Shoot down all who do not obey, cashier officers on the spot, but take that ditch.'[16] By dusk his orders were finally carried out.

Hiller now was poised for the kill and could have rolled up the French line of resistance from left to right. Inexplicably, however, this was not done. He already had issued orders to bring up guns and additional battalions when suddenly Wimpffen accompanied by

Colonel Stutterheim of the staff arrived and told him 'to halt and not to start a new battle.' And when Hiller insisted that this was the time for the final assault there was a violent scene with insults exchanged.[17] Wimpffen, with the weight of the archduke's authority behind him, made his point and there was no effective pursuit as the French rearguard fell back to the bridge and then to the Lobau after dark. Elsewhere pockets of French troops still held on to the river bank south of Aspern and to the granary in Essling. The last French troops did not leave the north bank until the next day, 23 May.[18]

It had been a bloody battle. The Austrians lost 5200 dead and 21,500 wounded, French losses, despite Napoleon's claims, were about the same. But the French had retired in good order and the Austrians captured only three guns, one pair of colours, and seven ammunition wagons. As usual, French senior officer casualties were heavier than the Austrian. Besides Marshal Lannes who died of his wounds some days later, three generals were killed in action and 18 generals were wounded. Two were captured. Austrian losses included one general killed and 13 high-ranking officers wounded.[19]

There was no effective pursuit. Some claimed that with 30,000 men who had not seen action and with pontoons available near Vienna, Charles should have followed the French to the Lobau where, with the bridge down again and the waters still rising, some 60,000 were stranded. Pursuit across a rising river might have been difficult, probably impossible, but a bombardment might have been effective and the argument that the Austrian batteries were out of ammunition seems unfounded.[20] The real reason for not following up success was that Charles refused to take any risks. He had fought a defensive battle aimed at exhausting and debilitating the enemy.[21] His success was not due to brilliant strategy but to personal bravery and to his careful husbanding of resources against an opponent who had gambled.[22] Apparently he believed that a repulse was enough to fan the embers of revolt in Europe and he expected that the fear of such developments would induce Napoleon to come to terms. Also he hoped that a tactical victory would push Prussia and Russia to join Austria.

The fact remains that Napoleon would have exploited this undoubted victory.[23] In the end, a partial success could not achieve definitive results. The enemy was able to recover and neither Prussia nor Russia were convinced that the time was ripe to risk intervention.[24] Even so, Aspern-Essling changed Napoleon's perceptions of the Habsburg army. Soon after Ratisbon he told a Swiss nobleman that the 'Austrians fight poorly; they are a mere mob,' while in

September he said to General Bubna that 'the Austrians not only are strong, they also fight very well.'[25] For the first time in 13 years Napoleon had been worsted in the field. His next attempt to attack the Austrians was to be well planned and prepared, and would see the use of greatly superior numbers.

From Aspern-Essling to Wagram

While Napoleon prepared for his next attempt, the Austrians wasted the next six weeks and did almost nothing to prevent Napoleon from converting the Lobau into a fortified base and to summon all possible reinforcements. Charles continued to be preoccupied with the search for peace and was losing control over his subordinates, his generals as well as his extraordinarily self-willed and uncooperative brothers.

Wimpffen was preening himself as the hero of Aspern-Essling and was ever more arrogant and condescending, while Hiller was sulky and told all who would listen how the French could have been annihilated. Among them was Emperor Francis. The day after the battle Charles took Francis, Stadion, and other dignitaries on a tour of the battlefield, apparently to impress them with the horrors of war and make them more amenable towards peace. The effort was rather spoiled when the impetuous Hiller suggested to the emperor that on the contrary this was the very moment to 'ring the tocsin, mobilize every available man and attack the enemy with your courageous army.' In a week, so the general maintained, 'the enemy will be destroyed and Your Majesty can dictate peace terms.' The emperor seemed impressed; the archduke remained silent. Three days later, on 26 May, during a conference at general headquarters Hiller again pleaded for an offensive. If a crossing at the Lobau appeared too risky, then let the army march to Pressburg and cross the river there, while 30,000 men would make a diversion from their present positions. This time Wimpffen objected. If the army was defeated at Pressburg, he maintained, it would have to retreat into Hungary leaving Bohemia, the richest province, uncovered.[26]

Nothing was resolved. A few days later, with many corpses still unburied, the main Austrian body was pulled back to the line of the Russbach. Only burial parties, outposts, and some pioneers remained along the river to bury the dead, observe the French, and begin work on a number of redoubts in the battle zone.

Beyond that the Austrians did very little. Charles appears to have been waiting for a great German uprising and for the approach of the Army of Inner Austria. He was in no mood for making military ventures. A few days after Aspern-Essling he wrote to Duke Albert, with whom he maintained close touch throughout his career, that he hoped to 'strike one more blow against the French, though you may rest assured that I shall risk nothing or as little as possible.'[27]

It was, however, problematical whether John's army would really provide a considerable accession of strength. At the end of May he passed out of Styria into Hungary, leaving behind a small garrison in Graz and detaching IX Corps under Ignatius Count Gyulai, who also held office as *Ban*, that is governor of Croatia, to defend that country against Marmont and to harry Eugene's line of communications. Chasteler's division, minus Buol's brigade still in the Tyrol, also had reached Styria but had failed to combine with the Army of Inner Austria. And that army now was much reduced, though John had managed to pick up some 10 *Landwehr* battalions, about 4000 all ranks, which were willing to fight. His army now comprised 35 battalions and 25 squadrons.

In Hungary, Palatine Archduke Joseph had collected a few supplies, mainly boots and ammunition, and somewhat belatedly had called out the *insurrectio*.[28] To be sure, this noble array did not amount to much. Latently hostile to Habsburg rule, the country did not rally and only about 12,000 including 3800 horsemen mustered at Raab, a fortress near the confluence of the Raab river and the Danube. While poorly organized, trained, and armed this still would have boosted John's strength to over 30,000 men, but the employment of the Hungarians became problematical when Archduke Joseph claimed that as Palatine he and not John should control all forces in Hungary. It required a sharply worded letter from the emperor to put an end to these ill-timed military ambitions.[29]

Meanwhile John also proved a difficult corps commanders who sometimes acted as if he was leading an independent army. Despite orders to march at all possible speed, he delayed his progress for five days, from 1 to 5 June at Körmend, a town 80 miles from Raab, to rest his troops. This evoked an angry communication from Charles. 'I regret,' the message went, 'the irreparable loss your non-compliance with my orders has caused.'[30] John received the letter when he finally arrived in Raab on 13 June. He also was told to detach 8000 men to Pressburg where Davout's corps was threatening a crossing into Charles's rear. With the remainder of his army, John was ordered to delay Eugene as long as possible and then join the main body. While he was pondering these admittedly difficult orders, Eugene

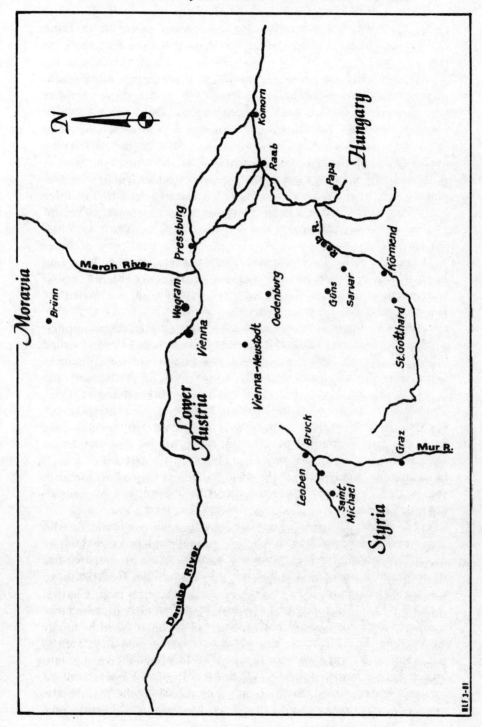

approached with 24,000 supported by another 9000 under Mac-Donald which, however, took no active part in the battle the next day.

Although Austrian forces outnumbered Eugene's, they were inferior in training and cohesion. John, however, had the advantages of a good defensive position and superior artillery. He placed his infantry, on the Szabadhegy plateau where a number of stone farmhouses and a church provided outlying strongpoints. The Hungarians stood on the right and his regulars and *Landwehr* on the left. A small body of Hungarian horse was stationed to the right of the plateau and the main cavalry force on the plain to the left. The guns were sited on the heights. Figures vary though at the least, John had 28,000 men, 51 battalions and 85 squadrons, supported by 32 guns.[31]

The Battle of Raab commenced shortly after eleven on 14 June. Eugene advanced with infantry against the plateau while his French and Italian horse charged the Austrian, actually for the most part Hungarian *insurrectio* cavalry, on the plain to the left. The infantry advance was repulsed, but on the Austrian left flank the charge combined with horse artillery fire caused the untrained horsemen to break. The French commander then threw in his reserve and with his flank disintegrating, John decided to break off the battle. Leaving behind some *insurrectio* units not engaged in the battle to defend Raab fortress, he retreated in fair order and the next morning crossed the Danube at Komorn. Austrian losses had been heavy. According to Bodart they amounted to 3500 killed or wounded, a significant 6500 missing or taken prisoner. The French lost about 4000 in all.[32] In his report John blamed the Hungarian cavalry 'which neither could ride or manoeuvre' for the defeat, a contention that did not impress Charles who replied that the real cause of the debacle had been the delay in Körmend and that John had failed to make proper use of his superior artillery.[33] When John finally reached Pressburg at the end of the month, relations between the brothers had become strained and it appears possible that this affected his actions during the Battle of Wagram.

During June Marmont had reached Styria, though he had been unable to intercept Chasteler who managed to combine with Gyulai on 13 June. Reinforced to almost 20,000 Gyulai attacked toward Graz but on 25 June he was repulsed in an epic fight by a single French light infantry regiment. When Napoleon called Marmont to Vienna, Gyulai entered the town on 3 July. Chasteler meanwhile had marched off again but failed to catch up with John and in early July

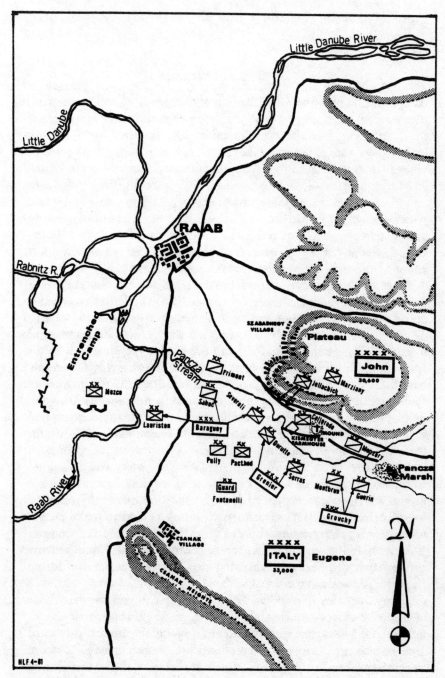

Battle of Raab, 14 June 1809. (Map courtesy Robert Epstein, Prince Eugene at War, 1809.)

ended up near Lake Balaton in Hungary where he rallied some of the units dispersed at Raab.[34]

On the eve of Wagram

At the end of June there had been few changes in the dispositions of the Austrian main army. Most of the troops remained in the positions they occupied since the withdrawal soon after the battle. Infantry camped on the escarpment beyond the Russbach, cavalry in the villages of the plain below. Army headquarters first was established at Markgrafneusiedl and then moved to Wagram. Hiller's VI Corps and the Army Advance Guard were deployed along the Danube from Aspern down to Gross-Enzersdorf, working on a series of redoubts and fieldworks. V Corps remained stationary near Nussdorf, but III Corps, except for one division, had been recalled from opposite Linz and was joining the main body for the coming battle.[35]

There still remained considerable fragmentation of the army. Ferdinand's corps was bogged down in Galicia, Gyulai was off in Styria, and in June about 12,000 men had been sent from Bohemia to raid into Saxony and the Main region. However, Charles was able to find reinforcements from the *Landwehr* of Lower Austria, Bohemia and Moravia. Individuals were used as filler replacements and battalions were brigaded with regular formations. At first there were some jurisdictional problems because the Bohemians and Moravians quite properly objected to serving outside the boundaries of their kingdom, but after being assured of equal treatment with the line they came willingly enough and in the end fought well. On the other hand, Charles found it difficult to replace lost horses and his cavalry remained understrength. By the first week of July, not counting V Corps which would not participate in the fighting or John's army which arrived too late, Charles had about 130,000 effectives, 160 battalions, 150 squadrons, and 414 guns.[36]

As was, and is, common in armies, commanders utilized the pause before battle to smarten up their troops. There was much drilling and many inspections, and to deal with what appeared a deterioration of discipline, Charles reintroduced corporal punishments abolished only in 1807. Not too much should be made of this. Napoleon also tightened up discipline and threatened draconian punishments in his army at this time. More important was that despite the shortcomings exhibited by the army both around Ratisbon and at Aspern-Essling, no effort was made to improve skirmishing tactics, control of large formations, or staff procedures. The instructions for the employment

AUSTRIAN TROOPS ENGAGED AT WAGRAM, 5–6 JULY 1809

Formation	Infantry battalions	Cavalry squadrons	Guns	Remarks
Advance guard	23	22	48	
I Corps	22	8	68	
II Corps	26	6	68	
III Corps	22	6	58	
IV Corps	24⅓	8½	60	
VI Corps	25⅓	16	64	
Reserve Corps	18	84	48	Cavalry and Grenadier Corps comb.
Totals	160⅔[1]	150½[2]	414	

In the vicinity of battlefield but not engaged

V Corps	15	8	32	
Army of Inner-Austria	20[3]	21	50	
Totals	35	29	82	

[1] Includes 21 *Landwehr* and 12⅓ volunteer battalions, not counting individuals integrated into other units.

[2] Includes 12 Hungarian *insurrectio*, ½ free corps squadron.

[3] Includes four Grenadier battalions.

of horse and foot issued on 5 June merely restated points already made in the respective regulations. Masses were to be used for fighting in open terrain; cavalry charges were to be made with gradually increasing speeds, and commanders always should take care not to expose closed formations needlessly to artillery fire. Perhaps the most important point was that while column commanders, the word now meaning corps, were to keep aligned with adjoining formations, they also were reminded that this should not be followed blindly. If a neighbouring formation was forced back, they were not to conform but to attack the front of an enemy pursuing the retiring column. 'If this is not done,' the instructions pointed out, 'the enemy only has to compel one of our columns to retire in order to push the entire front back ... as unfortunately happened on several occasions during the last battle.'[37]

Instructions for the artillery were published the next day. These too did not provide anything startling. Except in rare circumstances, guns were not to waste their fire on skirmishers or counter-battery work and concentrate on the enemy infantry. Fire, the instructions stated, was most effective when delivered by several batteries against a single point.[38]

At the same time, the Austrian command did not come up with a single battle plan, though it was agreed that if the enemy crossed from the Lobau, VI Corps and the Advance Guard were to delay him as long as possible while the main army was to advance and press against his flanks. Should the enemy advance against one wing of the army, then the other wing was to attack.[39] However, the question of where to fight was unresolved. While there were fieldworks and redoubts in the Aspern-Essling sector these, as Hiller repeatedly and vehemently pointed out, were not strongly armed and as the weeks passed it became clear to the Austrian command that the French superiority in cavalry and artillery, especially the heavy batteries now emplaced on the Lobau, made fighting close to the river an extremely risky undertaking.[40] Finally, there were intelligence reports that the enemy intended to cross at Pressburg while making a simultaneous, of much weaker, effort from the Lobau. The reports estimated quite accurately that the French now had 162,500 men, including 20,200 cavalry.[41]

Overriding all his other concerns was the archduke's continued preoccupation with the need for peace. On 23 June Charles sent a long letter to his brother Francis asserting that Austria could not continue to fight a multi-front war without allies. 'None of the assumptions on which hopes for a favourable outcome of this war were based have materialized.' Russia had turned hostile and might be joined by Prussia. The entire Confederation of the Rhine was fighting for Napoleon; Italy was lost, and the Bosnians were raiding the Military Border. He conceded that a great victory could still reverse the situation.[42] Stadion disagreed. Throughout Europe, the chancellor claimed, anti-French agitation was spreading; a British fleet was harassing the Italian coast and pinning down Murat in Naples. In England a strong amphibious force almost was ready to sail for the German coast. In short, Stadion argued, the situation was much brighter than pictured by Charles. If the main army was not prepared to challenge the enemy, at least it could send reinforcements to Saxony and to Galicia.[43] The issue was not resolved. By 30 June there was clear evidence that the French were about to undertake a major operation. Charles placed his army on an increased alert and sent warning orders to John.

The Austrians had excellent information regarding Napoleon's growing capabilities but could only guess at his intentions. There was considerable traffic between Napoleon's camp and the other side of the Danube and outposts close to the river could observe French preparations. 'The steady work of carpenters and shipwrights,' one contemporary, Varnhagen von Ense, observed, 'the arrival of artillery and ammunition wagons – none of this escaped our notice.' Nothing, however, was done to interrupt the French in their work. Lobau island and the adjoining lesser islands were converted into an impregnable base of operations armed with 129 heavy guns, for the most part captured pieces from the Vienna arsenals, and linked to the mainland by three permanent and well protected bridges. A fleet of gunboats, including two captured from the Austrians, patrolled the Danube. Supplies from Austrian depots fed and clothed the troops; additional guns of Austrian provenance served to fill out Napoleon's field batteries, and provided regimental pieces reintroduced to bolster the raw infantry. Including the Lobau garrison and batteries, he had a total of 188, 965 men available during the coming battle, 260 battalions, 207 squadrons, and 617 guns.[44]

Napoleon's plan was based on deception, the demonstrated slow reaction of the Austrians, and the sheer weight of numbers and firepower. Beginning 30 June he demonstrated against the Mühlau salient and four bridges were openly constructed on the north side of the Lobau. The real crossing was to be from the eastside to the Marchfeld just below Gross-Enzersdorf. Landing on a broad front, with ten bridges in operation, the entire army, except for Marmont, was to be across the Danube by noon on 5 July. If the archduke had formed up behind the Aspern-Essling-Gross-Enzersdorf line of field works, the Austrian army, pivoting on Gross-Enzersdorf, would be outflanked immediately after the crossing, and if he pulled back to the Bisam Hill-Russbach position, the landing would be unopposed and superior manpower would break through or envelop the enemy.[45]

On the Austrian side there was divided opinion as to the next move. At first Charles could not make up his mind whether the enemy was in earnest and for two days he did nothing. On 1 July he moved the army forward to within a thousand yards behind VI Corps and the Advance Guard, deployed to meet a frontal attack. The next day, however, he changed his mind apparently because of the threat of the heavy guns on the Lobau. The army returned to the Russbach line where a number of small redoubts were hastily thrown up in front of I Corps. This left VI Corps exposed and Hiller very unhappy.

He had argued for several days that his weak corps could not possibly carry out its assigned mission of delaying a French advance, and that his field works were incomplete because he had not been given enough men and material. On 4 July he took leave on the grounds of ill health.[46] Although his departure was unlamented, his behaviour must be seen in vivid contrast to Massena's who, badly hurt by a fall from his horse and in pain, led his corps from a light carriage. Hiller's action was symbolic of the self-centred feuding, unchecked by a strong central authority, which so frequently impaired the functions of the Austrian high command. Klenau took over VI Corps and *Feldmarschall Leutnant* Nordmann, an able officer, the army Advance Guard. Aware that a major French attack was imminent, at seven in the evening of 4 July, Charles sent an urgent message to John. 'The battle here on the Marchfeld will determine the fate of our Dynasty ... I request that you march at once, leaving behind all baggage and impedimenta, and join my left wing.'[47] The archduke confidently expected John to arrive the next day. In the event, the message arrived only at six the next morning and then it took John 18 hours to get his troops moving at no particular speed.

Wagram: the first day

On 4 July the Lobau batteries began to bombard the front from Aspern to Gross-Enzersdorf, demolishing redoubts and inflicting heavy casualties. About two in the afternoon there was a heavy thunderstorm and rain continued on and off into the early part of the night. With Austrian observation hampered, troops from II (Oudinot) and IV (Massena) Corps crossed into the Hanselgrund southeast of Gross-Enzersdorf driving back Austrian *Jägers*. Additional troops followed and attempts by Austrian guns to harass the crossing were silenced by the heavier French batteries. By dawn Napoleon had major elements of IV, II, and III (Davout) Corps across the river. There was violent fighting, but Nordmann was unable to hold Gross-Enzersdorf against IV Corps. He fell back north towards Austrian IV Corps while with his line compromised, Klenau putting up a stubborn defence at Aspern, retired towards Leopoldau just below the eastern slope of the Bisam Hill. With adequate space to wheel north and west, by ten in the morning the French, 134,000 infantry, 27,600 cavalry, and 433 guns strong that first day, were deployed in two curved lines. From left to right in the first line was IV Corps, followed by II and III Corps. The second line consisted of the Saxon Corps (Bernadotte), the Army of Italy, and the Imperial Guard. The planning that had brought such a vast array across the river in such a short period had paid off.

Across the Marchfeld, the Austrian left was deployed behind the Russbach from Wagram to Markgrafneusiedl with I Corps on the right, II Corps in the centre, and IV Corps on the left. With steep banks on the far side the Russbach was a substantial obstacle, but to the right of this six mile wide position, around Gerasdorf, the terrain provided no defensive assets. Here Charles stationed the larger part of the Cavalry Corps, with the grenadiers in reserve. He also issued orders that Klenau was to pull back to Stammersdorf in the foothills of the Bisam Hill and for III Corps to take up positions on his left. The Austrian line therefore formed a sharp angle, though its apex was weakly held.[48]

As the French advance had progressed, gaps had opened in the first line which were filled. In the late afternoon the French army made an irregular wedge. On the right Davout, Oudinot, Eugene and Bernadotte faced the Russbach; Massena the Bisam Hill. The Imperial Guard and 8000 cavalry were in reserve, and to guard against John, Napoleon had pushed another 8000 light horse together with a division of infantry east to Glinzendorf. Marmont and Wrede were in the process of crossing. Fighting had continued throughout the afternoon in the plain in front of the Austrian IV Corps position and Nordmann's forces suffered substantial losses.

The Austrians were not expecting any more major action. Napoleon, however, wanted to gain a quick victory by breaking the Austrian left and centre on the Russbach. About seven in the evening the French columns advanced to the assault. Napoleon had ordered Oudinot to attack II Corps, Eugene was to hit between I and II Corps, while on the flanks Bernadotte, supported by 36 horse guns of the Imperial Guard, was to take Wagram and Davout was to take Markgrafneusiedl. After some initial successes the attack failed. MacDonald's corps of the Army of Italy was on the point of breaking through the Austrian line when Charles appeared and at considerable personal risk rallied the wavering troops. When additional Austrian reinforcements came into action the Italians broke in panic. Bernadotte's rather feeble attack on Wagram was repulsed, and with his troops exhausted, even the reliable Davout made only minor skirmish attacks against Markgrafneusiedl. Night had fallen and when French troops fired accidentally on the white-coated Saxons, these too panicked and streamed back across the field. Fighting on good defensive ground, resolutely led by Charles, the Austrians clearly outfought the attackers when combat ended about ten that night.[49]

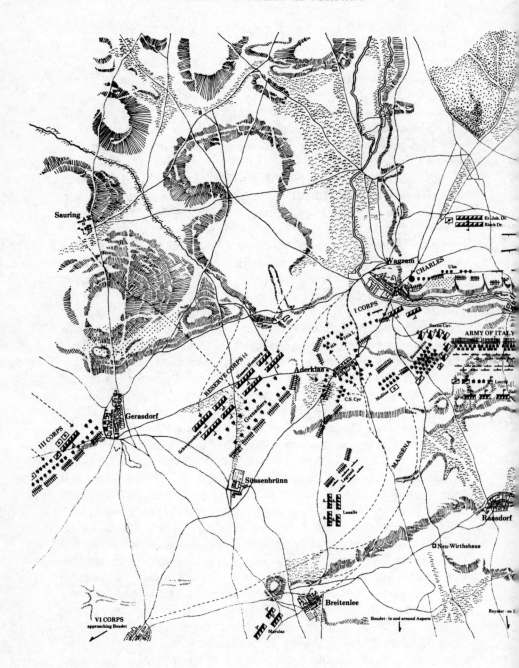

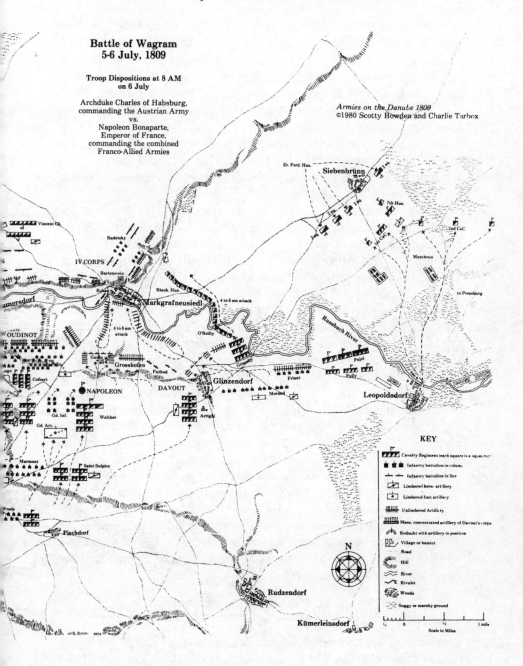

Battle of Wagram
5-6 July, 1809

Troop Dispositions at 8 AM
on 6 July

Archduke Charles of Habsburg,
commanding the Austrian Army
vs.
Napoleon Bonaparte,
Emperor of France,
commanding the combined
Franco-Allied Armies

Armies on the Danube 1809
©1980 Scotty Bowden and Charlie Tarbox

Er. Ferd. Hus.
Siebenbrünn

7th Hus.

2nd CaC

Monthrun

to Pressburg

Vincent Ch.

Radetzky

IV. CORPS

Bartenstein

Rokas   Blank. Hus.

Markgrafneusiedl   4 to 6 am attack

OUDINOT   4 to 6 am
attack   O'Reilly

Russbach River

Pajol

Grosshofen   Pally

Colbert   Gud   Grünne

Grosshofen   Putbod   Friant

NAPOLEON   DAVOUT   Glinzendorf

Morand

Gd. Inf.   Walther   Leopoldsdorf

Gd. Art.   Arrighi

Marmont   Saint Sulpice

Vrede

Pischdorf

Rudzendorf

Kümerleinsdorf

KEY

▧▧	Cavalry Regiment (each square is a squadron)
▪▪	Infantry battalion in column
—	Infantry battalion in line
⚏	Limbered horse artillery
⚏	Limbered foot artillery
▥▥	Unlimbered Artillery
▥▥	Mass, concentrated artillery of Davout's corps
⌂	Redoubt with artillery in position
⬚	Village or hamlet
- -	Road
⌢⌢	Hill
∿	River
∿	Rivulet
♣	Woods
⋯	Soggy or marshy ground

N

Scale in Miles

¼   0   ½   1 mile

211

For the next day, Napoleon planned to reinforce his right flank with Davout turning the enemy's left around Markgrafneusiedl while Oudinot, Bernadotte, and Eugene were to neutralize the centre. Holding the central position, Napoleon retained the Guard, Marmont's corps, Wrede's Bavarians, and the Reserve Cavalry at his disposal and moved Massena's IV Corps closer to Aderklaa, leaving only Boudet's division near Aspern to guard the approaches to the Lobau and its vital bridges. The French left had been weakened but the army was stronger. Having been reinforced during the day, and not counting losses, the emperor disposed of 159,000 infantry, 29,000 cavalry, and 448 guns.

Charles also made plans and shortly after midnight issued orders for a general attack soon after sunrise, that is about four in the morning. The French left was to be driven in by VI and III Corps, supported to the north by a simultaneous advance by part of the Cavalry Corps and by an attack delivered by I and IV Corps. To avoid congestion, II Corps was instructed to stand in place during the initial stages and provide artillery support. Actually, IV Corps was relatively weak, but then Charles confidently expected that this wing would be reinforced by John. No attempt was made to bring V Corps into action. Its role was to remain in place so as to protect a retreat by the army across the Bisam Hill if this became necessary. It was a bold plan with success depending on synchronized movements, something at which the Austrians had never excelled and which was made more difficult by the 12-mile front. Its eventual failure was due because of Napoleon's ability to use his interior position and his superior numbers to reinforce threatened points.

Anxious to preserve the archduke's reputation, Habsburg historians have alleged that the archduke initially wanted to bring III and VI Corps into line with I, II, and IV Corps and sweep Napoleon into the Danube in a frontal attack. Grünne and Wimpffen allegedly foisted the more complicated scheme on Charles. This, however, is a legend. What was true was that the plan was issued too late and did not provide for a battle reserve.[50]

Wagram: the second day

Given the distance from headquarters, III and VI Corps could not receive their orders before 3 a.m. and therefore could not possibly be in place one hour later. In turn, this delayed the movements of the cavalry. Even so, III and IV Corps moved out on time. About four, IV Corps advanced, driving in the French outposts and by five was preparing to assault Davout's main position at Glinzendorf. At this point the archduke became aware that his right wing had not come into action and issued orders to halt the attack and to return to the original line. Meanwhile I Corps under Bellegarde also had made progress. Advancing on Aderklaa it found the village almost deserted and occupied it without much fighting. However, further movement was halted when Bernadotte's artillery opened heavy fire. Napoleon ordered in Massena's IV Corps to retake the village. Leading his troops from a light carriage, the marshal managed to retake Aderklaa and almost broke through the hinge between the Austrian left and right wing. An Austrian counterattack, supported by two Grenadier brigades and some cavalry, recaptured the village by eight in the morning. At this point, Bernadotte's corps was seized by a panic, the Saxon infantry leaving the field in droves, but Napoleon, having his troops open fire on the fugitives, finally restored order, aided by the arrival of elements dispatched by Massena.

Shortly after 8 a.m., III and VI Corps finally arrived, though III Corps had to be moved somewhat to the north to help fill in the gap developing towards Süssenbrunn. Still, opposed only by one French division, (Boudet), Klenau's VI Corps made rapid advances towards the vital bridges. By ten in the morning it had retaken some of the redoubts lost the previous day, stormed Aspern and Essling, and arrived in Breitenlee. Thus it was in position to strike into Napoleon's rear. Klenau, however, did not act. His orders made no provisions for such a move and so he waited for further instructions. Also waiting for orders to advance was the bulk of the Austrian cavalry north of Süssenbrunn.

The Austrians were slow to exploit their opportunity and Napoleon was at his best. Bessières' cavalry charged to delay the Austrians' horse forming up, while the emperor rushed a massed battery, 112 guns, forward to provide cover for Massena's corps to disengage and march south to bolster the sagging left. Moving in column across the III Austrian Corps front was a dangerous manoeuvre, but Kolowrat remained passive. Only his artillery attempted to impede Massena's progress.[51] By noon the French, assisted by heavy artillery fire from the Lobau raking Klenau's flank, had brought the Austrian advance in this sector to a standstill.

Davout meanwhile was making good progress. Shortly after noon his columns took Markgrafneusiedl after a bitter struggle in which two Austrian generals fell at the head of their troops. Rosenberg repeatedly had called for reinforcements, but had been told that he would have to wait for John. And the army of Inner Austria still was not in sight. Judging the moment opportune, Napoleon launched MacDonald in a massive attack against the juncture of III Corps and the Grenadiers in the direction of Gerasdorf. MacDonald moved forward in a huge hollow square of 21 battalions with 8000 men, supported by heavy cavalry on each flank. The dense mass suffered enormous casualties and by the time it reached the Austrian line it had slowed to a crawl, reduced to 1500 men. Napoleon reinforced MacDonald with the Bavarians and now had only two regiments of Old Guard infantry left in reserve. At this point, intervention by John might have turned the battle around, though the Austrian left flank already was compromised and the front broken on other parts of the field.

While MacDonald's column had been sacrificed, Massena had retaken Aspern and the Army of Italy was fighting in Wagram. Archduke Charles, determined to preserve his army, gave orders for a phased withdrawal at 2.30 that afternoon.[52] The French were too weary to pursue and the Austrians got away in good order with their army still combat capable. Napoleon had won the largest battle in Europe with over 320,000 men engaged. His losses, however, were heavy and exceeded those of the Austrians. French losses included five generals, 238 officers, and 6568 men killed, 27 generals, 883 officers, and 25,847 men wounded. They also lost 12 eagles or standards, 21 guns, and about 4000 prisoners. The Austrians suffered four generals, 120 officers, and 5507 men killed, 13 generals, 616 officers, and 17,490 men wounded. Lost to the enemy were 10 flags and 20 guns. However, the French also took 18,000 prisoners.[53] Napoleon is supposed to have exclaimed that 'war was never like this. Neither prisoners nor guns. This day will have no result.' He was wrong. Charles and many high-ranking officers now regarded peace as essential and there was little enthusiasm for continuing the war.

Immediately and for well over a century, there has been a debate as to who was responsible for the defeat. Among the scapegoats were Grünne and Wimpffen and above all Archduke John who had only reached the battle area at four in the afternoon when it already was too late.[54] On 9 July, Archduke Charles sent him an angry message. 'I am sorry to note that your appearance a few hours earlier and even with only a few thousand men would have been decisive for the outcome of the battle.'[55] Yet, this remains speculation. Up until the last minute Napoleon retained the ability to disengage Marmont's corps for action on his right, and by two, when he had committed almost all reserves, it is doubtful that any development on the right wing would have changed the situation in the centre. What is clear, however, is that John had been dilatory in executing his orders. After marching out too late, he moved with slow deliberation. He had heard the sound of the guns but failed to hurry.[56]

Of course, if John had arrived on the first day, the Austrian left wing would have been strengthened, though whether this would have affected the ultimate outcome remains doubtful. As it was, the archduke's bitterness concentrated on Rosenberg whom he blamed for losing the battle by his poor handling of troops. The other corps commanders, Bellegarde, Kolowrat, Hohenzollern-Hechingen, and Klenau, all were promoted or decorated, though none of them had showed much distinction. It should be noted that some of the blame must be attributed to Charles's system of command and control. Always concerned with safeguarding his position as a member of the dynasty, he never took his commanders into his confidence. There were no joint conferences before battle and relations between the archduke and his corps commanders were formal. He did not reveal his overall plan of battle to his subordinates, and with orders issued only a few hours before fighting commenced on the second day, this would have been difficult. Therefore each corps commander fought according to his instructions, with little flexibility or initiative when circumstances changed. Kolowrat did not attack when Massena's corps marched across its front and Klenau, having reached the Aspern-Essling line, did not continue to press against the French communications. Finally, it can be argued that from the outset, Charles regarded the coming battle with trepidation and left too large a reserve, V Corps, to cover the retreat. Handling a major battle, with a frontage of over 12 miles, according to the rigid Theresian command system at best was cumbersome and at worst led to hesitation, lack of co-ordination, and missed opportunities.

Rather ungenerously, Archduke Charles felt that his troops had let him down. In a message to his corps commanders he complained that the 'troops on the left wing have not achieved the task assigned to them, one which considering their numbers, their position, and the importance of the day, I had every right to expect being carried out. These troops are responsible for the unhappy outcome of the battle.' There had been confusion and disorder, and the withdrawal had been too rapid. 'In general,' the archduke continued, 'with some exceptions I am not satisfied with the conduct of the infantry.' The officers, he complained, had not done their best to stem disorder and 'shouting was so general that the commanders could not be heard.' In the future, the colonels should either keep their regiments quiet, or the regiment would be decimated and the remainder distributed among other regiments. The commanders would be cashiered and the officers dismissed.[57] The message, to say the least, showed Charles at his worst. The troops had more than done their duty. Napoleon who was in a good position to judge on more than one occasion reprimanded those who belittled the Austrian army by stating, 'it is obvious that you were not at Wagram.'[58]

The armistice of Znaim and the end of the war

Napoleon only began a serious pursuit of the Austrians late on 7 July and he was not sure about the exact direction of their retreat. He divided his forces directing Massena towards Znaim and Davout and Marmont towards Brünn, keeping the Imperial Guard and Oudinot in central reserve. On 8–9 July there were a series of sharp rearguard actions, notably the encounter at Hollabrünn, an indication that the Austrians could still fight. Charles, however, merely continued fighting to preserve the army; he had no more hope and continued to press for peace. The emperor, who meanwhile had moved to Hungary, still talked about continuing the fight perhaps by rallying the *insurrectio* and the Bohemian *Landwehr*.[59] This, of course, was totally unrealistic. On 11 July Massena caught up with Charles and after several hours of sharp fighting in the streets, with Austrian losses at about 6200, the archduke decided to sign an armistice on his own responsibility. 'My army which had not been able to cook for several days was much fatigued and further retreat in the face of the enemy risky, while an attack against his strong positions was even more dangerous. Under these circumstances I sought an armistice.'[60] The agreement was signed early in the morning of 12 July and ended the active phase of the war.

The emperor and his entourage was furious about Charles's initiative and imperial disapproval resulted in a series of letters demoting him from the rank of *Generalissimus* and reducing his authority to the troops under his immediate command. In addition, the emperor demanded the removal of Grünne who was widely disliked. On 23 July the weary archduke resigned his command. 'A commander who has aroused Your Majesty's displeasure to such a degree can no longer have your confidence and therefore can no longer hold command of the army. These considerations lead me to lay the command of the army at the feet of Your Majesty.'[61] The emperor accepted the resignation. By this time many highranking officers no longer wanted to serve under Charles, though he was missed by the troops. The archduke never again held active command.[62]

Peace negotiations dragged on for several months. The Austrian emperor delayed proceedings because he still hoped to reverse the verdict of Wagram. At imperial headquarters in Komorn the various factions fought each other. On 19 July, Metternich maintained that Austria still had 250,000 effectives and that the people were willing to continue the war. He did, however, propose that this strength should be used to obtain the best possible terms.[63] Others in the war faction had even bigger aspirations and Archduke John, suddenly adventurous, talked of a general revolt spreading from the Tyrol into Upper Austria. The army was less inclined to such wild schemes. Charles had left behind a plan to resume operations along the left bank of the Danube west of Vienna, but this was rejected as totally impractical by Liechtenstein whom the emperor had placed in command.[64] On 15 August, Wimpffen submitted a sober assessment to the emperor. Without going into the question of war or peace, he pointed out that army morale was shaken and discipline deteriorating. There was no transport or ammunition for a major offensive and little had been done in the way of preparing fortified positions for defensive operations.[65] It mattered little if Benjamin Bathurst, the newly arrived British emissary in Komorn, reported to Canning that 'intelligence of the arrival of His Majesty's forces in the North of Germany ... has infused animation in the Austrian councils.'[66] The British landing, not in Germany but in Holland, was slowed down by French and Dutch troops and decimated by fever. In September the British evacuated. It was a humiliating failure and Bathurst reported that 'from what I can learn the Emperor appears to have Peace constantly on his mind.'[67]

Peace was signed at Schönbrunn on 14 October 1809. Austria ceded western Galicia to the Grand Duchy of Warsaw, made territorial concessions to Russia, and ceded parts of Carinthia, Carniola, the Military Border, the Hungarian Littoral, and Croatia south of the Save which became the Illyrian Provinces under French rule. Austria had to pay a heavy indemnity and reduce her army to 150,000 men. Never before had such restrictions been placed on the proud army. In Vienna, however, news of the humiliating peace was cheered in the streets.

On 27 November 1809, Archduke Charles returned to the capital, unaccompanied, dressed in the uniform of a colonel of Hussars, and riding in a simple coach. There was no official reception. His brother, the government, and even the people were only too willing to ignore him and he never was able to resume his military career. In 1812 and 1813 his name was mentioned for high command, but neither the emperor nor his ministers were willing to let him play a major role. He briefly returned to active duty in 1815 when he served as commandant of Mainz, hardly a position appropriate for a man who had outfought the French and had held his own against Napoleon. After Emperor Francis died in 1835, the archduke hoped to play a more important part in the state, but his hopes were dashed again and he remained in retirement until his death on 30 April 1847.

Charles found some consolation in his marriage to Henrietta of Nassau-Weilburg and in his six children, one of whom, Archduke Albrecht, had a distinguished military career. In 1866 he was victorious at Custozza and thereafter served as Inspector General of the reconstituted Austro-Hungarian army. In this capacity he did much to revive the reputation of his father and it was under his auspices that the campaigns of Charles were studied by the historical section of the general staff. His military writings gained attention and in the end, Charles, together with Prince Eugene and Radetzky, entered the pantheon of heroes of the Habsburg dynasty.

IX

Perplexities and Recovery: the Army 1810–14

THE outcome of the war of 1809 imposed major changes on Austrian policy. Stadion, the champion of German nationalism and the war party, was dismissed and replaced by Metternich who, hoping to exploit the tensions between France and Russia, looked for a temporary rapprochement with Napoleon. At the same time, aware that the restoration of the Habsburg Monarchy as a great power required both arms and diplomacy, he endeavoured to improve the state's military posture. Despite the loss of territory, burdened with a heavy indemnity, and with the army restricted, Austria managed to preserve the framework for expansion and in the end it contributed a large field army, the strongest contingent on the allied side, to the final campaign against Napoleon.

Radetzky and the Hofkriegsrat

On 30 July 1809, Archduke Charles handed over command of the main army to Fieldmarshal Johann Prince Liechtenstein who requested the services of *Feldmarschall Leutnant* Joseph Count Radetzky as his chief of the Quartermaster General Staff.[1] However, Radetzky, an experienced soldier and not a theoretician, demurred, claiming that 'he did not think himself qualified for such an important assignment.' But Emperor Francis commanded him to accept, assuring the general that 'your character guarantees that you will not make stupid mistakes on purpose and if you merely make ordinary mistakes, that I am already used to.'[2] The conversation, reported in Radetzky's memoirs, illustrates the emperor's sharply lowered expectations and his disenchantment with the soldiers.

Radetzky accepted the post and until the final peace treaty was signed he worked together with Liechtenstein to raise the combat capabilities of the army in case hostilities were renewed. His position was extremely difficult. The chief of the Quartermaster General Staff was regarded as a subordinate of the *Hofkriegsrat* as well as the army commander and before Radetzky could take any action, he had to consult with Bellegarde, Duka and Bubna, consider their opinions, and then report the result of these deliberations to Liechtenstein. Then, after having gone through this entire process, Radetzky was required to submit his decision, with all relevant evidence, to the emperor in person. By December, he wanted to quit, and sent a long memorandum to the prince explaining why he had accepted the post 'only with the gravest misgivings.' The reason, he wrote, was Austria's chronic unpreparedness for war. Every defeat was followed by a 'great outcry for army reform' but at the same time there always was an 'even greater desire not to spend the necessary funds.' As a result, 'our armies never were strong enough or adequately equipped. After every battle won by the valour of the troops, the means to exploit success were lacking, while after every defeat, the army had to look for salvation in retreat and a hasty armistice.' Radetzky believed that the basic cause for this state of affairs was that the 'army never had been popular among the masses, while the higher classes too had little interest in a strong army.'[3]

The diagnosis was correct, even if it did not offer a cure. The real transformation in the nature of war since 1792 was not so much the result of new organization, fighting methods, or logistics, but, as Clausewitz perceived it, because of the 'participation of the people in this great affair of state.'[4] In Prussia, the reformers led by Scharnhorst, were pushing for wide political and social reforms, accompanied by a purge of the officer corps and major changes in the military command and control system. In Austria, however, popular participation was ruled out by the very nature of the multinational empire. Even the very modest beginnings of a people's army, the *Landwehr*, had frightened the ruling classes, while major changes in the administrative and command structure were ruled out by the emperor's suspicions of ambitious soldiers. Even after 17 years of war, he regarded his soldiers as nothing more than 'another group of uniformed servants,' and, always enamoured of paper work, he returned the administration of the army into the hands of the *Hofkriegsrat*.[5] Liechtenstein, who was accused of meddling into policy because he had advocated peace, was relieved of his position within the year.

Even so, it also was clear that the *Hofkriegsrat*, always primarily an administrative agency, could not possibly supervise the conduct of operations on the scale and at the pace that had emerged. Therefore it was attempted to improve the position of the Chief of the Quartermaster General Staff. In December 1809, Radetzky was appointed a full member of the council, a *wirklicher Hofkriegsrat*. Utilizing his new authority, Radetzky set about to make modest reforms. In 1810 he reorganized the staff into functional sections dealing with cartography, intelligence, archives, and service with the field armies. He also tried to remove incompetents whose only qualifications were a 'glib tongue, good horsemanship, and a ready vocabulary of technical jargon.'[6] To provide better qualified staff officers, Radetzky, who never had attended any military school, favoured a programme of systematic instruction and during the winter of 1810-11 he himself gave a series of lectures to selected officers in Vienna.[7] Unfortunately, as in all other contemporary armies, Radetzky conceived staff work as purely operational. Logistic functions were left in the hands of the poorly prepared and organized commissariat.

For all that, his relationship with the *Hofkriegsrat* remained ill defined and there was considerable overlap between the first section of the council, the Military Department, and the Quartermaster General Staff. Moreover, Radetzky, a bluff fighting soldier who first had seen action against the Turks in 1788, never became reconciled to working within the framework of a bureaucratic body which, he asserted, 'believed that an army could be led with office procedures alone.'[8] There was some truth in this statement, and yet it also did the agency injustice. In the years following the Treaty of Schönbrunn, the council had the unenviable duty of trying to maintain a military establishment under conditions of unprecedented economic hardship. For well over a decade, Austria had financed extensive campaigns on a hand-to-mouth basis, partially by subsidies from Great Britain and partially by issuing paper money. Resort to the printing press had led to inflation, aggravated by a flood of forged currency manufactured as an economic warfare scheme in France and French occupied Italy. In late 1810 the state literally had run out of money and had been forced to call in silver plate and other bullion in private hands.

In 1811, Joseph Count Wallis, governor of Bohemia, was made finance minister. On 20 February he issued a *Finanzpatent* in the form of a most drastic deflation. All existing paper money and small coins were called in to be exchanged by so-called redemption bonds at the rate of one new for five old. All taxation was to be paid in the new currency and the government also was to pay salaries, pensions and such in the new legal tender. The patent initially relieved much misery for those who had to live on fixed incomes, including junior officers, but its effects did not last for very long. In 1813, when Austria started to rearm, it once again resorted to printing money. Moreover, deflation did not bring down prices as much as Wallis had hoped. Even so, army expenditures were slashed from 253,202,864 florins in 1809, and 175,554,061 in 1810 to 30,393,768 the following year with a slight rise to 47,795,343 in 1811.[9] Count Colloredo, the president of the *Hofkriegsrat*, protested that he could not possibly operate with such a budget and resigned in 1811. His successor, Fieldmarshal Heinrich Count Bellegarde, managed by various manipulations, freezing pay and allowances, hiring troops out for public and even private labour, reducing rations, and freezing pay and allowances. Moreover, until 1812, there was no production of new weapons while remaining stocks of uniforms and boots were completely depleted.

Army organization and strength, 1810–12

Some economies were achieved through the reduction in the size of the army, limited by treaty to 150,000. Eight regiments of the line which had lost their recruiting districts as part of the territorial cessions made in the Treaty of Schönbrunn were disbanded while the six *Grenzer* regiments in Croatia were transferred to the French service. This left the army with 38 German, 15 Hungarian, and 11 *Grenzer* infantry regiments, and nine *Jäger* battalions. In the 53 line regiments the third battalions were placed on cadre status while companies in the first and second battalions were reduced to about 60 men in the German and about 100 in the Hungarian regiments. The nine *Jäger* battalions were cut back to one division each, though the *Grenzer* regiments, economically self-supporting, were kept at full strength. To provide cadres for quick expansion, redundant officers were retained as supernumeraries on half pay. For the same reason the 35 mounted regiments and the four artillery regiments were kept together, though the heavy cavalry regiments were reduced to four squadrons and the light to six. The *Artillery Handlanger Corps*, the engineers, and the pontooneers became skeleton units. Finally, all free corps, volunteer, and *insurrectio* formations were disbanded.[10]

Despite these substantial reductions, Austria did not fully comply with the restrictions of the peace treaty. In 1811, instead of the authorized 150,000 men, there actually were 259,918 on the rolls, though with men on leave, only 171,066, including 22,444 considered fit for limited duty only, were available.[11] The well-informed

John Harcourt King, a British agent sent by the Foreign Office to Vienna, placed the number of effectives even lower. 'The army,' he reported in early 1812, 'has been so extremely reduced and what remains of it is so badly paid, clothed, and equipped that 60,000 men would be the most that the Government could at the present employ on active service.'[12]

Additional manpower was to be provided by the *Landwehr* and the reserves. Napoleon had demanded the immediate deactivation of the *Landwehr* and within weeks after peace had been concluded these units had been stood down. Also, neither Metternich nor any of the senior generals favoured this popular force, but if Austria was to rearm, its manpower would be needed. Therefore, the *Landwehr* obligations were kept on the books, registers were maintained, and in 1811 it was decreed that on mobilization these men would constitute the fourth battalions of the German line regiments. At the same time, the conscription laws remained in force even though after 1812, when the duration of active service was set at a uniform 14 years in all branches and arms, the number of eligible men exceeded requirements. This excess was used to form reserves. *Hofkriegsrat* instructions dated 12 September 1812 ordered that reserves were to be provided for the German infantry, the *Jäger*, and certain other units. Infantry reservists would undergo two annual training periods, while cavalry and artillery reservists merely were to be enrolled until called. Training periods varied. Reservists for the line infantry regiments were to be trained for four weeks initially, followed by three weeks thereafter; *Jäger* reservists, on the other hand, had to serve only two weeks. During training the reservists would receive pay and allowances of the line, but would have to bring their own clothing. In Galicia, however, they were issued linen smocks and forage caps.[13] None of these arrangements applied to Hungary which continued to carry a lesser military burden than the Hereditary lands.[14]

The French alliance and the Auxiliary Corps in Russia

In December 1810, Radetzky compiled his first annual appreciation of the political-strategic situation. Austria, he concluded, had become a middle power situated between two super-powers, France and Russia. France still represented the most immediate threat, but Russia also could not be trusted. He advised that Austria might gain territory in the Balkans, but he also felt that a rapprochement with France could be useful. Prussia, the general warned, was unreliable as a potential ally. In the final analysis, he concluded, Austria could only count on her own army, which, excluding the poorly trained *Landwehr*, could be expanded within three months to 156,000 effectives.[15]

The possibility of an Austro-French alignment already was in Metternich's mind, while Napoleon was thinking along similar lines. The French emperor had been chastened by his experience in 1809, he was worried about deteriorating relations with Russia, and vexed by efforts to place Bernadotte, the marshal disgraced after Wagram, on the Swedish throne. In Spain the war was not going well, and there was discontent in France where desertion and evasion of conscription reached a new height. Finally, there was the problem of a legitimate successor. For these reasons, early in 1810 Napoleon decided to accept Metternich's offer of marriage to the 18-year-old Archduchess Marie Louise, the eldest daughter of Francis I. The arrangement signalled an Austrian tilt against Russia and implied the assumption of territorial compensations.

In this fashion the Habsburgs 'returned to their old custom of securing by marriage what they had lost in war,' yet the arrangement was opposed by several archdukes, senior officers, and others. Encouraged by British promises of money and arms, there were a number of conspiracies culminating eventually in the grand scheme of the *Alpenbund* early in 1813. For the moment, however, nothing came out of these schemes, though when Austria concluded a formal military alliance in March 1812, some officers quit the service in protest.[16] Metternich, too, was disappointed with the treaty. Napoleon proved unwilling to provide major territorial adjustments, though he conceded that the Austrian auxiliary corps, 24,000 foot and 6000 horse, would not be counted in the treaty strength and that it would remain under his personal command. The French emperor would have liked to have the Archduke Charles as corps commander because his rank and status offered assurances of Austrian engagement to his cause, but the archduke refused. Undoubtedly, the refusal suited Metternich though it further annoyed Francis. The minister had no intention of getting deeply involved in war with Russia and already had informed the Tsar that Austria's role would be confined to a token force. To handle command under these circumstances required diplomatic talent and Prince Schwarzenberg, a soldier-diplomat with limited command experience, was chosen for the post.

At that, Austrian resources were hard pressed to provide the troops for the Russian enterprise, especially when, after some violent quarrels with Wallis, Radetzky managed to mobilize an additional corps of observation to provide a fall-back frontier defense. Altogether,

Austria mobilized 28 line, eight *Grenzer*, three Grenadier and three *Jäger* battalions, together with five heavy and 13 light cavalry regiments and 20 batteries.[17] However, the force was poorly equipped and units were not up to full strength. As King reported 'nothing could be more pitiful than the execution of these measures.' The troops assembling in Galicia, he continued, were 'in want of everything.'[18] Matters had not improved in early June when King painted a dismal picture of Austria's military prospects. If the French invasion failed and Austria in turn was threatened 'it could if driven to the last extremity put into motion 70 or 80,000 men,' but these would have to be collected from all the lands of the empire. And Hungary, he continued, could not be counted on. 'The ill-will of the Hungarians,' he wrote, 'is deeply rooted.'[19]

During the spring of 1812, Napoleon assembled an immense army, French, German, Italian, Austrian, and Polish troops, the most powerful army the world had ever seen or would see again until 1914. On 24 June, he crossed into Russia with 449,000 men, taking Smolensk on 18 August. On 7 September, at Borodino, Napoleon defeated the main Russian army, but lost about a quarter of his own men. Decimated by sickness and desertion, the French entered Moscow on 16 September, technically triumphant, but unable to bring the Russians to terms. On 18 October, amid signs of the approaching winter, the *Grande Armée* began its retreat.

Because of its size, the army had marched along parallel routes with the main force in the centre, its flanks protected by a Prussian corps in the north and the Austrians and a small Saxon corps under Reynier in the south. Schwarzenberg never penetrated deep into Russia. Reaching Lublin on 20 June, with Minsk as his major objective, he was diverted south where Reynier was hard pressed by Tormassov. On 12 August, together with Saxon elements, Schwarzenberg defeated the Russians at Gorodetshna and continued to pursue Tormassov until in early September he halted on the line of the Styr River. There followed a four week pause during which the Russians were reinforced by the Army of Moldavia under Admiral Tshitshagov which compelled Schwarzenberg to fall back along the Bug into central Poland. By this time the Austrian supply system had broken down. 'It is only with the greatest exertion,' the prince wrote, 'that I manage to keep my troops alive; heaven only knows how long I can do this.' Moreover, under deprivation, troop discipline began to falter and there were incidents of looting, sternly suppressed.[20]

Although the Austrian corps had not progressed very far east, Napoleon was well pleased with its performance. He subordinated

Reynier's corps to Schwarzenberg's control and recommended to
Emperor Francis that the prince be promoted to the rank of fieldmarshal. On the other hand, the Russians were displeased and protested
to Vienna that the auxiliary corps had not exercised the promised
restraint.[21]

At the end of October the good relations between Napoleon and
Schwarzenberg were strained when, to protect the French retreat, the
Austrians once again were ordered to Minsk. In the event, with the
Saxons suddenly under attack by a new Russian force under General
Sacken, Schwarzenberg was diverted and meanwhile Tshitshagov
captured Minsk and its valuable depots. Napoleon was enraged, and
accused Schwarzenberg of outright treachery, though in the end he
did not push the matter.[22] November came and weather conditions
deteriorated. While the French continued their retreat, reaching
Smolensk by 7 November, the cohesion of their army weakened
daily. At the same time, the Austrians too were exhausted. 'Man and
beast,' Schwarzenberg complained, 'are approaching complete disintegration.' Under a verbal agreement with the Russians, he now
withdrew his troops, including the Saxons, to winter quarters around
Byalistok. For the Austrians the campaign virtually was over.

Although the French army still was strong enough to force a
crossing of the Beresina on 27–28 November, its remnants became a
straggling mob. Napoleon left for France and only the rearguard,
commanded by Ney, maintained some semblance of order, straggling
into East Prussia in December. Schwarzenberg considered that Napoleon's departure had removed French control and he had received
instructions from the *Hofkriegsrat* to extricate his corps. Hoping to
detach Austria from her French alliance the Russians applied discreet
political and military pressure, and stranded in Poland without
supplies or hope of relief, with 7000 killed in battle and another
4000 dead of disease and exposure, Schwarzenberg, 'considering the
rigorous season and other circumstances equally pressing,' on 30
January 1813 signed a formal convention neutralizing his corps.
Interpreting the conditions liberally, he also tried to bring back the
Saxons when in February he began his withdrawal to Galicia.[23]
Recalled to Vienna at the end of the month, Schwarzenberg, his
mission completed, handed over command to General Frimont.
Technically, Austria remained Napoleon's ally; in reality, however,
Vienna had adopted a policy of armed neutrality.

Armed neutrality and mobilization

The French disaster in Russia changed the entire political-military situation. Many patriots felt that Austria should at once declare war on Napoleon and together with Great Britain, Russia, and Prussia overthrow the usurper. To force the issue, Archduke John and others tried to promote a major uprising by the *Alpenbund* in the Tyrol, Salzburg, Carinthia and other areas. Metternich did not share their feelings and had no intention of unleashing popular emotions. In March 1813, the main conspirators were arrested and John temporarily banished from court.

Metternich acted out of an aversion against popular potentially uncontrollable insurrections, but he also feared that with Austria poorly armed and financially depleted, premature action would lead to the replacement of French by Russian hegemony in Germany. Therefore, he continued to negotiate while engaging in a covert and later open mobilization.

In January 1813, the council of ministers authorized increases in effectives and in February orders were issued to assemble a strong corps of observation in Bohemia. The corps became operational in April. At the same time two additional corps, one on the Danube to watch Bavaria and the other in Inner Austria to guard the Italian frontier and, if possible, to recover Croatia, were activated.[24] As King noted with satisfaction, 'by the end of April therefore, Austria will have disposable 100,000 men complete and provided with everything.'[25] Actually the numbers were closer to 160,000 though the supply situation remained difficult.

Keeping up the guise of neutrality, Austria continued to negotiate both with Napoleon and his enemies. These now included Prussia which on 16 March had declared a 'war of liberation' and Sweden which was preparing to send troops to northern Germany. The Austrian military diplomats, Schwarzenberg and Bubna, demanded that Napoleon should abandon his conquests east of the Rhine, requests which the emperor indignantly refused. Instead, with a hastily raised army of 145,000 men, including many raw recruits, the emperor moved east to deal with the approximately 80,000 Prussians and 120,000 Russians. He intended to push through Saxony in the direction of Berlin and then on to the Oder where some 50,000 troops under Eugene still held important fortresses. If successful this would have eliminated Prussia and deprived the Russians of their base. On 2 May he encountered the allies at Lützen and defeated them. He continued to Dresden and on 21 May again defeated the allies at Bautzen. But the two victories, bought at high cost, were tactical successes only. Shortage of cavalry prevented effective pursuit and the allied armies remained intact. Austria, however, effectively renounced her alliance and proposed an armistice which was signed on 4 June, later extended to 10 August. Both sides used the delay to reorganize and reinforce, but in the nature of things the allies had more to gain than Napoleon.

The major accession to the allied strength would be the intervention by the reconstituted Austrian army. In early May, the corps of observation in Bohemia was officially designated as an army and Schwarzenberg named its commander with Radetzky as his chief of staff.[26] Convinced after Lützen that the allies were in poor shape and that 'one may assume that our army will have to fight the enemy's main body while the Russo-Prussian army will be contained by a few corps,' Radetzky urged immediate full mobilization.[27] However, Metternich, supported by Schwarzenberg, Bellegarde, and Duka, acting as the emperor's representative, meeting in a hasty conference at army headquarters, rejected this idea. They still hoped for a diplomatic solution. Moreover, arms and equipment were not available in the quantities required. Undeterred, Radetzky a week later told his chief that 'the hope that there will be no war cannot outweigh the disadvantage if it does come and we are not prepared.' This time Schwarzenberg agreed and on 14 June, another conference decided on full mobilization.[28] On 22 June the *Hofkriegsrat* issued orders for reservists to report to their units and on 6 July the *Landwehr* was called up.[29] Although there developed shortages in manpower, forcing the lifting of exemptions and the call-up of underage men, and complaints that Hungary did not carry a load comparable to the Hereditary lands by August a very considerable army, almost 200,000 men had been assembled in Bohemia. In addition, the Army of Inner Austria mustered about 37,000 and the army on the Danube stood at 39,000.[30] By the end of August, Austria had 479,000 men under arms, with 298,000 combatants, and eventually would mobilize a total of 568,000.[31]

Though men were available, arms, equipment, and provisions were lamentably deficient. Army headquarters continually requested muskets, uniforms, boots, and ammunition, but the *Hofkriegsrat* could only reply that the last reserve stocks had been used up in the Russian campaign and that no major deliveries could be expected until autumn.[32] When hostilities opened, the Austrian army was the worst equipped among the combatants. On 26 August, General Wilson, the British observer with the main army, reported troops marching in a pelting rain storm 'drenched to the bones, most of them without shoes, many without greatcoats,' and a month later he warned that 'with the weather daily becoming worse, we shall soon have skeleton battalions, the more especially as the Austrians are ill-shod and clothed.'[33] Radetzky later remembered that during any army parade artillery and infantry units appeared in linen smocks and underpants, while about one third of the foot lacked cartridge pounches so that their ammunition was ruined if it rained.[34] Wilson, nonetheless, thought the Austrians looked rather good. 'It was,' he noted, 'a fine spectacle. . . . The infantry were active men in the best military order; the cavalry, both cuirassiers and hussars, superb,' but the artillery 'not so good as heretofore.'[35] To alleviate shortages, the British government in September promised that muskets, accoutrements, ammunition, uniform cloth, and shoe leather would be sent as soon as possible, but in the event transports did not sail for Fiume until November and some deliveries were made only after the campaign was over.[36] In November, Schwarzenberg complained to Metternich that 'we need shoes, pants, shirts and a bottle of wine to revive our energies, but no one listens to our requests.'[37]

Allied command and strategy

With mobilization going slower than expected, Metternich made a last ditch diplomatic effort. On 26 June he met with Napoleon in Dresden to negotiate an extension of the armistice until 10 August and to explore the chance of the emperor accepting Austria's terms. The interview ended with an exchange of insults. The next day, at Reichenbach, Austria formally joined Prussia, Russia and Sweden and on 12 August entered the war. In round numbers, the coalition had 800,000 men against Napoleon's 600,000, which, when inflated returns, minor theatres of operations, garrison, and rear echelons were excluded, came to about 570,000 against 410,000. With Austria providing the largest contingent, Metternich insisted on naming the supreme commander, telling Schwarzenberg that 'the power placing 300,000 men in the field is the first power, the others are auxiliaries.'[38]

Metternich's choice was Fieldmarshal Schwarzenberg, a selection that already had caused some controversy in May when the Archduke Charles, the other archdukes, as well as senior generals such as Liechtenstein, had been passed over. Even Radetzky had misgivings about a man whom he regarded primarily as a well-connected court general and diplomat. Metternich, however, had his way.[39] The Tsar was bitterly disappointed. While willing to accept an Austrian supreme commander, he favoured Archduke Charles with General Antoine Henri Jomini, formerly chief of staff to Ney, as his assistant. But Metternich would not budge. He considered Charles too difflcult to control and allegedly declared that 'we need a general who makes war and not a politician.' It was ironic, perhaps, that Schwarzenberg was appointed not becuase of his military talents, though these have been underrated, but because his aristocratic background, diplomatic experience, and tact made him the ideal man to cope with the problems of coalition warfare.[40]

Even so, according to Wilson, 'the question of command has been one which threatened and still threatens much mischief,' and Schwarzenberg was accompanied into the field by the three allied rulers and their vast retinue of advisors all of whom insisted on putting forward their own schemes and on being briefed on all proposed operations.[41] Life at supreme headquarters became a continual war council, no fewer than 17 in the autumn of 1813 alone, with Schwarzenberg outvoted nine times and only in complete agreement with decisions taken on six occasions.[42] At Dresden interference became so great that the politic Schwarzenberg threatened to resign, complaining that 'it really is inhuman what I must tolerate and bear, surrounded as I am by feeble-minded persons, eccentric projectors, intriguers, asses, babblers, and niggling critics.'[43] Relations with the volatile and ambitious Tsar Alexander were the most strained, but the prince also had problems with his own sovereign who continued to rely on Generals Duka and Kutschera and constantly reminded him to be cautious with Austria's last army.[44] Finally, though Schwarzenberg was in supreme command, the allied armies under Blücher, Bernadotte, and Bennigsen tended to operate independently and conformed only reluctantly to the overall strategic plan.

In the strategic direction of the campaign, Schwarzenberg's main assistants were Radetzky and Major General Baron Langenau, a young Saxon officer who had defected to the allies in June and was appointed to head the Bohemian army's operations section. Vain, ambitious, and much overrated, Langenau established intimate relations with Schwarzenberg. By contrast, relations between Radetzky and Schwarzenberg, while correct and co-operative, never were close, though in the end they managed to form an effective partnership.[45] Radetzky was the author of the master plan – the so-called Trachenberg Plan – that guided allied strategy in the autumn of 1813. Expecting intervention, he handed over routine Quartermaster General Staff business to *Feldzeugmeister* Bienenthal in February and began planning for joint allied operations. In March he proposed a plan for destroying the remaining French forces in Germany followed by an advance to the Rhine.[46] Faced with Napoleon's rapid recovery, and realizing that no single allied commander was up to facing the emperor, he abandoned this plan and came up with a scheme based on the concept of attrition. Any allied army attacked by Napoleon in strength should retire, while the others closed in on French communications and detached corps. By keeping Napoleon constantly in motion, his forces would be weakened and the area under his control constricted. As Radetzky explained it to Wilson, he advocated a 'system of defence combined with offensive operations on a small scale over a general offensive movement which might win much, but also might lose all.'[47] Only after attrition had taken its toll and the enemy was too hemmed in to utilize his interior lines, would there be a final concentric advance.[48]

It was a sensible plan for which later both Russians and Swedes claimed credit. When in June Radetzky met with General Toll, the Tsar's chief of staff, that officer was in complete agreement and submitted the plan to an allied council held at Trachenberg in July, which accepted it.[49] On 17 August, the first allied war council with Austrian participation meeting at Melnik, endorsed the idea and further decided that three allied armies – Bernadotte with the Army of the North, Blucher with the Army of Silesia, and Schwarzenberg with the Army of Bohemia – should launch a concerted drive on Leipzig.

Austrian organization and tactics

In 1809 the Austrian army had abandoned the corps system and the Army of Bohemia was organized in a main body, led by Schwarzenberg, and a left-wing under Klenau. The very substantial artillery reserve, 23 batteries, was at the disposal of the army commander. Divisions of various sizes and composition constituted the largest tactical formations. In August 1813 the order of battle of the army in Bohemia was as follows:[50]

Formation	Battalions	Strength	Squadrons	Strength	Composition
Advance guard					
1st light division	4	3943	12	1544	2 brigades, 2 batteries
2nd light division	3	2987	18	2305	2 brigades, 2 batteries

Formation	Battalions	Strength	Squadrons	Strength	Composition
Main body					
1st line division	12	12,865	–	–	
2nd line division	13	12,872	–	–	
3rd line division	11	9175	–	–	3 brigades and 3 batteries per division
4th line division	12	12,620	–	–	
1st inf. res. div.	8	6175	–	–	2 grenadier brigades, 3 batteries
2nd inf. res. div.	12	10,285	–	–	3 brigades, 3 batteries
1st cavalry division	–	–	16	2402	2 heavy brigades
2nd cavalry division	–	–	18	2717	2 light brigades
3rd cavalry division	–	–	24	2780	2 light brigades
3rd light (reserve) division	5	5826	12	1659	1 light inf. brigade 1 light cav. brigade 1 cav. battery
Left wing (Klenau)	27	25,855	20	2663	1 light, 2 line divisions, 1 cav. brigade, 7 batteries
Total: includes 6030 artillerists.	107	109,173	120	16,070	

Also assembled was a very respectable artillery park, 52 batteries: three 3-pounder brigade batteries, twenty-two 6-pounder brigade batteries, fourteen 6-pounder position batteries, eleven 12-pounder position batteries, and two heavy 18-pounder positon batteries. The composition reflected the general desire for a more hard-hitting field piece than the 3-pounders already abolished in most armies. In compliance with the artillery organization of 1809, the brigade batteries had eight cannons, while the position batteries were mixed with two howitzers, predominantly 7-pounders, and four cannons.

Army headquarters, as in 1809, was structured into four major sections. The commander allocated divisions and batteries to the wings of the army as the situation warranted. When the army advanced into Saxony it was divided into the Advance Guard, Klenau's flank corps, and a right and left wing. The right wing, the Prince of Hessen-Homburg commanding, consisted of four infantry and three cavalry divisions; the left wing under I. Gyulai had two infantry and one cavalry divisions.[51] Marching separately were two Russian and one Prussian corps, 82,000 and 45,000 respectively, which crossed into Bohemia beginning 11 August. Schwarzenberg had mixed feelings about their arrival. While he welcomed the increased strength, he worried about supplying such numbers and feared, with good reason, that the allies were likely to plunder friend and foe alike.[52]

Command and control of the army in its original organization proved difficult and on 5 September 1813 the corps system was reinstituted, though the term 'corps' was not used and the formations were designated as *Armee Abtheilungen*. Still, they were corps formations and this name soon crept into official reports and will be used here. In addition to the two, later three, light divisions of the Advance Guard, commanded by Generals Moritz Liechtenstein and Bubna, there were four corps: I (H. Colloredo), II (Merveldt), III (I. Gyulai), and IV (Klenau). Normally they were to have one light and two line divisions. Merveldt's corps, however, had two line divisions. The light division was composed of one brigade of two line regiments and one brigade of *Grenzer* or *Jäger* battalions and some light cavalry. The line division had two brigades, each of two infantry regiments. Each brigade had its own battery, normally 6-pounders, though 3-pounders were provided for one brigade of IV Corps and for the light divisions. One 6-pounder cavalry battery and two 12-pounder batteries were available as corps artillery reserves. The additional light troops required for completing the corps were found by raising volunteer light infantry battalions, increasing the number of *Jäger* battalions to 12, and by the recovery of some *Grenzer* units when the French evacuated the Illyrian provinces. Light cavalry was provided by Hungarian volunteers, the *Veliten*. The Army Reserve, commanded by Hessen-Homburg, was composed of 20 Grenadier battalions and 33 squadrons of heavy cavalry. The Artillery Reserve (Reisner) consisted of about one third of the 394 available guns, and was organized in batteries as before.[53]

Austrian strength increased steadily throughout 1813, but less than one third of the troops could be considered fully trained, the bulk, in Radetzky's words, were 'peasants in uniform.' Clearly the regiments

ORDER OF BATTLE, ARMY OF BOHEMIA, SEPTEMBER 1813

	Battls	Sqdns	Men	3-pdr	6-pdr	6-pdr horse	6-pdr	12-pdr	18-pdr
				brigade batts			Position batts		
1st light division	4	16	6418	1	–	1	–	–	–
2nd light division	7	18	11,197	1	–	1	–	–	–
I Corps	21	11	26,232	–	4	1	1	2	–
II Corps	14	8	15,742	1	3	1	1	2	–
III Corps	20	12	23,800	–	4	1	6	2	–
IV Corps	24	14	30,056	–	4	1	1	–	–
Army Res.	20	33	24,988	–	4	4	–	–	–
Art. Res.	–	–	–	1	–	5	2	4	2
	110	112	138,433	4	19	15	6	12	2

Adapted from *Beiträge*, I, 234–5.

were unable to perform the complicated manoeuvres of the 1807 manual and simpler tactics had to be adopted making the column attack and not the fire of the line the main element of combat. Already at Wagram the Austrians had relied heavily on attack columns and Schwarzenberg and Radetzky continued this trend. On 12 August, the fieldmarshal issued new tactical instruction. 'While it must be left to each of the generals and independent formation commanders how to deploy his troops,' the instructions read, 'it is my wish to lay down certain basic principles.' In contrast to Charles who had considered the line as the normal combat formation both for the attack and the defence, Schwarzenberg preferred masses and columns for both situations. Offensively these should be screened by skirmishers, while for the defence he suggested deployment in chequer board formation so that the second line could provide both fire and shock support, and, if opportunity arose, the units of the first line not engaged could fall or fire on the flanks of an advancing enemy.[54]

To provide fire support, he advised that guns be brought forward as far as possible, though always covered by infantry, and that several batteries be combined for concentrated fire under the direction of a senior gunnery officer. Skirmishing was not given much weight in the new instructions. The Austrian high command remained convinced that poorly trained troops could not execute it properly. As Radetzky observed in September, 'fighting *en tirailleure* should be done only in very restricted fashion because neither the Russians nor we have mastered the *manière de tirailler*.'[55]

The Austrians at Dresden and Leipzig

When fighting commenced the front stretched from Hamburg to Prague. The allied plan called for Bernadotte's Army of the North to protect Berlin and, if possible, to threaten Hamburg. In the centre, Blücher's Army of Silesia was to enter Saxony, while the Army of Bohemia was to invade Saxony from the south. Napoleon sent one corps towards Berlin and moved his main force to dispose of Blücher. On hearing that Schwarzenberg had crossed the Bohemian mountains he turned back. Meanwhile, the Tsar's foreign advisors had induced Schwarzenberg to take Dresden before Napoleon could contermarch to its relief. By this time the allied forces already were in trouble, 'only three days march from their main base, the supply service had broken down and bread, ammunition, and clothing were short.'[56] On 26 August the army, with the Austrians on the left and centre, the Prussians on the right, and the Russians holding a refused right flank, attacked the city, turned into a fortified camp and defended by 20,000 men under St Cyr. The poorly co-ordinated allied attacks were beaten off and late that day, Napoleon materialized with the Guard and Mortier's Corps. The following morning two additional French corps arrived. Rain and lack of provisions had sapped Austrian morale and on the second day of the battle the left wing facing Murat's corps disintegrated. Some units broke; 11 battalions surrendered on the field. The losses reveal the tale. With only 32 officers and 1132 men killed and 142 and 5236 wounded, 74 officers and 3705 men were taken prisoners while four officers and no less than 5938 men were reported missing.[57] Overall, Schwarzenberg lost 38,000 men and ordered a retreat to Bohemia.[58]

If the Austrians were no match for French troops inspired by Napoleon, they had except for part of the left wing fought well enough. Wilson declared that the 'intrepidity of the Austrians could not be excelled, nor the perfection of their disposition; but they were required to do that which was physically impossible.'[59] In any case, they still were able of fighting back. On the day of Dresden, Blücher defeated MacDonald at the Katzbach. Napoleon now turned against him, sending one single corps, Vandamme's, to follow the Bohemian army. But the allies no longer were sheep to be gathered by a pursuer. On 30 August Vandamme found himself cut off at Kulm and Nollendorf and forced to surrender with a large part of his corps.

Meanwhile, according to plan, Blücher retreated before Napoleon while the Army of Bohemia and the Army of the North prepared to march on Saxony. To gain room for manoeuvre, Napoleon took up positions around Leipzig in September, but found himself the target of converging allied armies. Although Ney, fighting against the Army of the North, scored some successes, the scales were tipping. Napoleon's German allies were becoming unreliable. Bavaria changed sides on 8 October.

With his communications threatened, Napoleon either had to retreat or stand to fight.

He took his stand at Leipzig where the 'Battle of Nations,' 16–19 October, was a series of bloody actions as the allies, ultimately 300,000 against 190,000 French, closed in from three sides. Before dawn on 19 October, undefeated but fearing encirclement, Napoleon began an orderly retreat to the west. At this point his Saxon and Baden troops went over to the enemy and in the confusion the last remaining bridge was blown up prematurely, leaving some 50,000 trapped in the city. It had been a bloody battle. French losses numbered around 60,000 with 325 guns; the allies lost 53,834, including 15,148 Austrians.[60] Schwarzenberg and Radetzky's strategy had been vindicated, though the performance of certain Austrian commanders was much criticized. Gyulai, Klenau, and Merveldt had shown little aggressiveness; Merveldt, in particular, failed to bar the French withdrawal and even managed to be captured with part of his command. However, allegations that the Austrians deliberately left a route for Napoleon to escape were untrue.[61]

In any case, it was victory and forced the French to evacuate Germany. During the retreat Napoleon defeated 17,000 Bavarians under Wrede, who had not waited for the 23,000 strong Austrian corps, at Hanau, some ten miles east of Frankfurt on 30–31 October and reached France with some 60,000 men still in formed units and with 40,000 stragglers. To attempt to bar the French, the Austrians had marched from the Inn to Hanau in record time, almost 15 miles per day, an enormous increase over the pace of 1805 and 1809.

The other allied armies proceeded at a slower pace. As usual, supplies had given out and there was much looting. Despite Schwarzenberg's watchful eye discipline weakened. Wilson observed that the Cossacks were the worst offenders, though 'the Prussians tread on their heels, and the Hungarians affiliate fast with the band.'[62] Overall, the Austrian army had done its duty, but it certainly was no longer animated by the patriotic feelings, such as they were, of 1809. The fieldmarshal wanted to conduct a professional campaign without the excesses of a popular war, and much to the disgust of his Prussian allies, but following Metternich's instructions, he reverted to the old-fashioned pattern of careful marches and manoeuvring. He fully shared Metternich's desire to reach a suitable accommodation with Napoleon. 'Austria,' he had proclaimed in his army order of 16 August 1813, 'enters the war not against France, but only against French domination beyond her frontiers.'[63] He always realized that he commanded an army scraped together only by a last supreme effort and had no intention to risk it. He was careful not to overreach himself and to spare his troops needless exertion.

Once the French were across the Rhine, Metternich became fearful that Russia might predominate in central Europe and persuaded the allies to offer Napoleon the 'natural frontiers' of France – that is the Alps, Pyrenees and the Rhine. With Wellington's army already in the south of France and allied armies on the Rhine it was a generous offer. But when Napoleon finally accepted in December, the allies deemed it too late and in January entered France.

The campaign in the south

Beginning in May 1813, an army of one cavalry and six weak infantry divisions, 32 battalions, 40 squadrons, and 120 guns was assembled under the command of *Feldzeugmeister* Hiller in Inner Austria.[64] Hiller arrived in Graz on 2 August under orders to protect Austrian territory and recover Illyria, the parts of Carinthia, Carniola, Croatia and the Military Border ceded in 1809.[65] At the same time, he was instructed to avoid any action that might antagonize the Bavarians. Opposing Hiller were a few French battalions in Croatia, the Military Border, and Dalmatia, as well as the Italian army under Eugene. This now was in poor shape. It had dispatched 40,000 men to Russia, followed in 1813 by two additional corps to reinforce Napoleon's main army in Germany. On 18 April, Napoleon ordered his stepson to raise another army to defend his kingdom and French Illyria. Eugene faced enormous difficulties. Most of the French troops had been withdrawn and there were few Italian officers, non-commissioned officers or cadres available; arsenals and depots were empty. In the end, he managed to gather some 55,000 foot, 1800 horse, and 130 guns. Most of his men were raw recruits.[66]

While the bulk of Hiller's troops faced Bavaria and Italy, recovery of the Military Border and Croatia was entrusted to a detached corps under *Feldmarschall Leutnant* Paul von Radivojevic, six battalions of infantry and six squadrons of cavalry. Once the *Grenzer* regiments had been returned to Austrian control, they were to be rearmed and made operational as soon as possible. For this purpose the *Hofkriegsrat* provided 12,000 muskets and lists of reliable officers.[67] The actual takeover of the Military Border was handled by Major General Laval Nugent, an Irishman in the Austrian service, with less than 2000 men. Upon his arrival, the *Grenzer* deserted the French and returned to their old allegiance. Only in several coastal forts where some officers remained loyal to the French was there any resistance. By mid-September the Austrians were in control of Croatia, Istria, and the Military Border. Fighting continued in southern Dalmatia, where Cattaro and Ragusa held out until January 1814. However, these operations were conducted by a provisional *Grenzer* detachment assisted by a British squadron, and after some confusion, the area was secured in the summer of 1814.[68]

Meanwhile Radivojevic and Nugent had rejoined Hiller's main force trying to break into Italy by way of the Carinthian mountain passes. Eugene, now a mature commander, managed to put up a very creditable defence and even pushed the Austrians back at several points. It wasn't until October that Hiller managed to drive the viceroy back across the Isonzo. Never a popular officer or an easy subordinate, Hiller was criticized for making so little progress and after some sharp exchanges with the *Hofkriegsrat*, he was relieved of his command on 3 November, Bellegarde himself taking over his army. In the end, it was the threat from the south where Murat, after fighting for Napoleon at Dresden and Leipzig, had begun negotiations with the allies, that forced Eugene to fall back later that month. He fought a determined rearguard action at Caldiero on 15 November in which he inflicted a sharp rebuff on the pursuing Austrians. The year ended with Eugene having managed with small resources to effectively defend his most important provinces, while the Austrians had recovered their lost territories. The following year, even though Murat deserted Napoleon on 11 January and sent 20,000 Neapolitans to join the 70,000 Austrians, Eugene and his Italians successfully defended the Mincio line and held the major fortresses. Following Napoleon's abdication, he concluded an armistice, abdicated and went into exile in Bavaria. The Austrians then occupied Lombardy. Overall, their effort in Italy had been lacklustre, showing neither strategic inspiration nor tactical finesse.

The campaign in France, 1814

After arriving on the Rhine in November, the allied armies deployed on a broad front from Holland to Basle. While the monarchs and their ministers met in Frankfurt to try and reconcile their positions about the future of France, the commanders tried to bring up reserves and improve their logistic situation. At this point the allies numbered 350,000–360,000 men with 1238 guns. The Main Army under Schwarzenberg was deployed between Basle and Mannheim; Blücher was encamped around Mannheim, Mainz, and Coblenz, while the Army of the North had been split. Bernadotte with his Swedes and some north German contingents blockaded Davout in Hamburg and threatened Denmark, Napoleon's last remaining ally, while a Prussian corps under Bülow, reinforced by a Russian corps under Wintzingerode had entered Holland. An additional Prussian detachment under Kleist was marching to join the Silesian army.

The Austrian army now was in poor shape, its ranks decimated by disease made worse by its lack of winter clothing. With Klenau's corps detached to besiege Dresden, held until 11 November by St Cyr, and few reserves available, it no longer was the largest contingent. In late November 1813, the composition of Schwarzenberg's army was as follows:

MAIN ARMY – SCHWARZENBERG, END OF 1813

1. Light Division (Bubna) 5 battalions, 30 squadrons, 3 batteries	6000–7000 men
2. Light Division (Liechtenstein) 5 battalions, 18 squadrons, 2 batteries	4000 men
I Corps (Colloredo) 27 battalions, 12 squadrons, 8 batteries	15,000–16,000 men
II Corps (Liechtenstein) 27 battalions, 12 squadrons, 8 batteries	15,000 men
III Corps (Gyulai) 26 battalions, 13 squadrons, 8 batteries	15,000 men
IV (Württemberg) Corps (Prince of Württemberg) 13 battalions, 12 squadrons, 4 batteries	12,000 men
V (Austro-Bav.) Corps (Wrede) 41 battalions, 54 squadrons, 14 batteries	48,000 men (18,000 Austr., 30,000 Bav.)
VI (Russian) Corps (Wittgenstein) 30 battalions, 28 squadrons, 5 batteries, and 5 Cossack regiments	20,000 men
Austr. Reserve Corps (Hessen-Homburg) 35 battalions, 28 squadrons, 5 batteries	20,000 men

Russ.–Pruss. Guards and reserves	7000 Pruss.
	31,000 Russ.
Cossack Corps (Platov)	2000 men
5 Cossack regts, 1 battery	

Adapted from Horsetzky, p. 278 about 200,000 men and 682 guns.

The two other armies were much smaller. Blücher's Army of Silesia had about 80,000 men with 312 guns, while Kleist and Winzingerode together numbered about 70,000 men with 228 guns. Altogether, the allies outnumbered French effectives by more than three to one.

Beset by military, political, and economic problems, Napoleon hoped that the allies would not invade until spring, giving him time to rebuild strength. His strategic options were restricted by the fact that Paris was his centre of operations and main arsenal. It was here that he intended to organize and arm the 963,000 conscripts, veterans, pensioners, foresters, customs guards and others he called up or alerted in late 1813 and early 1814. While these were readied, he intended to delay the allies by stirring up guerrilla warfare in the frontier districts and then to rely on his interior lines, superior mobility, and allied disunity to defeat their armies individually. It was but a scheme that had no real chance for success. Most of the men called never showed up; less than one eighth saw service, and, except in Lorraine, there was no guerrilla resistance. Napoleon would have been wise to accept the repeated offers of a negotiated settlement put forward by the allies, but he no longer was capable of thinking in realistic terms.

Nonetheless, in December 1813 his preparations worried the Austrian commanders, and though Schwarzenberg and Radetzky rarely challenged their government's policies, they pressed for permission to enter France. Schwarzenberg informed the emperor that because of the lack of local provisions the army either would have to advance or retreat, while Radetzky declared that 'by delaying operations we give the enemy time to convert 100,000 demoralized men into 300,000 soldiers.'[69] At first, supported by Duka who objected that even the great Eugene had not ventured deep into France, the emperor refused, but by the middle of the month he and Metternich acceded to Schwarzenberg's request. The decision was made easier because Schwarzenberg did not propose a headlong offensive against the frontier fortresses, as advocated by the Prussians, but a careful advance by the Bohemian Army in a great arc through northern Switzerland to the plateau of Langres from where it could threaten Napoleon's communications, while at the same time the Army of

Silesia would move through the Palatinate to Metz and ultimately combine with Schwarzenberg on the Marne. Altogether, the plan exemplified classic eighteenth century manoeuvre strategy designed to avoid bloody actions while exerting pressure on the enemy to come to terms. To avoid antagonizing the population and to prevent the irruption of a people's war, Schwarzenberg gave strict orders to his troops to avoid looting and any other misbehaviour.[70]

The plan was sound, and if Prussian historians have criticized it as 'timid, hesitant, and old-fashioned,' it served the political ends of Austrian policy that neither desired to rout Napoleon totally nor to achieve needless and costly military triumphs.[71] For that matter, the plan succeeded initially. After violating Swiss neutrality, Schwarzenberg reached the Langres Plateau in late January with only 25 miles separating him from Blücher. At this point Schwarzenberg was ordered to halt to permit a new diplomatic initiative, while Napoleon arrived at the front and immediately attacked. He struck first at Blücher and forced him to retire, but when reinforced by Schwarzenberg, and with a numerical superiority of three to one, he defeated Napoleon at La Rothière on 1 February and drove him back with the loss of 73 guns. However, Schwarzenberg did not keep the armies united and this allowed Napoleon to renew the offensive against Blücher whose corps he defeated in a number of engagements. But continual reinforcements made up losses and Schwarzenberg now was advancing in turn, pushing them back to Troyes and then to Bar-sur-Aube. Again, the allies offered Napoleon terms which he refused and even Metternich no longer could save Napoleon. On 1 March 1814 the allies signed the Treaty of Chaumont pledging to restore the Bourbons and reduce France to her ancient limits.

In March the allied armies were on the move again, following the Trachenberg scheme of attacking where Napoleon was not, and retreating where he was. At this point their superiority was so great that nothing short of a miracle could have saved Napoleon. An attack against the main body of the Army of Silesia, heavily reinforced by elements of the Army of the North, in a good defensive position near Laon, failed. Napoleon now was tired and his attack in two unco-ordinated columns on 8–9 March was repulsed. In the meantime, Schwarzenberg had advanced towards Paris and Napoleon gave hasty orders to defend the capital. Turning against the Austrians, he was defeated on 20 March at Arcis-sur-Aube, 100,000 allies against 30,000 French. Clearly such odds were unsurmountable and Napoleon staked everything on a last gamble. Leaving Marmont and Mortier to cover Paris, he marched east with some 40,000 men, hoping to gather new troops en route, and by cutting off allied communications with Germany, forcing Schwarzenberg and Blücher to withdraw their forces.

The allies, ignoring the threat to their rear, saw their opportunity and seized it. After detaching some cavalry to shadow Napoleon, Schwarzenberg directed the bulk of his combined armies on Paris, over 200,000 men. An attempt by Marmont and Mortier to bar the way with 17,000 collapsed on 25 March. In the early hours of 31 March Marmont deserted with the remnants of his corps and the allies entered Paris later that day. The emperor still hoped to mount a counter-stroke that would rally the country, but his commanders, eager to salvage their positions and wealth, refused to follow him. And when Napoleon asserted that the army would still follow him, Ney informed him that, 'the army will only obey its generals.'

Nothing more was left to be said. Napoleon abdicated on 11 April and was exiled to Elba.

The balance sheet

The wars were not yet finished; in a few months Napoleon would return – for 'one hundred days.' But in 1815 the Austrian army would see little fighting. In Belgium, Wellington and Blücher defeated Napoleon before the main army under Schwarzenberg could be brought up from Germany; in Italy where Murat again changed sides in March 1815, and attempted to unify the peninsula under his leadership. The attempt failed and on 3 April 1815, 30,000 Neapolitans were defeated at Tolentino by a mere 11,000 Austrians under *Feldmarschall Leutnant* Bianchi. Other Austrian forces from Italy entered southern France in June, but encountered little opposition and fought only minor skirmishes. Essentially, the balance sheet of the wars that had begun in 1792 could be drawn up for the Austrian army already in 1814.

Contrary to often-expressed opinion, this balance came out in favour of the army. The main purpose of any armed force is to serve the political ends of the state, and this the Habsburg army did. Austria had entered the war against the French Revolution not to achieve military glory but to defend and restore the dynastic order of the eighteenth century. On this objective there was agreement between the generals and the politicians. Even the conflict between the Archduke Charles and Emperor Francis was more one of personalities and methods than of ultimate aims. At the same time, the political and military leadership realized that radical innovations in the military sphere were linked to changes in government and society that neither of the parties desired. Therefore, albeit with some administrative, strategic, and tactical improvements, they retained a military establishment resembling that of the pre-revolutionary period. Basically the Habsburg army remained a dynastic force, relying on its corporate spirit and not on enthusiasms or on engaging popular emotions. Its remarkable recuperative powers indicated that this spirit still was to be reckoned with.

In purely military terms, it is clear that neither the Austrian commanders nor the troops ever equalled the French at their best. For all his achievements, Charles never could match Napoleon of whom he stood in awe and the other generals, Radetzky included, always preferred not to confront him directly. Staff work, administration, and movement control also remained inferior to that of the French, though by 1813 the gap was closing fast. Throughout the wars, the army suffered from constant, and often petty, feuding within the higher echelons, but this also was true in France, Prussia, and Russia. The failure of a major purge of senior officers, prevented by political and social circumstances, undoubtedly had ill effects. Finally, Austrian strategy remained tied to the eighteenth-century concepts of strategic positions and did not look to the destruction of the enemy forces as its major objective. In tactics too, the reluctance to place emphasis on open order fighting proved a major handicap to the very end.

As for the Austrian troops, they fought much better than could be expected. Enduring great hardships and losses, they displayed fortitude and professionalism. Undoubtedly their discipline was of the highest order and, despite their polyglot character, the reliability of the regulars never was in doubt. The Austrian Army Cross, the first decoration distributed to all ranks, summed up their achievement. On its front the medal bore the inscription '*Libertate Europae asserta 1813-1814*,' while on the reverse side it read '*Grati princeps et patria*.' Europe had regained its liberty from French hegemony and the army had earned the gratitude of its sovereign and state. The ultimate settlement at Vienna restored Austria's great power position, while the experiences of 1792-1814 confirmed the Habsburgs' faith in the traditional military system.

Notes

Notes

Abbreviations

HHStA	Haus, Hof- und Staatsarchiv, Vienna
KA	Kriegsarchiv, Vienna
FA	Feldakten
HKR	Hofkriegsrat
MkkKA	*Mitteilungen des k.k. Kriegsarchius*
PRO	Public Record Office, London

CHAPTER I

1 As Holy Roman Emperor, of course, he was Francis II until 1806, but in 1804 he took the title Emperor of Austria, becoming Francis I. To avoid confusion he has been called Francis I throughout.

2 M. v. Angeli, 'Die Heere des Kaisers und der französischen Revolution im Beginn des Jahres 1792,' *MkkKA*, New Ser, IV (1889), 19.

3 A. Sorel, *L'Europe et la révolution Française* (8 vols, Paris, 1885–1904), I, 455.

4 Figures from C. A. Macartney, *The Habsburg Empire 1790–1918*, London, 1968, p. 82. An extensive description of the Monarchy during the last decade of the eighteenth century on pp. 2–119.

5 B. K. Király, *Hungary in the Late Eighteenth Century*, New York, 1969, pp. 104–5.

6 A. v. Arneth, *Geschichte Maria Theresias*, 10 vols, Vienna, 1863–79, IV, 87, and from the collection of memoranda known as 'Maria Theresa's Political Testament,' in C. A. Macartney ed., *The Habsburg and Hohenzollern Dynasties in the Seventeenth and Eighteen Centuries*, New York, 1970, pp. 125–6.

7 W. C. Langsam, *Francis the Good. The Education of an Emperor 1768–1792*, New York, 1949, pp. 126–31.

8 J. Cognasso, *Freymüthiger Beytrag zur Geschichte des österreichischen Militairdienstes*, Frankfurt and Leipzig, 1798, p. 18, and A. Ellrich, ed., *Humoristische und historische Skizzen aus den Jahren der Revolutionskriege. Aus den hinterlassenen Papieren eines verstorbenen Soldaten*, Meissen, 1844, pp. 251–2. J. M. Schweighofer, *Betrachtungen über die Ursachen und Folgen des geganwärtigen Türkenkrieges*, Frankfurt-Vienna, 1788, n.p.

9 O. Regele, *Der österreichische Hofkriegsrat 1556–1848*, Vienna, 1949, p. 25; 'Betrachtungen über die österreichische Kriegsverfassung,' quoted in Angeli, p. 24.

10 Macartney, *Habsburg and Hohenzollern Dynasties*, pp. 125–6.

11 C. Duffy, *The Army of Maria Theresa*, New York, 1977, pp. 19–20.

12 E. Kotasek, *Feldmarschall Graf Lacy*, Horn, 1956, pp. 173–8.

13 A. Wandruszka, *Leopold II*, 2 vols, Vienna-Munich, 1961, II, 304.

14 KA, FA 1792, Deutschland and Niederlande, 13–82.

15 M. Rauchensteiner, *Kaiser Franz und Erzherzog Carl*, Munich-Vienna, 1972, pp. 11–13; Langsam, pp. 65, 69, 80–81.

16 G. A. Craig, 'Command and Staff Problems in the Austrian Army, 1740–1866,' in *War, Politics, and Diplomacy: Selected Essays*, New York, 1966, pp. 4–7.

17 Österreichisches Staatsarchiv, *Inventare österreichischer Archive*, 2nd Series, *Inventar des Kriegsarchivs*, 2 vols in 1, Vienna, 1953, I, 141.

18 Regele, p. 25.

19 Duffy, p. 21.

20 G. E. Rothenberg, *The Military Border in Croatia, 1740–1881*, Chicago, 1966, pp. 18–90.

21 Regele, pp. 21–5.

22 Rothenberg, pp. 44–5.

23 K. Peball, 'Das Generalsreglement der Kaiserlich-königlichen Armee vom. 1. September 1769,' in *Schriften des Heeresgeschichtlichen Museums in Wien*, III (1867), 80–128.

24 C. J. Prince de Ligne, *Mélanges militaires, littéraires et sentimentaires*, 15 vols, Dresden, 1795–1802, II, 131.

25 O. Criste, *Erzherzog Carl von Österreich*, 3 vols, Vienna-Leipzig, 1912, I, 206.

26 O. Regele, *Generalstabschefs aus vier Jahrhunderten*, Vienna-Munich, 1966, pp. 26–7.

27 Kriegsgeschichtliche Abteilung des k.u.k. Kriegsarchivs, *Krieg gegen die französische Revolution 1792–1797*, Vienna, 1905, I, 227–8. (Hereafter cited as KA, *Krieg 1792–1797*.)

28 *Ibid.*, pp. 249–50.

29 *Ibid.*, pp. 481–2.

30 Duffy, pp. 24–8. Compare G. E. Rothenberg, 'Nobility and Military Careers: The Habsburg Officer Corps, 1740–1918,' *Military Affairs*, XXXX (1976), 182–3.

31 E. Guglia, *Maria Theresia*, Munich-Berlin, 1917, II, 22–3.

32 J. C. Allmayer-Beck, 'Wandlungen in Heerwesen zur Zeit Maria Theresias,' *Schriften des Heeresgeschichtlichen Museums in Wien*, III (1867), 21–2.

33 G. E. Rothenberg, 'Some Observations on the Evolution of Technical and Scientific Education in the Austrian Army during the Eighteenth Century,' *Science, Technology and Warfare, Proceedings of the Third Military History Symposium USAF Academy*, Washington, 1969, pp. 78–80.

34 Karl Fürst Schwarzenberg, *Feldmarschall Fürst Schwarzenberg*, Vienna-Munich, (1964), p. 25.

35 M. Ritter v. Thielen, *Erinnerungen aus dem Kriegserleben eines 82 jährigen Veteranen der österreichischen Armee*, Vienna, 1863, pp. 5–6.

36 KA, Hofkommission Nostitz-Rieneck, 'Gedanken über das Kauffen und Verkauffen der Chargen in der Armee,' F II–8. KA, *Krieg 1792–1797*, I, 217.

37 KA, *Krieg 1792–1797*, I, 218.

38 Allmayer-Beck, pp. 19–21.

39 F. Walter, *Männer um Maria Theresia*, Vienna, 1951, p. 106.

40 FML Leopold Unterberger, KA Mem. VII–49.

41 J. Zimmermann, *Militärverwaltung und Heeresaufbringung in Österreich bis 1806*, Vol. III of *Handbuch zur deutschen Militärgeschichte 1648–1939*, Frankfurt, 1965, 105–14.

42 Angeli, pp. 19–21; H. Meynert, *Geschichte der k.k. österreichischen Armee*, 3 vols, Vienna, 1852–54, III, 47–9.

43 K. J. v. Gruber, *Lebenserinnerungen eines Reiteroffiziers vor hundert Jahren*, Vienna, 1906, pp. 9–11.

44 Rothenberg, *Military Border*, pp. 84–5, 93.

45 KA, *Krieg 1792–1797*, I, 205–6.

46 Compare Angeli, pp. 28–9 with KA, *Krieg 1792–1797*, I, 231–7.

47 *Ibid.*, pp. 231–2, 236; Rothenberg, *Military Border*, pp. 67–68.

48 KA, Hofkommission Nostitz-Rieneck, FIX-9.

49 KA, Schriftgut Militärgrenze, F30, Maj. Gen. Klein, 'Gedanken über Eigenschaften und Widmung der k.k. Militair Gränzer.' Compare Rothenberg, *Military Border*, pp. 94–5, and KA, *Krieg 1792–1797*, I. 421–3.

50 Angeli, pp. 7, 31.

51 KA, *Krieg 1792–1797*, I. 237; Angeli, p. 5.

52 A. Dolleczek, *Geschichte der Oesterreichischen Artilllerie*, Vienna, 1887,

pp. 362–3, 440–41. For artillery material, types of projectiles, and tactics see G. E. Rothenberg, *The Art of Warfare in the Age of Napoleon*, London-Bloombington, Ind., 1977, pp. 24–7, 74–80.

53 For a discussion see the introduction by E. Peball to the new edition of G. F. v. Tempelhof, *Geschichte des sieben jährigen Krieges in Deutschland*, Osnabrück, 1977, pp. v–xlviii. Compare Duffy, p. 208.

54 Among others Angeli, pp. 99-101.

55 *Exerzitium und Regelement für die sämmtliche k.k. Infanterie*, Vienna, 1769.

56 *Exercitii Regelement für die gesammte k.k. Kavallerieregimenter*, Vienna, 1769; *Neuabgeändertes Exerzierreglement für die gesammte k.k. Kavallerieregimenter*, Vienna, 1772, and 'Reglement für die k.k. Cavallerie,' ms 1784, KA, Bibliothek. Compare J. Gallina, *Beiträge zur Geschichte des österreichischen Heerwesens*. Vol. 1, *Der Zeitraum von 1757–1814*, Vienna, 1872, pp. 76–8, hereafter cited as *Beiträge*. Also F. N. Maude, *The Ulm Campaign*, London, 1912, pp. 38–9.

57 KA *Krieg 1792–1797*, I, 257–9, and M. v. Angeli, *Erzherzog Carl als Feldherr und Heeresorganisator*, 5 vols., Vienna-Leipzig, 1896–7, V, 88. Compare Maude, pp. 12–13.

CHAPTER II

1 J. M. Sherwig, *Guineas and Gunpowder. British Foreign Aid in the Wars with France 1793–1815*, Cambridge, Mass., 1969, p. 75.

2 An overview of the campaigns in A. V. Horsetzky, *Kriegsgeschichtliche Übersicht der wichtigsten Feldzüge in Europa seit 1792*, 6th ed., Vienna, pp. 58–110.

3 C. Falls, *The Art of War from the Age of Napoleon to the Present Day*, London, 1961, pp. 34–5.

4 *Beiträge*, I. 81–97, gives mobilization scales.

5 *Ibid.*, pp. 109–10.

6 Criste, *Erzherzog Carl*, I. 62.

7 KA, *Krieg 1792–1797*, I. 218–19.

8 *Beiträge*, I. 149.

9 M. Ritter v. Thielen, *Erinnerungen aus dem Kriegserleben eines 82 jährigen Veteranen der österreichischen Armee*, Vienna, 1863, pp. 19–22.

10 KA, *Krieg 1792–1797*, I. 253–4.

11 *Exercitium und Regelement*, 1769, p. 73.

12 Cited in Angeli, 'Die Heere des Kaisers,' p. 47.

13 KA, *Krieg 1792–1797*, I. 113–19.

14 *Ibid.*, pp. 275–6.

15 *Ibid.*, II, 96–7.

16 J. W. Fortescue, *A History of the British Army*, London, 1915, IV, 92; Maude, pp. 22–6.

17 Criste, *Erzherzog Carl*, I. 80–83, 90.

18 Rothenberg, *Art of Warfare*, pp. 98–110.

19 *Ibid.*, and S. Ross, *From Flintlock to Rifle. Infantry Tactics, 1740–1866*, London, 1979, pp. 66–71.

20 See the observations in Fortescue, IV, 224.

21 Criste, *Erzherzog Carl*, I, 117–19.

22 Fortescue, IV, 221–2.

23 Valenciennes, 12 March 1794, *Beiträge*, I, 131–4.

24 James Craig, Major General and chief of staff to the Duke of York, Fortescue, IV, 279.

25 E. Kotasek, *Feldmarschall Graf Lacy*, Horn, 1956, p. 207. Compare R. Lorenz, *Volksbewaffnung und Staatsidee in Österreich, 1792–1797*, Vienna, 1923, pp. 49, 53–5.

26 W. Wickham ed., *The Correspondence of the Right Honourable William Wickham*, London, 1870, I, 153–4, 158–9.

27 Fortescue, IV, 498.

28 R. W. Phipps, *The Armies of the First French Republic*, London, 1926–9, II, 402–4.

29 Criste, *Erzherzog Carl*, I, 6–29; Rauchensteiner, *Kaiser Franz*, pp. 15–23, 28–9.

30 A. Freiherr v. Waldstätten ed., *Erzherzog Carl. Ausgewählte militärische Schriften*, Berlin, 1882, pp. 4–11.

31 KA, Mem. B/473, Nr. 56 of 4 Apr. 1796. Compare Criste, *Erzherzog Carl*, I, 192–3.

32 Rauchensteiner, *Kaiser Franz*, pp. 24–5.

33 Wickham to Grenville, 8 April 1796, *Correspondence*, I, 333.

34 Criste, *Erzherzog Carl*, I, 198.
35 *Beiträge*, I, 137–9.
36 *Ibid.*, pp. 141–2.
37 An analysis of operations in E. B. Hamley, *The Operations of War*, 6th ed., Edinburgh and London, 1907, pp. 161–74.
38 Criste, *Erzherzog Carl*, 294–5, 301–2.
39 Rauchensteiner, *Kaiser Franz*, pp. 26-8.
40 Criste, *Erzherzog Carl*, I, 202, 339–40.
41 Letter of 20 August 1796, Thomas Graham, Baron Lynedoch Papers, Scottish National Library. A. Brett-James, *General Graham Lord Lynedoch*, New York, 1959, pp. 66, 77.
42 Bern, 14 December 1796, Wickham, *Correspondence*, I, 493.
43 To Alvinczy, 30 December 1796, 'Dagobert Sigmund Reichsgraf von Wurmser,' *MkkKA*, XXXI (1878), 96.
44 'Erinnerungen aus dem Leben des Feldmarschall Grafen Radetzky. Eine Selbstbiographie,' *MkkKA*, New. Ser. I (1887), 49.
45 Lorenz, pp. 83–5.
46 KA HKR IX–1119.
47 Criste, *Erzherzog Carl*, I. 497.
48 Eden to Graham, 17 February 1797, Graham Papers.
49 To Francis I, 20 March 1796, Criste, *Erzherzog Carl*, I. 411.
50 To Francis I, 24 March 1797, *Ibid.*, pp. 510–11.
51 Radetzky, 'Selbstbiographie,' p. 51.
52 Criste, *Erzherzog Carl*, I. 533–4.
53 Lorenz, p. 137.
54 Rauchensteiner, *Kaiser Franz*, pp. 35–6. Compare the account in H. Rössler, Österreichs Kampf um Deutschlands Befreiung, Hamburg, 1940, I, 113–15.
55 Anon. (Archduke Charles), *Die Grundsätze der Strategie, erläutert durch die Darstellung des Feldzugs von 1796 in Deutschland*, 3 vols, Vienna, 1814, III, 357.
56 Radetzky, 'Selbstbiographie,' pp. 8–10.
57 Compare Criste, *Erzherzog Carl*, I, 330, and H. Ommen, *Die Kriegsführung des Erzherzogs Carl*, Berlin, 1900, p. 129.
58 Zach to Alvinczy, 18 April 1798, 'Eine Denkschrift Zach's aus dem Jahre 1798,' *MkkKA*, 3rd Ser. II (1903), pp. 173–7, 179–83.
59 Maude, pp. 15–16.

CHAPTER III

1 Morton to Grenville, 1 Nov. 1797, Public Record Office (PRO), FO 7/50.
2 KA, Nachlass Mack, B/573–3.
3 Rauchensteiner, *Kaiser Franz*, pp. 40–41; compare Francis to Charles, 4 Febr. 1798 cited in E. Wertheimer, 'Erzherzog Carl und die zweite Coalition bis zum Frieden von Lunéville 1798–1801,' *AöG*, 67 (1886), 196–7.
4 Charles to Francis, 3 May 1708, *Ibid.*, p. 197.
5 Criste, *Erzherzog Carl*, II, 11; M. v. Angeli, *Erzherzog Carl als Feldherr und Heeresorganisator*, Vienna-Leipzig, 1896, II, 508.
6 Zach, 'Denkschrift,' pp. 166–7, 172–3, 179–83, 190. For the tensions within the officer corps see also J. Rauch, *Erinnerungen Eines Offiziers aus Altösterreich*, ed. A. Weber, Munich, 1918, pp. 358–9.
7 Criste, *Erzherzog Carl*, II, 12.
8 A. Dolleczek, *Monographie der k.u.k. österrung blanken and Handfeuerwaffen*, Vienna, 1896, pp. 79–81.
9 A. B. Paget and J. R. Green eds, *The Paget Papers. Diplomatic and Other Correspondence of the Right Hon. Sir Arthur Paget, GCB, 1794–1807*, New York, 1896, II, 25–6.
10 Criste, *Erzherzog Carl*, II, 11, 50.
11 *Ibid.*, II, 49.
12 Ellrich, pp. 156, 236–9.
23 KA, HKR, FA 1798, Innerösterreich 5–52 1/2.
14 K. Peball, 'Zum Kriegsbild der österreichischen Armee und seiner geschichtlichen Bedeutung in den Kriegen gegen die Französiche Revolution und Napoleon I. In den Jahren von 1792 bis 1815,' in W. v. Groote and K. J. Müller, *Napoleon I und das Militärwesen seiner Zeit*, Freiburg, 1968, pp. 145–6.
15 J. Rauch, *Erinnerungen eines Offiziers aus Altösterreich*, A. Weber ed., Munich, 1918, pp. 346–7.
16 *Beiträge*, I, 143–4.
17 A. B. Rodger, *The War of the Second Coalition, 1798–1801: A Strategic Commentary*, London, 1964, pp. 151–4, 157.
18 Criste, *Erzherzog Carl*, II, 15, 17, 33–5;

Wertheimer, pp. 201–2, and Angeli, *Erzherzog Carl*, II, 508.

19 Horsetzky, p. 114.

20 Regele, *Hofkriegsrat*, p. 63; Rauchensteiner, *Kaiser Franz*, pp. 44–5, Criste, *Erzherzog Carl*, II, 34.

21 *Ibid.*, pp. 45–6. KA, MNFK. B/473–58.

22 Friedberg, 19 Hornung (February) 1799, printed in Rauchensteiner, *Kaiser Franz*, pp. 115–16.

23 Zurich, 5 July 1799, To Grenville, Wickham, *Correspondence*, II, 121–2.

24 KA, MNKF B/473–50 copy.

25 28 March 1799, in Criste, II, 59–60. *Erzherzog Carl*, II, 59–60.

26 To Albert, 31 March 1799, Wertheimer, p. 208.

27 *Die Feldzüge von 1799 in Italien und in der Schweiz*, Vol. V of Hinterlassene Werke des Generals Carl von Clausewitz über Krieg und Kriegsführung, Berlin, 1632–7, pp. 334–5.

28 Wertheimer, p. 211; Criste, *Erzherzog Carl*, II, 71–2; Wertheimer, 210–13.

29 Rothenberg, *Art of Warfare*, pp. 21–2. The picture in A. A. Lobanov-Rostovsky, *Russia and Europe, 1789–1825*, Chapel Hill, N.C., 1947, pp. 31–3, 43–64 is far too favourable to the Russians.

30 To Grenville, 17 Oct. 1799, Wickham, *Correspondence*, II, 272–3.

31 To Sir Charles Whitworth, 3 Nov. 1799, *Ibid.*, 324–6.

32 *Ibid.*, p. 261.

33 Paret, pp. 202–3.

34 Wertheimer, p. 231.

35 Lt Col. Clinton, cited by Wickham to Grenville, 10 Oct. 1799, Wickham, *Correspondence*, II, 258–9.

36 Criste, *Erzherzog Carl*, II, 79–86.

37 To Grenville, 29 June 1799, Wickham, *Correspondence*, II, 110–11.

38 Criste, *Erzherzog Carl*, II, 95–5, 104–6.

39 Wickham to Suvorov, Zurich 22 Aug. 1799, *Correspondence*, II, 165.

40 Wangen, 18 Oct. 1799, *Ibid.*, p. 279.

41 Augsburg, 3 Nov. 1799, to Sir Charles Whitworth, *Ibid.*, 324–6, and 9 Dec. 1799 to Lord Minto, *Ibid.*, p. 354. Criste, *Erzherzog Carl*, II, 130–32.

42 To Grenville, 29 June 1799, Wickham, *Correspondence*, II, 117–18.

43 Augsburg, 31 Oct. 1799, *Ibid.*, p. 321.

44 Grenville to Whitworth, 8 Febr. 1800, cited in Sherwig, pp. 125–6.

45 29 Oct. 1799, Wertheimer, p. 238.

46 Rössler, I, 118–20.

47 For a subaltern's account of the battle see Rauch, pp. 374–6.

48 20 June 1800, KA, FA 1800, VI ad 326.

49 Criste, *Erzherzog Carl*, II, 153–6.

50 Wertheimer, pp. 240–41.

51 KA, FA 1800, Deutschland, VII–291.

52 Sherwig, p. 131.

53 Criste, *Erzherzog Carl*, II, 158–60.

54 *Ibid.*, pp. 165.

55 Grüber, p. 16.

56 Wertheimer, pp. 246–7.

CHAPTER IV

1 KA, MNKF, B/473–55.

2 Angeli, *Erzherzog Carl*, V, 92 has the appointment *in toto*.

3 Criste, *Erzherzog Carl*, II, 182–3.

4 Haus, Hof-und Staatsarchiv, Vienna, Fassbender Akten, XXXII–1. (Hereafter cited as HHStA, Fassbender.)

5 Public Record Office, Foreign Office Papers, 7/65. (Hereafter cited as PRO, FO.) Compare A. B. Paget and J. R. Green eds, *The Paget Papers, Diplomatic and other Correspondence of the Right Hon. Sir Paget, G.C.B., 1794–1807*, New York, 1896, II, 16–17.

6 KA, B/573–20. Also printed in excerpt in Rauchensteiner, *Kaiser Franz*, p. 67.

7 Radetzky, 'Autobiographie,' p. 63; Rauchensteiner, *Kaiser Franz und Erzherzog Carl*, pp. 65–6.

8 Criste, *Erzherzog Carl*, II, 276, 80.

9 Instruction printed in Rauchensteiner, *Kaiser Franz*, pp. 60–61.

10 KA, Kriegsministerium Akten, 1810, 30–186.

11 Rauchensteiner, *Kaiser Franz*, p. 63.

12 Cited in Criste, *Erzherzog Carl*, II, 219–20.

13 *Ibid.*, pp. 263–7.

14 *Ibid.*, 206–7. Compare O. Regele, *Generalstabschefs aus vier Jahrhunderten*, Vienna-Munich, 1966, p. 26.

15 *Ibid.*

16 *Ibid.*, pp. 201–2.

17 J. C. Allmayer-Beck, 'Die Allezeit

Getreuen,' in H. Siegert, ed. *Adel in Österreich*, Vienna, 1971, p. 314.

18 KA, Memoirs, VII-49.

19 Criste, *Erzherzog Carl*, II, 208–9.

20 KA, HKR, 1804, G-10/143 of 2 Oct. 1804.

21 To Francis, 18 Aug. 1802, in Criste, *Erzherzog Carl*, II, 215–16.

22 MaCartney, pp. 175–6; A. Springer, *Geschichte Oesterreichs seit dem Wiener Frieden*, Leipzig, 1863, I, 66–7.

23 J. Zimmermann, *Militärverwaltung und Heeresaufbringung in Österreich bis 1806*, Vol. III of *Handbuch zur deutschen Militärgeschichte*, Frankfurt, 1965, pp. 114–19.

24 Criste, *Erzherzog Carl*, II, 211–12; Angeli, *Erzherzog Carl*, V, 141–3.

25 KA, HKR, 1802, G 9/3-6284.

26 Zimmermann, p. 118; Memorandum of 5 March 1804, in Criste, *Erzherzog Carl*, II, 257.

27 Cited in E. v. Frauenholz,*Das Heerwesen des XIX. Jahrhunderts*, Munich, 1941, pp. 424–30.

28 Documentation for the section on the Military Border in Rothenberg, *Military Border*, pp. 83–96.

29 KA, Nachlass Mayer v. Heldenfeld, B/857–80.

30 O. Stolz, *Wehrverfassung und Schützenwesen in Tirol*, Munich-Vienna, 1960, pp. 124–31.

31 A Fournier, *Gentz and Cobenzl. Geschichte der österreichischen Diplomatie in den Jahren 1801–1805*, Vienna, 1880, p. 36.

32 *Ibid.*, p. 110.

33 *Ibid.*, p. 112.

34 Anon. 'Zur Characteristik des Erzherzogs Carl und der österr. Armee in den Jahren 1801 bis 1804,' *MkkKA*, 5 (1881), 106–21. Compare O. Regele, *Feldmarschall Radetzky*, Vienna-Munich, 1957, p. 66.

35 Gruber, pp. 35–6.

36 Rauchensteiner, *Kaiser Franz*, p. 67.

37 KA, FA (CA), F 11–16. Printed in Criste, *Erzherzog Carl*, II, 252–7.

38 9 March 1804, Fournier, pp. 215–19.

39 To Lord Harrowby, Vienna, June 1804, Paget, II, 134.

40 Criste, *Erzherzog Carl*, II, 259.

41 Fournier, pp. 241–2.

42 Harrowby to Paget, 11 September 1804, Paget, II, 149.

43 Fournier, pp. 153–4.

44 Letter in Criste, *Erzherzog Carl*, II, 530–31.

45 Draft in KA, MNKF, B/473, 29. Letter dated 29 January in Criste, *Erzherzog Carl*, II, 534–5.

46 *Ibid.*, pp. 304–5.

47 To Lord Mulgrave, 13 March 1805, Paget, II, 163.

48 Fassbender to Charles, 21 April 1805, Criste, *Erzherzog Carl*, II, 563–7.

49 Charles to Francis, 22 April 1805, *ibid.*, pp. 569–70.

50 Fournier, pp. 156–7.

51 Paget to Mulgrave, 19 March 1805, Paget, II, 167.

CHAPTER V

1 Rauchensteiner, *Kaiser Franz*, p. 74.

2 C. Duffy, *Austerlitz 1805*, Camden, Conn., 1977, p. 37.

3 Fournier, pp. 303–4.

4 'Report on the political situation in Europe,' KA, MNKF, B/473-7.

5 'Allerunterhänigster Bericht,' KA, HKR, 1805-4–8.

6 KA, MNKF, B/473-22.

7 C. R. V. Schönhals, *Der Krieg 1805 in Deutschland*, Vienna, 1873, pp. 13–14.

8 Paget, II, 175, 179.

9 Sherwig, pp. 160–61, 170.

10 KA, FA 1805, Deutschland, 7/29-30. Compare Criste, *Erzherzog Carl*, II, 317–18.

11 KA, FA 1805, Deutschland, F/8-34 1/2.

12 Criste, *Erzherzog Carl*, II, 319–21.

13 Fournier, p. 184; Duffy, *Austerlitz*, p. 38.

14 W. Rüstow, *Der Krieg von 1805 in Deutschland und Italien*, Frauenfeld, 1853, p. 56.

15 Latour to Army Command Germany, 31 Aug. 1805, KA, FA 1805, Deutschland, F/8-29 1/2.

16 Schönhals, pp. 22–3.

17 To Lord Mulgrave, 24 Oct. 1805, Paget, II, 224–5.

18 Rüstow, pp. 89–90.

19 Cited in A. Beer, *Zehn Jahre Österreichische Politik, 1801–1810*, Leipzig, 1877, p. 132, n. 1.

20 Rüstow, pp. 57–8; Schönhals, pp. 45–7.

21 Beiträge, I, 187; KA, B/573–17, 18.

22 'Suggestions for the drill and evolutions of foot,' Ibid., B/573–9.

23 Criste, Erzherzog Carl, II, 321.

24 Vorschrift welche Gegenstände des Exercitiums und der Evolutionen der Infantrie abzuschaffen oder zu vereinfachen sind, Vienna, 1805, p. 14.

25 Duffy, Austerlitz, p. 27; Schönhals, p. 69.

26 Rauch, p. 436.

27 Dollezcek, p. 448.

28 'Proposals for reductions of trains and baggage . . .,' KA, B/573–13. Compare Beiträge, I, 184–5.

29 Duffy, Austerlitz, p. 29.

30 Schönhals, pp. 23–4, 26.

31 Rüstow, pp. 75–7.

32 Ferdinand to Francis, 20 Sep. 1805, KA, FA 1805, Deutschland, F/9–24–1.

33 Ibid., 66 1/4.

34 Latour to Francis 23 Sept. 1805, ibid., 43.

35 Paget, 1 Nov. 1805, PRO, FO 7/75.

36 Charles to Francis, 9 Sep. 1805, printed in W. Nemetz, 'Erzherzog Karl,' in W. Hahlw ed., Klassiker der Kriegskunst, Darmstadt, 1964, pp. 289–91.

37 Schönhals, p. 43; KA, FA 1805, Deutschland, F/9–45 1/2.

38 Duffy, Austerlitz, pp. 40–44.

39 Horsetzky, pp. 144–5.

40 Kienmayer to Mack, 5 Oct. 1805, KA, FA 1805, Deutschland, F/5–40 a, b, c.

41 Schönhals, pp. 69–70.

42 A. Krauss, 1805. Der Feldzug von Ulm, Vienna, 1912, p. 154.

43 Schönhals, p. 102.

44 Ibid.

45 A general discussion in O. Regele, 'Karl Freiherr von Mack und Johann Ludwig Graf Cobenzl. Ihre Rolle im Kriegsjahr 1805,' MŠTA, 21 (1968), 144–5.

46 Fournier, p. 185.

47 Charles to Francis, 23 Sep. 1805, Padua, KA, FA 1805, Italien F/22–245 1/4.

48 Rauchensteiner, Kaiser Franz, p. 74.

49 KA, FA 1805, Italien, F/27–285 1/2. Compare Criste, Erzherzog Carl, II, 337–9.

50 Ibid., pp. 575–6.

51 Ibid., p. 338.

52 Ibid., p. 345.

53 After action report, KA, FA 1805, Italien, F/27–289–93. Analysis in Rüstow, pp. 105–9.

54 Thus L. A. Thiers, Histoire du Consulat et de l'Empire, 20 vols, Paris, 1845–62, vol. VI.

55 R. Egger, Das Gefecht bei Dürnstein-Loiben 1805, Vienna, 1965.

56 Paget, II, 230.

57 Schönhals, pp. 120–22.

58 W. Hummelberger and K. Peball, Die Befestigungen Wiens, Vienna-Hamburg, 1974, pp. 73–4.

59 Paget, II, 239, 241–2.

60 M. V. Creveld, Supplying War. Logistics from Wallenstein to Patton, London, 1977, pp. 59–61.

61 R. Egger, Das Gefecht bei Hollabrunn und Schöngrabern 1805, Vienna, 1974, p. 7.

62 Ibid., pp. 5–12.

63 Duffy, Austerlitz, p. 64.

64 Count Nostiz's account, written in 1820, KA, FA 1805, Deutschland, F/13–182. Compare the account of Maj. Mahler, 6th Bat., 49th Infantry, 'Tagebuchblätter aus dem Jahre, 1805,' MkkKA, 6 (1881), 499–523.

65 KA, FA 1805, Deutschland, F/11–106 1/2.

66 Rüstow, p. 317.

67 Charles to Francis, KA, FA 1805, Italien, F/12–57 1/4.

68 Schönhals, pp. 148–9.

69 Olmütz, 20 Nov. 1805, Pagett, II, 246.

70 K. Stutterheim, La bataille d'Austerlitz, Paris, 1806, p. 11.

71 Paget, II, 252–3.

72 Paget to Mulgrave, PRO, FO 7/71.

73 Criste, Erzherzog Carl, II, 372–3.

74 Rössler, I, 246–69.

CHAPTER VI

1 P. Paret, Yorck and the Era of Prussian Reform, 1807–1815, Princeton, N.J., 1966, pp. 73–4.

2 Rauchensteiner, Kaiser Franz, pp. 77–9.

3 Charles to Francis, 3 Jan. 1806, HHStA, Kaiser Franz Akten, F/78a.

4 Criste, Erzherzog Carl, II, 380–83.

5 Rauchensteiner, Kaiser Franz, pp. 79–81.

6 *Ibid.*, Criste, *Erzherzog Carl*, II, 385-7.
7 *Ibid.*, p. 388; Regele, Hofkriegsrat, pp. 30-31, 87.
8 Rauchensteiner, *Kaiser Franz*, pp. 83-8 *passim*.
9 Kriegsgeschichtliche Abteilung des k.u.k. Kriegsarchivs, *Krieg 1809*, Vienna, 1907, I, 17-18. (hereafter KA, Krieg 1809)
10 *Ibid.*, pp. 19-21.
11 To Friedrich v. Gentz, in Maj. Jacubenz, 'Gentz und Fassbender. Ungedruckte Briefe aus der Zeit von 1802 bis 1808,' *MkkKA*, 3rd Ser. VII (1911), 57-102.
12 KA, *Krieg 1809*, I, 28-9. Compare Rauchensteiner, *Kaiser Franz*, pp. 82-3.
13 Mayer to Francis, 22 March 1808, KA, MNKF, B/473, 43. Compare *ibid.*, Nr. 44.
14 *Grundsätze der höheren Kriegs-Kunst für die Generäle der österreichisch-Armee*, Vienna, 1806.
15 KA, Nachlass Mayer v. Heldenfeld, B/857-5.
16 KA, *Krieg 1809*, p. 116.
17 *Grundsätze der höheren Kriegs-Kunst*, pp. 1-2, 8-9.
18 *Ibid.*, pp. 19-22.
19 *Ibid.*, pp. 43-4.
20 *Ibid.*, pp. 85-8.
21 *Ibid.*, pp. 89-91.
22 Anon., 'Die Armee Napoleon I. im Jahre 1809 mit vergleichenden Rückblicken auf das österreichische Heer,' *MkkKA III* (1881), 371-408 and passim. Compare C.v.W. (Carl v. Müffling), *Marginalien zu den Grundsätzen der höheren Kriegskunst für die Generäle der österreichischen Armee*, Weimar, 1810, p. 72. Lindenau's comment in KA, B/619-61.
23 H. Delbrück, *Geschichte der Kriegskunst im Rahmen der politischen Geschichte*, Berlin, 1920, IV, 503-4.
24 K. Peball, 'Zum Kriegsbild der österreichischen Armee und seiner geschichtlichen Bedeutung in den Kriegen gegen die Französishce Revolution und Napoleon I. in den Jahren von 1792 bis 1815,' in V. v. Groote and K. J. Müller ed., *Napoleon I. und das Militärwesen seiner Zeit*, Freiburg, 1968, pp. 149-51.
25 *Beiträge zum practischen Unterricht im Felde für die Offiziere der österreichischen Armee*, Vienna, 1806-13.
26 W. Wagner, *Von Austerlitz bis Königgrätz. Österreichische Kampftaktik im Spiegel der Reglements, 1805-1864*, Osnabruck, 1978, pp. 6, 21-5.
27 *Ibid.*, pp. 4-5.
28 *Grundsätze der höheren Kriegs-Kunst*, pp. 3-4.
29 To Archduke Joseph, 8 Dec. 1805, Criste, *Erzherzog Carl*, II, 370; *Exercier-Reglement für die kaiserlich-königliche Infanterie*, Vienna, 1807, Book II, para. 13.
30 KA, *Krieg 1809*, I, 102.
31 Wagner, pp. 7-13.
32 KA, *Krieg 1809*, I, 74-5.
33 *Exercier-Reglement 1807*, Book I, section 3, paras 1 and 2.
34 KA, *Krieg 1809*, p. 111.
35 *Exercier-Reglement 1807*, Book II, section 2, preamble and paras 1-3.
36 *Ibid.*, Book III, sections 1 and 2.
37 *Ibid.*, preamble to sections 1 and 2.
38 KA, *Krieg 1809*, pp. 101-2, 112-13.
39 KA, FA 1813, Deutschland, F/10-436b.
40 C.v.W., *Marginalien*, pp. 93-4.
41 KA, *Krieg 1809*, I, 113.
42 *Exerzierreglement für die k.k. Grenzinfantrie*, Vienna, 1808.
43 *Belehrung der Plänkler*, Vienna, 1810 (?)
44 KA, *Krieg 1809*, I, 76-7.
45 *Ibid.*, *Exercier-Reglement für die k.k. Cavallerie*, Vienna, 1806, Book I, Sec. 1, paras 7-8.
46 *Ibid.*, Book III, para. 2; Cf. KA, *Krieg 1809*, I, 104-5.
47 *Beiträge*, I. 228.
48 KA, *Krieg 1809*, I, 114-15. Compare H. Ommen, *Die Kriegsführung des Erzherzogs Karl*, Berlin, 1900, pp. 81-2.
49 Major Semek, 'Die Artillerie im Jahre 1809,' *MkkKA*, 3rd Ser. III (1904), 74-5. Compare KA, *Krieg 1809* I, 106-7.
50 Dolleczek, pp. 449-50; *Beiträge*, 198-200.
51 KA, *Krieg 1809*, I, 78-9, 106-7.
52 Wagner, p. 21.
53 Österreichisches Staatsarchiv, *Inventar des Kriegsarchivs*, I, 40-41.
54 Duffy, *Army of Maria Theresa*, pp. 44-5.

55 Casualty figures from G. Bodart, *Militärisch-historisches Kriegs-Lexikon*, Vienna-Leipzig, 1980, pp. 902–4.
56 Cited in Duffy, *Army of Maria Theresa*, p. 108.
57 *Dienst-Reglement für die kaiserlich-königliche Infanterie*, 2 parts, Vienna, 1807–8.
58 *Ibid.*, Part 1, preamble, p. 1.
59 *Ibid.*, Part 1, para. 5.
60 Frauenholz, pp. 432–4.
61 Criste, *Erzherzog Carl*, II, 404–5; Macartney, *Habsburg Empire*, pp. 184–5.
62 C.v. Clausewitz, *On War*, trans. O.M. Jolles, New York, 1943, p. 568.
63 6 Aug. 1806, Criste, *Erzherzog Carl*, II, 400.
64 Karl Fürst Schwarzenberg, *Feldmarschall Fürst Schwarzenberg*, Vienna, 1964, p. 97; Regele, *Radetzky*, p. 394.
65 Cited in Rössler, I, 319.
66 KA, *Krieg 1809*, I, 84–8. Compare Zimmermann, pp. 116–19.
67 On this paragraph see Rothenberg, *Military Border*, pp. 96–101.
68 To Francis, 6 July 1808, KA, KM 1808–1/29.
69 Criste, *Erzherzog Carl*, II, 452–3.
70 To Francis, KA, MNKF, B/473–6, 46.
71 A. Beer, *Zehn Jahre österreichischer Politik, 1801–1810*, Leipzig, 1877, pp. 316–35. For a detailed breakdown of French strength see HHStA, Staatskanzlei, Vorträge 1808, F/267.

CHAPTER VII

1 Rauchensteiner, *Kaiser Franz*, p. 94.
2 KA, *Krieg 1809*, I, 168–9.
3 *Ibid.*, pp. 169–70.
4 Sherwig, pp. 210–12.
5 G. C. Bond, *The Great Expedition*, Athens, Ga., 1979, pp. 6–12.
6 Angeli, *Erzherzog Carl*, IV, 10; KA, *Krieg 1809*, I, 178–80.
7 Karl, *Ausgewählte Schriften*, VI, 357.
8 KA, FA 1809, Hauptarmee, F/1–15.
9 H. Delbrück, *Erinnerungen, Aufsätze, und Reden*, Berlin, 1902, p. 605.
10 KA, *Krieg 1809*, I. 170.
11 To Mayer, KA, FA 1809, Hauptarmee, F/1–9 ad.
12 *Ibid.*, F/2–30.
13 *Ibid.*, 39.
14 *Ibid.*, F/14–3/4.
15 Rauchensteiner, *Kaiser Franz*, p. 91; Criste, *Erzherzog Carl*, III, 9–13.
16 Rauchensteiner, *Kaiser Franz*, p. 92.
17 KA, *Krieg 1809*, I, 178–9, 188–9.
18 *Ibid.*, p. 118.
19 KA, MNKF B/473–46.
20 *Beiträge*, I,203–4; Dolleczek, p. 449.
21 Karl, *Ausgewählte Schriften*, V, 153.
22 Maude, pp. 40–41. Compare KA, *Krieg 1809*, I, 97–100.
23 Horsetzky, pp. 189–90.
24 F. L. Petre, *Napoleon and the Archduke Charles*, New York-London, 1976, pp. 11–24. Compare Criste, *Erzherzog Carl*, III, 23.
25 A comprehensive order of battle and evaluation of troops in S. Bowden and C. Tarbox, *Armies on the Danube 1809* (Arlington, Texas, 1980, pp. 38–9, 42–4).
26 Criste, *Erzherzog Carl*, II, 462.
27 KA, FA 1809, Hauptarmee, F/2–31, 32.
28 KA, *Krieg 1809*, I, 190–92.
29 Radetzky, p. 65; compare Delbrück, *Erinnerungen*, pp. 585–6; and the discussion C. Binder v. Krieglstein, *Der Krieg Napoleon's gegen Österreich*, 1809, Berlin, 1906, pp. 95–6; Petre, pp. 71–3.
30 KA, *Krieg 1809*, I, 190–92.
31 *Ibid.*, pp. 194–5.
32 KA, FA 1809, Hauptarmee, F/3–132, 146, 165.
33 *Armeebefehl*, 6 April 1809, actually issued 9 April.
34 M. Rauchensteiner ed., 'Das sechste österreichische Armeekorps im Krieg 1809,' *MÖSTA*, XVI–XVII (1964–5), 154.
35 KA, FA Hauptarmee, F/4–121. Compare Criste, *Erzherzog Carl*, III, 24–5.
36 KA, *Krieg 1809*, I, 227; Criste, *Erzherzog Carl*, III, 25–6.
37 KA, *Krieg 1809*, I, 263–4.
38 Col. H. Hess, 'Gedrängte Darstellung des Feldzuges in Bayern,' KA, FA 1809, Hauptarmee, F/13–402.
39 *Ibid.*,F/4–198.
40 Criste, *Erzherzog Carl*, III, 69–70.
41 The account of the engagements and battles follows KA, *Krieg 1809*, I, 542–69, and Bowden and Tarbox, pp. 50–54.
42 KA, *Krieg 1809*, I. 578.

43 *Ibid.*, pp. 581–2; Angeli, *Erzherzog Carl*, IV, 180–81.
44 Text in Criste, *Erzherzog Carl*, III, 79–80; Petre, p. 227.
45 Rauchensteiner, *Kaiser Franz*, pp. 99–100.
46 Creveld, p. 75.
47 KA, *Krieg 1809*, I. 596–8.
48 Karl, *Ausgewählte Schriften*, VI, 357.
49 Criste, *Erzherzog Carl*, III, 108.
50 Rauchensteiner, 'Das sechste österreichische Armeekorps,' pp. 167–8. Compare R. W. Litschel, *Das Gefecht bei Ebelsberg am 3. Mai 1809*, Vienna, 1968, pp. 6–8.
51 *Ibid.*, pp. 8–9.
52 Karl, *Ausgewählte Schriften*, VI, 336.
53 R. W. Litschel, *Lanze, Schwert und Helm*, Linz, 1968, p. 109.
54 *Ibid.*, pp. 121–6; Petre, p. 240 Hiller's report KA, FA 1809, Hauptarmee, F/5–68.
55 Rauchensteiner, 'Das sechste österreichische Armeekorps,' p. 173.
56 Report of FML Thiery Baron de Vaux, 12 May 1809, KA, Kartensammlung, Inland C1, Envelope D. Compare Hummelberger and Peball, p. 72.
57 Petre, pp. 254–6; Angeli, *Erzherzog Carl*, IV, 260.
58 Hiller's account Rauchensteiner, 'Das sechste österreichische Armeekorps,' pp. 175–7.
59 O'Reilly's report on capitulation, 13 May 1809, KA, FA 1809, Hauptarmee, F/5–624. Petre, pp. 323–4.
60 E. Wertheimer, 'Zur Geschichte Wiens im Jahre 1809,' *AöG*, 74 (1889), 164, 194.
61 For these and other details concerning Eugene I am indebted to my former student Robert Epstein, unpublished PhD dissertation, *The Viceroy at War*, Temple University, Philadelphia, Pa., 1980.
62 *Ibid.*
63 KA, *Krieg 1809*, II, 474–6.
64 I have followed figures in G. Bodart, *Militärhistorisches Kriegs-Lexikon*, Vienna-Leipzig, 1908, p. 397.
65 Epstein, *op. cit.*, and F. Vanicek, *Specialgeschichte der Militärgrenze*, Vienna, 1875, IV, 130–31. KA, *Krieg 1809*, II, 374–99 has extensive details.

66 Horsetzky, pp. 123–4; Petre, pp. 301–4.
67 Rothenberg, *Military Border*, pp. 108–9, and KA, Mem III/135, 'Feldzug in Dalmatien 1809.'
68 Horsetzky, pp. 216–19.

CHAPTER VIII

1 D. Chandler, *The Campaigns of Napoleon*, New York, 1966, p. 735.
2 H. v. Zwiedeneck-Südenhorst, *Erzherzog Johann von Österreich im Feldzug von 1809*, Graz, 1892, p. 23. Compare M. Rauchensteiner, *Die Schlacht von Aspern am 21. und 22. Mai 1809*, Vienna, 1969, pp. 3–4.
3 KA, FA 1809, Hauptarmee, F/13–17.
4 Angeli, *Erzherzog Karl*, IV, 311.
5 Criste, *Erzherzog Carl*, III, 126–8, and A. Menge, *Die Schlacht von Aspern am 21. und 22. Mai 1809*, Berlin, 1900, pp. 160–64.
6 Dolleczek, p. 451.
7 Chandler, pp. 696–9.
8 I have here followed the order of battle given in Rauchensteiner, *Aspern*, pp. 7, 28–30.
9 *Ibid.*, pp. 8–9; Chandler, p. 700.
10 Rauchensteiner, *Apsern*, pp. 9–10.
11 Criste, *Erzherzog Carl*, III, 134–6.
12 Chandler, pp. 702–3.
13 Rauchensteiner, 'Das sechste österreichische Armeekorps,' p. 187.
14 Criste, *Erzherzog Carl*, III, 143–4; Chandler, p. 704.
15 Rauchensteiner, *Aspern*, pp. 18–19, Criste, *Erzherzog Carl*, III, 146–7.
16 Rauchensteiner, 'Das sechste österreichische Armeekorps,' p. 187.
17 *Ibid.*, p. 188.
18 KA, FA 1809, Hauptarmee, F/5–410, 416.
19 Bodart, p. 405.
20 Dolleczek, p. 451.
21 Delbrück, *Erinnerungen*, pp. 588–9; Menge, p. 186.
22 Rauchensteiner, Aspern, pp. 15, 21.
23 F. M. Kircheisen, *Napoleon*, London, 1931, p. 466.
24 Menge, pp. 188–95.
25 F. M. Kircheisen, *Gespräche Napoleons*, Stuttgart, 1912, II, 62, 69.
26 Rauchensteiner, 'Das sechste österrei-

chische Armeekorps,' pp. 189–93, 199–200.

27 Criste, *Erzherzog Carl*, III, 163–4.

28 Joseph to John, 23 May 1809, in Zwiedeneck-Südenhorst, pp. 29–30.

29 Criste, *Erzherzog Carl*, III, 168–70.

30 Charles to John, 11 June 1809, in Zwiedeneck-Südenhorst, p. 71.

31 *Ibid.*, pp. 248–54. Compare M. v. Angeli, 'Wagram. Novelle zur Geschichte des Krieges von 1809,' *MkkKA*, 5 (1881), 87.

32 Bodart, p. 407.

33 John's after action report, 16 June 1809, Komorn, KA, FA 1809, Ungarische Insurrektion 1809, F6/100. Compare Zwiedeneck-Südenhorst, pp. 86–90, 93–4.

34 Horsetzky, pp. 204–6.

35 M. Rauchensteiner, *Die Schlacht bei Deutsch Wagram am 5. und 6. Juli 1809*, Vienna, 1977, pp. 7–8, 10–11.

36 *Ibid.*, pp. 8–9; Angeli, *Erzherzog Carl*, IV, 299; Horsetzky, p. 211.

37 *Beiträge*, I, 224–5.

38 *Ibid.*, pp. 225–7, Dolleczek, pp. 454–5.

39 *Ibid.*, pp. 7–8; Chandler, p. 718.

40 H. Hertenberger, 'Die Schlacht bei Wagram,' Diss. Univ. of Vienna, 1950, pp. 71–2; Rauchensteiner, *Wagram*, p. 8.

41 Koller to Charles, 11 and 20 July 1809, KA, FA 1809, Hauptarmee, F/6–29.

42 Criste, *Erzherzog Carl*, III, 176–9.

43 *Ibid.*, pp. 184–7.

44 I have accepted here the high figure given by Bowden and Tarbox, 155–61, based on documents in the archives at Vincennes. Petre, pp. 351–2 makes the figures much more equal. Chandler, p. 709, gives Napoleon 'close on 160,000 men ... and more on the way.'

45 *Ibid.*, pp. 710–11.

46 Rauchensteiner, 'Das sechste österreichische Armeekorps,' pp. 203–5.

47 KA, FA 1809, Hauptarmee, F/7–103–1.

48 Rauchensteiner, *Wagram*, pp. 17–19; Chandler, pp. 713–19.

49 *Ibid.*, and Petre, pp. 357–61.

50 Rauchensteiner, *Wagram*, pp. 22–25. Compare Criste, *Erzherzog Carl*, III, 232–4.

51 Criste, *Erzherzog Carl*, III, 228.

52 Rauchensteiner, *Wagram*, p. 32.

53 *Ibid.*, p. 34. As usual, figures fluctuate widely.

54 H. Hertenberger, 'Die Schlacht bei Wagram,' Diss. Univ. Vienna, 1950, pp. 226–33; Criste, *Erzherzog Carl*, III, 246.

55 KA, FA 1809, Hauptarmee, F/7–103–33 of 9 July 1809.

56 Rauchensteiner, *Wagram*, p. 32.

57 KA, FA 1809, Hauptarmee, F/7–123. Printed in Peball, 'Zum Kriegsbild,' pp. 166–7.

58 L. Madelin, *Histoire du consulat et de l'empire*, Paris, 1945, VIII, 238.

59 Criste, *Erzherzog Carl*, III, 276–7. Francis to Charles, 11 July 1809, KA, FA 1809, Hauptarmee, F7/153.

60 *Ibid.*, p. 261.

61 *Ibid.*, pp. 276–7.

62 Rauchensteiner, *Kaiser Franz*, pp. 109–10.

63 In E. H. Kraehe, *Metternich's German Policy*, Princeton, 1963, I, 100.

64 H. Rössler, *Österreichs Kampf um Deutschlands Befreiung*, Hamburg, 1940, pp. 71–3.

65 Komorn, 15 August 1809, in Criste, *Erzherzog Carl*, III, 502–7.

66 Bathurst to Canning, 23 July 1809, FO 7/50.

67 Bathurst to Canning, 30 September 1809, *Ibid.*, 88.

CHAPTER IX

1 Criste, *Erzherzog Carl*, III, 277.

2 Radetzky, 'Selbstbiographie,' p. 69.

3 Radetzky, 'Eine Memoire Radetzky's das Heerwesen Österreichs beleuchtend aus dem Jahre 1809,' *MkkKA*, 10 (1884), 361–70. Compare Regele, *Radetzky*, pp. 86–7.

4 Clausewitz, *On War*, O.M. Jolles trans., New York, 1943, p. 568.

5 Springer, I, 124.

6 Regele, *Radetzky*, pp. 392–7.

7 *Ibid.*, pp. 399–700.

8 Regele, *Radetzky*, pp. 88, 397.

9 A Beer, *Die Finanzen Österreichs im XIX. Jahrhundert*, Prague, 1977, p. 14.

10 KA, *Befreiungskrieg 1813 und 1814*, Vienna, 1913, II, 1–5.

11 KA, *Befreiungskrieg*, II, 4–5.

12 King to Wellesley, Vienna, 2 March 1812, PRO FO 7/99.

13 KA, HKR 1812 (G/9–2–17).
14 Regele, *Radetzky*, p. 102.
15 *Ibid.*, pp. 98–9.
16 Springer, I, 200, 202–3.
17 KA, *Befreiungskrieg*, II, 11–15.
18 To Castlereagh, Vienna, 29 April 1812, PRO FO 7/99.
19 *Ibid.*, Vienna, 2 June.
20 Schwarzenberg, pp. 162–3.
21 *Ibid.*, pp. 165, 170.
22 Chandler, p. 829.
23 KA, *Befreiungskrieg*, pp. 34–9. Compare King to Castlereagh, Vienna, 7 February 1813, PRO FO 34/6.
24 KA, HKR 1813, B/I–23–16, 17, 19; G/I–69, 63.
25 To Castlereagh, Vienna, 14 February 1813, in C.S.B. Buckland, *Metternich and the British Government from 1809 to 1813*, London, 1932, pp. 468–9.
26 KA, FA 1813, Hauptarmee, F/5–1, 5.
27 KA, FA 1813, Hauptarmee, F/5–21 of 10 May 1813.
28 *Ibid.*, F/6–88, 90.
29 KA, *Befreiungskrieg*, II, 86–9.
30 *Ibid.*, pp. 101, 121–2.
31 *Regele*, Radetzky, p. 118.
32 KA, *Befreiungskrieg*, II, 65–9. Compare KA, FA 1813, Hauptarmee, F/VI–32.
33 R. K. Wilson, *Private Diary of Travels, personal services and public events during missions and employment with European armies in the campaigns of 1812, 1813, 1814*, London, 1860, II, 89, 114, 137.
34 E. Glaise-Horstenau, *Die Tage von Dresden 1813*, Leipzig, 1911, p. 31.
35 Wilson, II, 84.
36 Sherwig, p. 306.
37 Regele, *Radetzky*, p. 157.
38 *Ibid.*, p. 118.
39 Glaise-Horstenau, pp. 42, 51; Schwarzenberg, pp. 200–2, 222–4.
40 G. A. Craig, 'Problems of Coalition Warfare: The Military Alliance against Napoleon, 1813–14,' in G. A. Craig, *War, Politics, and Diplomacy*, New York–Washington, 1966, pp. 26–8.
41 Wilson, II, 86.
42 Glaise-Horstenau, pp. 45–6. Compare the eyewitness account in Thielen, p. 133.
43 Regele, *Radetzky*, p. 136.
44 Craig, p. 29; Glaise-Horstenau, pp. 45–6.
45 *Ibid.*, pp. 52–5.
46 Radetzky, *Denkschriften militär-politischen Inhalts aus dem handschriftlichen Nachlass*, Vienna, 1859, pp. 90–93.
47 Wilson, II, 84–5.
48 Regele, *Radetzky*, pp. 121–3.
49 *Ibid.*, pp. 124–5.
50 Beiträge, I, 229–31. Compare F. L. Petre, *Napoleon's Last Campaign in Germany*, London, 1912, pp. 27–8.
51 *Ibid.*, p. 232.
52 KA, *Befreiungskrieg*, III, 7, 14–15.
53 KA, FA 1813, Hauptarmee, F/9 27–100; KA, *Befreiungskrieg*, V, 2–3.
54 KA, FA 1813, Hauptarmee, F/8–99, 208. Printed in extenso in *Beiträge*, I, 265–8; discussion in Wagner, pp. 30–31.
55 KA, FA 1813, Hauptarmee, F/10–436b.
56 KA, *Befreiungskrieg*, III, 241.
57 Glaise-Horstenau, pp. 183–5.
58 Bodart, p. 455.
59 Wilson, II, 94.
60 KA, HKR 1813, G-1–69/317.
61 Regele, *Radetzky*, pp. 146–7.
62 Wilson, II, 191.
63 KA, FA 1812, Hauptarmee, F/8–281.
64 J. Sporschil, *Feldzug der Österreicher in Illyrien und Italien* in den Jahren 1813 und 1814, Brunswick, 1844, p. 7.
65 KA, FA 1813, Hiller, F7/105.
66 *Ibid.*, 38a, 45a.
67 Rothenberg, *Military Border*, pp. 119–21.
68 Sporschil, pp. 46–61.
69 Regele, *Radetzky*, p. 160.
70 Schwarzenberg, pp. 267–8.
71 G. Ritter, *The Sword and the Scepter*, trans, H. Norden, Coral Gables, Fla., 1969, p. 68.

Select Sources and Bibliography

Select Sources and Bibliography

Manuscript sources

Kriegsarchiv (KA) Wien:
  Feldakten (FA) for 1792-1813.
  Hofkriegsrat Akten (HKR) for 1788–1814.
  Memories (Mem) occasional memoranda on various subjects.
  Militär-Hof-Commission Nostitz-Rieneck, 1791–9.
  Militärischer Nachlass Kaiser Franz I (MNKF), B/473.
  Nachlässe, including Lindenau (B/619), Mack (B/573), Mayer (B/857), Radetzky (A/1), and Zach (B/852).
Public Record Office (PRO) London:
  Reports from Wickham, Paget, and others.

Printed regulations and instructions

Regulament für das Kais. Königl. Ingenieurs-Corps, Vienna, 1748.
Exercitium für die sämmentliche Kaiserich-Königliche Infanterie, Vienna, 1769.
Instructionspunkte für gesammte Herren Generals der K.K. Armee, Frankfurt a.M., 1795. Mack's army instruction for 1794.
Grundsätze der höheren Kriegskunst für die Generäle der österreichischen Armee, Vienna, 1806.
Exercier-Reglement für die kaiserlich-königliche Infanterie, Vienna, 1808.
Schematismus der kaiserl.-königl. Armee für das Jahr 1790, Vienna, 1790. Appeared yearly with slightly varying titles.

Contemporary memoirs, letters, and other works

Anon. *Das Heer von Innerösterreich unter den Befehlen des Erzherzogs Johann im Kriege 1809 in Italien, Tyrol, und Ungarn*, Leipzig, 1917. By a staff officer. Contains numerous excerpts from official records.
Carl, Archduke of Austria, *Ausgewählte Schriften*, F.X. Malcher ed., 6 vols, Vienna-Leipzig, 1893–4.
— *Warum benutzten die Österreicher den Sieg von Aspern nicht zu einer offensiven Operation auf das rechte Donauufer*, Pest, 1811.
Cognazzo, J., *Freymüthiger Beytrag zur Geschichte des österreichischen Militairdienstes*, Frankfurt-Leipzig, 1789. The late Theresian army as seen by an officer.
Ellrich, A. ed., *Humoristische und historische Skizzen aus den Jahren der Revolutionskriege. Aus den hinterlassenen Papieren eines verstorbenen Soldaten*, Meissen, 1844. A rare glimpse of life in the ranks.

Gruber, K. J., *Lebenserinnerungen eines Reiteroffiziers vor hundert Jahren*, Vienna, 1906.

Jacubenz, Major, 'Gentz und Fasbender. Ungedruckte Briefe aus der Ziet von 1802 bis 1808,' *Mitteilungen des k.u.k. Kriegs Archivs*, 3rd Ser., VII (1911), 57–102.

Paget, A. B. and Green, J. R., *The Paget Papers. Diplomatic and other Correspondence of the Right Hon. Sir Arthur Paget, G.C.B.*, 1794–1807, 2 vols, New York, 1896.

Radetzky, J. V., *Denkschriften militär-politischen Inhalts aus dem handschriftlichen Nachlass des k.k. österreichischen Feldmarschalls Grafen Radetzky*, Vienna, 1858.

— 'Eine Memoire Radetzky's das Heerwesen Österreichs beleuchtend aus dem Jahre 1809,' *Mitteilungen des k.k. Kriegs Archivs*, VIII (1884), 361–70.

— 'Erinnerungen aus dem Leben des Feldmarschalls Grafen Radetzky. Eine Selbstbiographie,' *Mitteilungen des k.k. Kriegs Archivs*, 2nd Ser., I (1887), 3–82.

Rauch, J., *Erinnerungen eines Offiziers aus Altösterreich*, A. Weber, ed., vol. XXI of *Denkwürdigheiten aus Altösterreich*, Munich, 1918. Another glimpse of life in the ranks.

Schönhals, C.v., *Der Krieg 1805 in Deutschland*, Vienna, 1873. Author served as a junior officer in Ulm campaign.

Thielen, M.v., *Erinnerungen aus dem Kriegserleben eines 82 jährigen Veteranen der österreichischen Armee*, Vienna, 1863.

Unterberger, L., *Nöthige Kenntnisse von dem Geschütz und dessen Gebrauch*, Vienna, 1807.

Wickham, W., ed., *The Correspondence of the Right Honourable William Wickham* from the Year 1794, 2 vols, London, 1870.

Wilson, R., *Private Diary of Travels, Personal Services and Public Events during Missions and Employment with the European Armies in the Campaigns of 1812, 1813, 1814*, H. Randolph ed., 2 vols, London, 1861.

Zach, A.v., 'Eine Denkschrift Zach's aus dem Jahre 1798,' *Mitteilungen des k.u.k. Kriegsarchivs*, 3rd Ser., II (1903), 165–95.

Secondary materials

Several of the works contain substantial source material. These are indicated by an asterisk.

*Angeli, M.v., *Erzherzog Carl als Feldherr und Heeresorganisator*, 5 vols, Vienna-Leipzig, 1896–7. Much basic material, but to be used with caution. A commissioned biography.

*— 'Ulm and Austerlitz,' *Mitteilungen des k.k. Kriegs Archivs*, III (1878), 283–394.

— 'Wagram. Novelle zur Geschichte des Krieges von 1809,' *Mitteilungen des k.k. Kriegs Archivs*, V (1881), 41–105.

— 'Die Heere des Kaisers und der französischen Revolution im Beginn des Jahres 1792,' *Mitteilungen des k.u.k. Kriegsarchivs*, 2nd Ser., IV (1889), 112.

Anon. 'Zur Charakteristik des Erzherzogs Carl und der österreichischen Armee in den Jahren 1801 bis 1804,' *Mitteilungen des k.k. Kriegs Archivs*, V (1881), 106–21.

Baer, F. H., 'Napoleon was not afraid of it,' *Arms and Armor Annual*, I (1973), 250–57. On the repeating air rifle.

Beer, A., *Zehn Jahre österreichischer Politik 1801–1810*, Leipzig, 1877.

Binder v. Krieglstein, C., *Der Krieg Napoleons Gegen Österreich 1809*, 2 vols, Berlin, 1902–6.

Bowden, S. and Tarbox, C., *Armies on the Danube 1809*, Arlington, Tex. 1981.

Buckland, C. S. B., *Metternich and the British Government from 1809 to 1813*, London, 1932.

Chandler, D., *The Campaigns of Napoleon*, New York, 1966.

Craig, G. A., 'Problems of Coalition Warfare: The Military Alliance against Napoleon, 1813–1815,' in *War, Politics, and Diplomacy. Selected Essays*, New York, 1966, pp. 22–45.

*Criste, O., *Erzherzog Carl von Österreich*, 3 vols, Vienna-Leipzig, 1912. Standard biography with many valuable documents.

—— *Feldmarschall Johannes Fürst von Leichtenstein*, Vienna, 1905.

Delbrück, H. and Daniels, E., *Geschichte der Kriegskunst im Rahmen* der politischen Geschichte, 6 vols, Berlin, 1900–32. A classic, Volume V is pertinent here.

Delbrück, H., 'Erzherzog Carl,' in *Erinnerungen, Aufsätze, und Reden*, Berlin, 1902. A sharp attack.

Dolleczek, A., *Monographie der k.u.k. österr.-ungarischen blanken und Handfeuerwaffen*, Vienna, 1896.

—— *Geschichte der österreichischen Artillerie*, Vienna, 1887.

Duffy, C., *The Army of Maria Theresa*, New York, 1977.

—— *Austerlitz 1805*, Hamden, Conn., 1977. Duffy is one of the few writers to deal with the Austrian army in English.

Egger, R., *Das Gefecht bei Dürnstein-Loiben 1805*, No. 3 of the *Militärhistorische Schriftenreihe* of the Militärwissenschaftliches Institut, Vienna, 1965.

Ernstberger, A., *Böhmens freiwilliger Kriegseinsatz gegen Napoleon*, Vol. XIV of *Veröffentlichungen des Collegium Carolinium*, Munich, 1963.

*Fournier, A., *Gentz und Cobenzl. Geschichte der österreichischen Diplomatie in den Jahren 1801–1805*, Vienna, 1880.

Frauenholz, E.v., *Das Heerwesen des XIX. Jahrhunderts*, Vol. V of *Entwicklungsgeschichte des deutschen Heerwesens*, Munich, 1941.

Fuller, J. F. C., *The Conduct of War, 1789–1961*, New Brunswick, 1961.

*Gallina, J., *Beiträge zur Geschichte des österreichischen Heerwesens*, Vol. I, *Der Zeitraum von 1757–1814*, Vienna, 1872. Fundamental.

Geschliesser, O., 'Das Zeitalter der Koalitions- und Befreiungskriege,' in H. St Fürlinger and L. Jedlicka, eds, *Unser Heer. 300 Jahre österreichisches Soldatentum in Krieg und Frieden*, Vienna-Munich-Zurich, 1963.

Heller v. Hellwald, F., *Der Feldzug in Süddeutschland 1809*, 2 vols, Vienna, 1864.

Hertenberger, H., 'Die Schlacht bei Wagram,' Diss. Univ. of Vienna, 1950.

Horsetzky, A.v., *Kriegsgeschichtliche Übersicht der wichtigsten Feldzüge in Europa seit 1792*, 5th ed., Vienna, 1905. Classic summary.

Hummelberger, W. and Peball, K., *Die Befestigungen Wiens*, Vienna, 1974.

John, W. *Erzherzog Karl. Der Feldherr und seine Armee*, Vienna, 1913.

Kircheisen, F. M., *Feldzugserinnerungen aus dem Kriegsjahr 1809*, Hamburg, 1909.

Krauss, A., *Der Feldzug von Ulm*, Vienna, 1905.

*Kriegsarchiv, Wien, *Kriege unter der Regierung des Kaisers Franz: Krieg gegen die französische Revolution*, 2 vols, Vienna, 1905.

* —— *Krieg 1809*, 4 vols, Vienna, 1907–10.

* —— *1813–1815. Österreich in den Befreiungskriegen*, 10 vols, Vienna, 1911–14.

* —— *Befreiungskrieg 1813 und 1814*, 5 vols, Vienna, 1913. Not completed and ends with Leipzig.

Litschel, R. W., *Lanze, Schwert, und Helm. Beiträge zur oberösterreichischen Wehrgeschichte*, Linz, 1968.

—— *Das Gefecht bei Ebelsberg am 3. Mai 1809*, No. 9 of the *Militärhistorische Schrifteneihe* of the Militärwissenschaftliches Institut, Vienna, 1968.

Maude, F. N., *The Ulm Campaign 1805*, London, 1912, Chap. 1 contains considerable detail on the Austrian army.

Meynert, H., *Geschichte der k.k. österreichischen Armee*, 3 vols, Vienna, 1852–4.

Menge, A., *Die Schlacht von Aspern am 21. und 22. Mai 1809*, Berlin, 1900. Sharp attack on Archduke Charles.

Nemetz, W., 'Erzherzog Karl,' in *Klassiker der Kriegskunst*, W. Hahlweg ed., Darmstadt, 1960, pp. 285–304.

Ommen, H., *Die Kriegsführung des Erzherzogs Carl*, No. 16 of *Historische Studien*, Berlin, 1900.

Paret, P., *Yorck and the Era of Prussian Reform, 1807–1815*, Princeton, N.J., 1966.

—— *Clausewitz and the State*, London, 1976.

Peball, K., 'Zum Kriegsbild der österreichischen Armee und seiner geschichtlichen Bedeutung in den Kriegen gegen die Französische Revolution und Napoleon I. in den Jahren von 1792 bis 1815,' In Groote, W.v. and Müller, K.J., eds, *Napoleon I. und das Militärwesen seiner Ziet*, Freiburg, 1968.

Petre, F.L., *Napoleon and the Archduke Charles. A History of the Franco-Austrian Campaign in the Danube Valley 1809*, 1976. Classic.

—— *Napoleon's Last Campaign in Germany, 1813*, New York, 1974.

Rauchensteiner, M., *Feldzeugmeister Johann Freiherr von Hiller*, Vienna, 1972.

—— *Kaiser Franz und Erzherzog Carl*, Munich, 1972. Important corrective to Criste.

—— *Die Schlacht von Aspern am 21. und 22. Mai 1809*, No. 11 of *Militärhistorische Schriftenreihe* of the Militärhistorisches Institut, Vienna, 1969.

—— *Die Schlacht bei Deutsch Wagram am 5. und 6. Juli 1809*, No. 36 of *Militärhistorische Schriftenreihe* of the Militärhistorisches Institut, Vienna, 1977.

Regele, O., *Feldmarschall Radetzky. Leben, Leistung, Erbe*, Vienna-Munich, 1957.

—— *Generalstabschefs aus vier Jahrhunderten*, Vienna-Munich, 1966.

* —— 'Karl Freiherr von Mack und Johann Ludwig Graf Cobenzl. Ihre Rolle im Kriegsjahr 1805,' *Mitteilungen des österreichischen Staatsarchivs*, XXI (1969), 142–64.

Rodger, A. B., *The War of the Second Coalition, 1798–1801*, London, 1964.

Rössler, H., *Österreichs Kampf um die deutsche Befreiung. Die deutsche Politik der nationalen Führer Österreichs 1805–1815*, Hamburg, 1940. Often cited, but tendentious.

Rothenberg, G. E., *The Military Border in Croatia, 1740–1881*, Chicago, 1966.
—— *The Art of Warfare in the Age of Napoleon*, London, 1977.
Rüstow, W., *Der Krieg von 1805 in Deutschland und Italien*, Frauenfeld, 1853.
Semek, Major., 'Die Artillerie im Jahre 1809,' *Mitteilungen des k.u.k. Kriegsarchivs*, 3rd Ser., III (1904), 51–160.
Sherwig, J. M., *Guineas and Gunpowder. British Foreign Aid in the Wars with France, 1793–1815*, Cambridge, Mass., 1969.
Sporschil, J., *Feldzug der Österreicher in Illyrien und Italien in den Jahren 1813 und 1814*, Brunswick, 1844.
Stutterheim, F. H.v., *Der Krieg 1809 zwischen Österreich und Frankreich*, Vienna, 1811.
Van Creveld, M., *Supplying War. Logistics from Wallenstein to Patton*, Cambridge, 1977.
Vaudoncourt, F. F. G. de, *Histoire politique et militarie du Prince Eugène Napoleon*, 2 vols, Paris, 1828.
Wagner, W., *Von Austerlitz bis Königgrätz: österreichische Kampftaktik im Spiegel d. Reglements 1805–1864*, Osnabruck, 1978.
Wertheimer, E., *Geschichte Österreichs und Ungarns im ersten Jahrzehnt des 19. Jahrhunderts*, 2 vols, Leipzig, 1890.
—— 'Erzherzog Karl und die 2. Koalition bis zum Frieden von Luneville (1798–1801),' *Archiv für österreichische Geschichte*, LXVII (1886), 193–252.
Zimmermann, Jr, *Militärverwaltung und Heeresaufbringung in Österreich bis 1806*, No. 3 of *Handbuch zur deutschen Militärgeschichte*, Frankfurt a.M., 1965.
*Zwiedeneck-Südenhorst, H.v., *Erzherzog Johann von Österreich im Feldzug von 1809*, Graz, 1892. Inclines towards John.

Reference works, encyclopaedias, and atlases

Alten, G.v. ed., *Handbuch für Heer und Flotte. Enzyklopädie der Kriegswissenschaften und verwandten Gebieten*. 6 vols and 2 suppl. vols, Berlin-Leipzig-Vienna, 1911–14.
Bodart, G., *Militär-historisches Kriegs-Lexikon*, Vienna-Leipzig, 1908.
Chandler, D., *Dictionary of the Napoleonic Wars*, New York, 1979.
Esposito, V. J. and Elting, J. R., *A Military History and Atlas of the Napoleonic Wars*, New York, 1964.
Kircheisen, F. M., *Bibliographie des Napoleonischen Zeitalters*, 2 vols, Berlin, 1908–12.
Kriegsarchiv Wien, *Inventar des Kriegsarchivs Wien*, 2 vols in 1, Vol. VIII of *Inventare österreichischer Archiv*, Vienna, 1953.
Wrede, A.v., *Geschichte der k.u.k. Wehrmacht. Die Regimenter, Corps, Branchen und Anstalten von 1618 bis Ende des XIX. Jahrhunderts*, in 6 vols, Vienna, 1898–1903.

Index of Persons

Index of Persons

Index of Battles & Treaties etc.

Index of Battles & Treaties etc.

Index of Army, units, tactics, etc.

Index of Army, units, tactics, etc.

Index of States, Provinces, Miscellaneous